Orange

Is Our Color

The Tuberville Years
Through Navy-tinted Glasses

Orange Is Our Color

The Tuberville Years

Through Navy-tinted Glasses

to the Rudd Family,

WAR EAGLE!

Josh Dowdy

Josh Dowdy

Seven States Publishing
Auburn, Alabama

www.orangeisourcolor.com

ORANGE IS OUR COLOR: THE TUBERVILLE YEARS
THROUGH NAVY-TINTED GLASSES

ISBN-13: 978-0-6158712-9-5

ISBN-10: 0-6158712-9-1

Seven States Publishing
Auburn, Alabama

Cover design by Josh Dowdy.

Cover photo and back cover photo by Scott Fillmer.
www.scottfillmer.com

Acknowledgments

Thank you, firstly, to my wife, Sarah, who tolerated our prolonged houseguest—this book—with remarkable patience. Thank you more so for loving me and encouraging me to make the book good, and to get it done!

Thank you to everyone I attended a game with during the Tuberville era. Forgive me for naming here only those who directly contributed to this project. My Dad has taken me to Jordan-Hare to see our Tigers under every coach since Barfield. My Mom has been to a few games as well. She at least tried to get me to major in journalism. Had I listened, this book would be better, and it might be my tenth instead of my first.

Thank you to Jordan Dowdy, my brother, without whom the Tuberville years would have been far less interesting. Jordan also provided research and fact-checking assistance.

Thank you, Uncle Donnie, for reading the proposal and providing feedback. Thank you also for hosting so many game watching parties at Gerald's house.

Sam Lasseter! Sam is a complex individual. The reader will know but one side of him by the end of this book. Thank you, Sam, for being an Auburn man, and also for reading various versions of the manuscript and providing critical observations.

Auburn folksinger and 2012 National Fantasy Baseball Championship winner Dave Potts also read parts of the manuscript and provided invaluable perspective. Dave and his wife Lara have supported my Auburn addiction over the years on a level second only to my parents. War Eagle!

Thank you to Joshua and Katie Jackson. "Action" obliged multiple interviews to help reconstruct and provide understanding for many off-the-field events. His in-laws, the Hughes family, have shared their food and even tickets over the years, for which I am constantly grateful.

Thank you to Matt McGee for providing his Auburn football insights throughout the last 17 years, and also for driving me to the 2003 Arkansas and 2005 South Carolina games. Matt also provided primary source material for chapter 11. Thank you to Matt's wife, Kim, for teaching her children to call me "Auburn Josh!"

Thanks also to some folks at The War Eagle Reader (www.thewareaglereader.com) who helped me out. Ben Bartley provided feedback on the thesis. Van Allen Plexico shared his expertise on the publishing process. Jeremy Henderson (I presume!) provided general support and encouragement via Twitter. Thanks and War Eagle!

Table of Contents

The earth is the Lord's and everything in it,
the world, and all who live in it.

Psalm 24:1

1

Introduction

On a warm Auburn day in May 2012 I stepped into J&M Bookstore to buy a hat. I also picked up a wallet-sized football schedule. The schedule designates the first game of the season, against Clemson at the Georgia Dome, as a True Blue game. A note at the bottom explains, "Fans Asked to Wear Blue." The season opener is the only True Blue game on the schedule. The remaining games have no wardrobe instructions. None are needed; because by 2012 everyone knows that orange is our color. Anyone who's been an Auburn fan more than 15 years or so might respond to this assertion with a couple of questions: *Since when?* and, *Says who?* We will address both questions in detail below, but the short answers are: 2000; and Tommy Tuberville. These answers lead to more questions. If the Auburn Family's commitment to wearing orange starts with Tommy Tuberville, who has not been our coach since 2008, why are we still wearing orange today? Furthermore, what does it matter?

This book is primarily about the events that took place in the life of the Auburn football program and the Auburn Family from 1999–2008. It is not, however, strictly a review of that decade, but rather a history that seeks to understand the lasting influence of the Tuberville era. The survival of *Tuberville orange* symbolizes how the events of that decade still impact the Auburn Family today. I am not saying Auburn fans think about Tommy Tuberville even in 2013 when they pull on an orange shirt; only that there is always an underlying connection between Tuberville and our practice of wearing orange en masse. Before we go any further, let's take a look at just how direct that connection is.

Orange Advent

Auburn fans first began wearing orange on game day when Tuberville asked us to in 2000. The game day edition of the Opelika-Auburn News for the 2000 season opener includes the following note.

> Auburn head coach Tommy Tuberville is urging Auburn fans to wear orange to tonight's game rather than blue or white. "We want everyone to show off their colors on national television," Tuberville said of the opener.[a]

The next day's edition of the O-A News reported the response.

> . . . the team was greeted with a sea of orange as they ran onto the field. Head coach Tommy Tuberville had asked the fans to dress in orange for the nationally televised game, and they obliged in large numbers.[b]

After the second home game of the season, the Birmingham News reported both the response to Tuberville's request and its significance.

> It seems Tuberville decided Auburn fans needed to have more of a presence on national television

games, so he decided fans should wear orange to Jordan-Hare. Never mind that Auburn fans had never been much into this school color thing at games, he thought wearing orange would be good for his team and for Auburn's image. So he suggested it a few days before this season began.

Almost all of the 86,000 fans who showed up for last week's LSU game were in the color of his choice. He has asked them to do the same for Saturday's 4 p.m. game against Northern Illinois. Wearing orange is a simple thing. But it demonstrates Tuberville's influence. "The head football coach at Auburn is not just the football coach—he's the leader of the people," said Housel. "I think that's why you saw Auburn people respond to Tommy's request to wear orange."[c]

The above reports make the connection between Tuberville and the origin of All Auburn All Orange very clear.[1] Furthermore, David Housel's comment suggests the Auburn people were already recognizing Tuberville in a role that transcends the field of play. We also see that Tuberville's reasoning behind wearing orange was to make an impression on the television audience. It was a marketing strategy, but, what were we selling? We will come back to that question later. For now we will note that the desired television effect explains why we wore an orange that is not even an official Auburn color.

---

[1] Here and elsewhere we will use the term *All Auburn All Orange* to mean the idea and practice of displaying school spirit through uniformity; that is, everyone wearing orange on game day. In a later chapter we will discuss the official All Auburn All Orange charitable fundraising program.

Auburn's colors are burnt orange and navy blue.[2] The color we wear on game day is neither. Burnt orange simply would not provide the pop on TV that Tuberville wanted. So, someone developed an alternative, brighter orange to use for Auburn apparel. Clothiers initially struggled to find the right balance between burnt and don't-shoot-me-I'm-not-a-deer orange. Consider this observation by Kevin Scarbinksy after the 2000 Vanderbilt game.

> Auburn coach Tommy Tuberville wants Auburn fans to wear orange. Shows up better on TV. Tuberville himself has changed colors, but what was the shade of that golf shirt he wore Saturday? Neon orange? Tangerine? Mango? Save it for night games, coach. It might glow in the dark.

It all the more shows Tuberville was not merely the Auburn football coach—he was, in some sense, the head of the Auburn Family. He convinced us not only to all wear the same color to Jordan-Hare Stadium, but even to wear a non-Auburn color. In 2001, Tuberville wanted to take our new monochromatism to a higher level.

I began my research with a vague memory of a pep talk Tuberville once gave on our commitment to wearing orange. He started off talking about the positive impact on team spirit, and then says we are going to wear orange even more than we did in 2000. He gets on a roll and says something to the effect of *everything's gonna be orange*! My friend Heath Neal, formerly a manager for the Auburn basketball team, remembers Tuberville getting carried away and saying, "We're gonna paint the goal posts orange." According to Heath, this message somehow got

---

[2] I have known this fact all my life but found it surprisingly difficult to document. Among other places, it is stated on page 53 of the 2013 Auburn Football Media Guide.

communicated to facilities management as an official directive, and the goal posts were actually painted orange. They were soon repainted to the florescent yellow that was standard at the time.[3] Back to my own recollection, I thought that just maybe in this discourse Tuberville had said, "Orange is our color!" I found direct documentation of the utterance nowhere. I wondered in what venue Tuberville might have made this pep talk, and then I got an idea— Tiger Talk. Perhaps Tuberville delivered his call to orange arms on his weekly, call-in radio show. I was unable to obtain recordings of the show from 2001 but found indirect evidence that makes the case.

The Auburn Football Illustrated for the 2001 opener against Ball State contains an advertisement for the Auburn Network Store. The Auburn Network produced Tiger Talk at the time. The ad features an item titled *Tuberwear T-Shirt ("Orange Is Our Color")*. The description reads, "Support the tigers by wearing orange this season in your official Tuberwear T-shirt." The front of the shirt reads, "Orange Is Our Color."

So, we have shown the connection between Tuberville and the beginning of Auburn fans wearing orange. We will later show how this connection only grows stronger. Of course, it makes sense that we would wear what Tuberville asked us to in 2000 and 2001—the honeymoon was still in progress. But, what about five years after Tuberville's departure? As stated above, I interpret the continuation of All Auburn All Orange as symbolic of the Tuberville decade's lasting influence on the Auburn Family. Just what is that influence? How did the experiences of those ten years impact the Auburn Family on such a deep level that the effect is still visible today? These are the big questions that we are going to answer by examining the history of Auburn football—on the field

---

[3] The Apocryphal ring is strong, but, given our title, could we really leave this story out?

and off—from 1999–2008. Before we get started, you might be wondering—just what kind of neurotic barner wants to go down this road (and take me with him!)?

Dyed in the Wool: Growing Up Auburn in the 1980s

I suspect many readers of this book will have a story something like my own. I knew I was an Auburn fan long before I knew what an Auburn fan was. Throughout my formative years I learned what it means to believe in Auburn and love it. I also learned the place of Auburn football within that belief and love. My understanding of the latter developed as much on Sundays as it did on Saturdays.

I remember fondly our family routine for Sundays in the fall. We came home from church and ate lunch; after lunch—the *playbacks*! My Dad used this term for the Auburn Football Review with Head Coach Pat Dye. The start of the show was mystical. It began abruptly with footage from the previous day's game—no commentary; only the sound of the crowd, its dramatic crescendo narration enough for each highlight. After a few big plays the broadcast cut to a clip from Coach Dye's post-game locker room address.[4] Only after this immersion into the game day experience did the formal introduction begin, and later came the education: Coach Dye talking through the highlights (and lowlights), explaining various decisions and plays, and talking about the players who made it all happen. His commentary was often less about Xs-and-Os and more about preparation and opportunity.

The playbacks were the afternoon counterpart to the Sunday School lessons I received in the morning. The curriculum may have lacked structure, but the message, over time, was consistent and clear. When I read Coach Dye's book, *In the Arena*, in 1992, I already knew by heart the philosophy it contains. Dye

---

[4] For me, nothing from today's increasingly invasive media coverage comes close to the intimacy of Coach Dye speaking to his players after a game.

had not spoken expressly on the playbacks about how sacrifice teaches discipline and how discipline leads to excellence, but the theme came across nonetheless; it underpinned everything he said and how he said it. Am I mythologizing a little this living patriarch of Auburn Football? Sure—how could I not? His record as Auburn's coach during the first four years I was really paying attention was 39 wins, 6 losses and 2 ties. What remains true beyond any romanticism is that Pat Dye was the head of the Auburn Family in the years when I learned what the Auburn Family is. That is why I saw the Tuberville decade through navy-tinted glasses firsthand. That background also colors my perspective looking back on the Tuberville years. Far from denying my bias, I will even claim it provides a degree of objectivity.

Tuberville was never *my* coach the way Dye was. For some younger fans Tuberville holds all the influence that Dye does for me. Some older fans appreciate Dye as greatly, or more, than I do, but they did not develop that appreciation at the same impressionable age; thus, they were free to more fully adopt Tuberville. Even some fans my own age are simply better adjusted adults, and live more so in the present; they, too, were All Auburn All Orange. I cannot claim to study the relationship between Tuberville and the Auburn people from the outside; but, in some regard, it was something happening all around me, rather than to me. With that confession, let's move on to how this book will examine that relationship.

We Still Wear Orange

The thesis of this book is that the events of the Tuberville decade impacted the Auburn Family at such a deep level that they actually altered how we understand our collective identity, and that the effect is still visible today. More specifically, the lasting impact of the Tuberville decade is due to the Auburn Family's experiences of three major events: *Jetgate*, the 2004 undefeated season, and the

Streak of six consecutive wins over Alabama. In our survey of all ten seasons of the Tuberville era we will see how these three events build upon each other to bring about lasting change for the Auburn Family. In the next chapter we will explore the story that brought Tuberville to Auburn. We will first close this chapter with a story from right after he got here.

I have attended many Auburn football games in my life, but I've been to the Auburn Christmas Parade only once. It was 1998. Tuberville had been hired just a few days before. As I walked across campus towards town I thought about the fact that I had shook hands with Pat Dye, and also with Terry Bowden, and now I wanted to shake Tuberville's hand. I had walked up Mell St. and was about to turn right on Thach when—there he was: Tommy Tuberville, standing among the gathering parade crowd. I approached him from behind and addressed him as if I had some business doing so. "Coach Tuberville!" This moment, of course, is long before he won 50 games over five seasons as Auburn's coach; before he won a BCS bowl game to finish an undefeated season; before he beat Alabama seven out of ten years. On this night, he was a man trying to make a good start at a new job. He snapped around as if I were a deeper-voiced Bobby Lowder and responded: "Yes!" He was holding a child—using both arms—so I didn't reach for his hand, but put mine behind his shoulder and said, "Welcome to Auburn." He said thank you, and I headed on to College Street. Almost ten years passed before we would meet again. A lot happens in between.

2012 FOOTBALL SCHEDULE

SEPT 1	vs. Clemson (Georgia Dome, Atlanta, GA)
SEPT 8	at Mississippi State
SEPT 15	vs. **LOUISIANA-MONROE**
SEPT 22	vs. **LSU**
OCT 6	vs. **ARKANSAS**
OCT 13	at Ole Miss
OCT 20	at Vanderbilt
OCT 27	vs. **TEXAS A&M**
NOV 3	vs. **NEW MEXICO STATE** (HC)
NOV 10	vs. **GEORGIA**
NOV 17	vs. **ALABAMA A&M**
NOV 24	at Alabama

Home Games in **BOLD**
(HC) = Homecoming

TRUE BLUE
- FANS ASKED TO WEAR BLUE -

FOLLOW US ON

FOR TICKET INFO
AUBTIX.COM
855-AUB-2010

—Why would anyone keep this?

—From page 178 of the 2001 Ball State game Auburn Football
Illustrated.

2

1999

"We're building a foundation to get us out of the
bottom. It's going to be bumpy—real bumpy."

Not exactly pep rally material, is it? In the summer of 1999
Tuberville made it clear there was work to be done.[a] Before we
really get into Tuberville's first season, let's set the backdrop and
review the tumultuous transition that ultimately brought Tommy
Tuberville to Auburn University.

It isn't pretty; but if we want to understand the beginning of
Tuberville's Auburn tenure, we have to take a look at the way his
predecessor's ended. To appreciate the darkness covering the end
of the Terry Bowden era, we have to remember how bright was the
beginning. So, below we will briefly revisit 1993–1998 to set the
stage onto which Tuberville stepped when he became Auburn's
24th head football coach.

On December 17, 1992—the day after Eric Ramsey
received his Auburn degree—the University named Terry Bowden
its next head football coach. Bowden had no previous Division I-A

coaching experience. What he lacked in credentials, of course, he made up in pedigree, being the son of Bobby Bowden. Terry was 36 years old when Auburn hired him, but he displayed the enthusiasm and energy of an even younger man. His unapologetic optimism proved contagious to players and fans alike.

Bowden chose *Attitude* as a keyword for the 1993 season. The motivational strategy worked, and Auburn won every game in Bowden's first season. The highlights were many, including an upset over fourth-ranked Florida and a come-from-behind victory over Alabama. Bowden also chose a motto for the 1994 season: *Audacity*; as in, could we be so audacious as to do it again? We almost did.

We won our first nine games in 1994. The season peaked on October 15, when Auburn played number-one-ranked Florida in The Swamp. The Gators had outscored their first five opponents of the season by a total of 254–60. They were favored over Auburn by 16 points. Bowden, however, brought a superb game plan to Gainesville, and Patrick Nix threw an eight-yard touchdown to Frank Sanders in the final minute, giving Auburn a 36–33 victory. After the game, Bowden lobbied for national championship contender status. "We come down here, 16-point underdogs, and beat them again . . . You tell me, should we be No. 1? I say yes."[b] We did not finish 1994 as No. 1, but Bowden's initial 20-game winning streak inspired high hopes for the future—hopes never fully realized.

The Tigers won eight games in each of the next two seasons. We saw improvement in 1997, and made our first appearance in the SEC championship game. Then came 1998. The beginning of the Bowden era was incredible; the end, regrettable.

Bowden had run out of slogans. In light of how 1998 began—with a 19–0 loss to unranked Virginia at home—*inauspicious* would have been appropriate. We won the second game of the season, 17–0 at Oxford, but then came four consecutive losses, after which Bowden abruptly resigned on Friday October 23. The situation was immediately bizarre. Over time it progressed to unfortunate; then embarrassing; and ultimately, lamentable.

It Gets Worse

Defensive coordinator Bill Oliver was named interim head coach. We then beat La. Tech. and Central Florida but lost our three remaining conference games. Oliver wanted to continue as the head coach beyond the interim period. When Tuberville was hired instead, Oliver sued the University, alleging he had been promised the job. He claimed to have secured a loan from Colonial Bank on assurances from the University that Auburn would pay off the loan over the course of his employment. As for Bowden, his severance included $620,000, five years' of mortgage payments and two cars. The settlement prohibited Bowden from making disparaging remarks against the University.

What had begun with such excitement and promise ended with a three-win season and two bitter, public disputes. The Auburn Family badly wanted to move on. Accordingly, off-the-field expectations for Tuberville's first season were just as important as expectations for on-the-field performance.

Meet Tommy Tuberville

The Auburn Family was embarrassed by the 1998 season and the bickering that outlived the final loss. We wanted a fresh start. In some regard, it mattered not so much who Tommy Tuberville was as who he was not—neither Terry Bowden nor Bill Oliver. Tuberville was legitimately an outsider. A new leader with no existing loyalties in a program has a distinct opportunity to encourage unity. The reaction of Auburn fan Connie Kanakis to Tuberville's hiring reflects this sentiment.

Like all Auburn people, we were devastated when all this came about. Now words can't describe how pleased I am with Auburn bringing in Tuberville. There are groups that would have loved to see Pat Sullivan down there, would have loved to see Bobby Wallace. I think what Tommy will do is bring all the groups together. I truly believe he will do that for us.[c]

There was hope Tuberville could heal the hurt of 1998 by fostering unity among the Auburn People. Doing so would require Tuberville to win over fans not as welcoming as Kanakis. Winning people over happened to be Tuberville's specialty.

When Ole Miss hired Tuberville in December, 1994, athletic director Pete Boone noted the coach's inspirational ability: "He can sell himself and he can sell the university."[d] Tuberville brought this ability to Auburn and immediately began selling his vision for the program—he intended to win national championships at Auburn. While his ambition to win was appealing, his potential for distancing Auburn from the recent past was just as important.

The annual pre-season Fan Day drew a crowd of about 4,500 people. Tuberville was scheduled to sign autographs for two hours, but pushed through to three hours and 45 minutes. "I went through five Sharpies; that was a record for me."[e] People were excited about moving on. They were buying into Tuberville's vision, and wanted to meet the man behind it. Expectations for returning the program to good repute were high, but what about on-the-field expectations?

When Tuberville said things would get bumpy, his warning wasn't aimed at the pundits—their expectations needed no tempering. In their season preview, The Sporting News ranked Auburn the 60th best team in the country. Tuberville was speaking to fans like me. When my friend Dave Potts asked for my honest prediction about the season, I lied. The honest answer would have been 13 wins. I had not known Dave very long at the time; so I decided to feign rationality and told him I thought Auburn would win nine regular-season games. I had misjudged the gap between my ideology and Dave's grounding in reality. He looked at me with as much disbelief as if I had told the truth. It must have been the first time he understood I was that kind of fan. I was not alone, however; at least one other person thought nine wins was possible.

Sophomore fullback Heath Evans provided a simple formula for success: "If we score 14 points a game, I think we'll win nine of the 11 games, just because teams aren't going to be able to score on our defense."[f] I wish he had been right. We scored 14 or more points in all but two games. Against Evans' optimism and my belief system stood the chief reason for Tuberville's grim assessment—lack of personnel.

We lost four running backs before the season began. The leading rusher from 1998, Michael Burks, transferred. The second-leading rusher, Demontray Carter, was ruled academically ineligible in June. Brandon Johnson and Casinious Moore were both expected to contribute. Johnson suffered a knee injury in the Alabama-Mississippi All-Star Game—at least he was playing football; Moore fell victim to the dreaded "pick-up basketball." Our receivers cupboard was equally bare.

Our only returning receiver who had ever caught a collegiate pass was Clifton Robinson; we were lucky to have him. Robinson was suspended from the team in April after being arrested for second-degree rape. He pleaded down to a lesser charge and was reinstated. Robinson spoke highly of Tuberville after his return. "He was a great supporter of me . . . He was just like a dad would be to his son in a situation like this. It was very comforting for me."[g] Robinson gave us at least some experience at receiver. Experience was the deciding factor in the quarterback competition; or, at least it was in the summer.

"I want to make this very clear . . . there is a possibility, if things don't work out in practice, or our offense doesn't respond to the guy, there could possibly be a change before the first game."[h] Ten days before the season opener, "the guy" was Gabe Gross. His conditional starter status sounds something like, "we've got two other guys who can sit the bench better than he can." Tuberville explained that Gross had not won the position outright—the choice was based strictly on him having more game experience than the other candidates. Tuberville did not make a quarterback change before the first game, but it didn't take long.

The Tuberville Era Begins

Tuberville's first opponent as Auburn's head coach was Division I-AA Appalachian State. The Mountaineers won ten games in 1998. I did not know that at the time, and expected the season opener would be an easy win, despite some mountain folk having tried to warn me.

Taco spent the summer of 1999 working at a camp in Black Mountain, North Carolina. Sam and I drove up from Alabama, and Matt came over from Raleigh to hang out for a weekend. We happened to meet some Appalachian State fans who kindly let us know the Mountaineers would beat our Tigers. I weighed the boldness of their speech against the good-heartedness of their naïveté. We judged them to be simple mountain folk and laughed off the affront. A month later, the prospect of losing to Appy State was not so funny.

Auburn struggled from the beginning. Starting quarterback Gabe Gross threw a touchdown in the first half, but also an interception. He threw another interception in the second half and ultimately completed only five of twelve attempts for 25 yards. We were trailing 12–7 when Ben Leard replaced Gross. The game remained undecided until Leard threw a 33-yard touchdown pass to Ronney Daniels with just 38 seconds left to play: Auburn 22 – Appalachian State 15. Disaster avoided.[1] The Tuberville era began with a win.

The second team on Auburn's 1999 schedule was Idaho. The Vandals scored three fourth-quarter touchdowns, but the Tigers held on for a 30–23 win. Tuberville played three quarterbacks: Leard, Gross and Jeff Klein. Leard outshone the others and was named the starter for the following week's SEC opener, at Baton Rouge.

"This Is Just the Start"

Tuberville's first conference game at Auburn was also his first upset victory. While neither team was ranked, LSU was favored by eight points. To win by eight, you have to score eight; on this night, LSU did not. The game's most memorable play came late in the first quarter. We lined up to attempt an 18-yard field goal, but our holder, walk-on quarterback Jacob Allen, tossed the ball over his shoulder to kicker Damon Duval, who was running behind Allen and raced into the end zone for a touchdown. The score seemed to juice up our team, and they never looked back. We beat LSU, 41–7.

After the game, spirits were high. Auburn safety Rob Pate described the victory as a landmark. "We've gone through so much as a team. To come out and prove ourselves on national

---

[1] A loss to App St. would have been doubly humiliating because the Mountaineers were a replacement opponent. The 1999 season opener was originally scheduled against Florida State, in Tallahassee. It was to be college football's first ever father-son coaching matchup. After Terry Bowden's departure, Auburn ultimately bought out the contract to play FSU. This action inspired accusations of cowardice by rival fans and critics. One writer opened his assessment of the cancellation with "War Chicken" (Clyde Bolton, "AU's Retreat a Cowardly Decision," *Birmingham News* (February 7, 1999): 1-B).

television—it's wonderful."[i] Wide receiver Ronney Daniels read a great deal of optimism into the result. "This shows us that we can beat anybody in the SEC."[j] Tuberville, too, drew confidence from the win. "They won't vote us in, but it's like everything else. We'll have to earn it."[k] David Housel was excited about being 3–0. "This is just the start." [l] What happened to climbing out of the bottom? Didn't Tuberville say it would be bumpy?

It Gets Bumpy

After the win at LSU, Auburn returned home only to suffer an overtime loss to Ole Miss. It was the beginning of a five-game losing streak that critically wounded our chances of making a bowl game in Tuberville's first season. What happened? Ben Leard suffered a dislocated shoulder in the third quarter against Ole Miss. He did not return until the eighth game of the season (against Arkansas). In the interim, Jeff Klein threw four touchdowns and seven interceptions.[2] After losing to Ole Miss we traveled to Knoxville. Damon Duval again the stole the show, this time by bickering with Tuberville after a botched fake punt. Tuberville sent Duval to the locker room. On the way, he flashed a peace sign and a goofy face to the TV audience. It was undignified. So was the outcome. The Vols beat us 24–0. The next week's game was closer, but, in a sense, uglier.

We slowly built a 16–0 lead against Mississippi State, but the Bulldogs kicked a field goal in the third quarter and scored a touchdown with 2:28 left in the fourth to make the score 16–10. Jackie Sherrill chose to kick deep rather than try an onsides. All we had to do was run out the clock, but we could not. We ran the ball three times and then faced fourth-and-eleven. Instead of punting,

---

[2] Any comparison between the two quarterbacks might be unfair. All the opponents for Auburn's five consecutive losses finished the season in the Top 25. The three teams Leard faced to begin the season were I-AA Appalachian State, Idaho from the WAC, and LSU, whose final record in 1999 was 3–8.

Tuberville had Duval run out-of-bounds in our end zone for an intentional safety, making the score 16–12. State responded by returning the free kick 41 yards. Four plays later they scored the winning touchdown.

This conclusion made me sick to my stomach, and I put all the blame on Tuberville. Afterwards, he said, "What makes it tough is these players practice hard and they fight hard. They got great character and great attitude and we should have won this game . . . ."[m] I agreed we should have won the game. Our team did not play very well, but State played worse; it looked like our coach found a way to give them the game. Over the next few years, whenever I was upset with Tuberville, I would say we should have fired him after the State game in 1999.

The losing streak ended with a win over Central Florida. The next week brought the most surprising and impressive victory of the season: a 38–21 win over 14th-ranked Georgia in Athens. Ben Leard looked like a Heisman candidate, completing passes to eight different receivers for 416 yards and four touchdowns with no interceptions. Unfortunately, we followed up this big win the same way we did the LSU game—by coming back down to earth.

Injustice at Jordan-Hare

Tuberville's first Alabama game was my final game as a student. Like Dye—and ultimately Tuberville—I ended with a loss to the Tide. The game was a tale of two halves: Auburn led 14–6 at the break, but Alabama outscored us 22–3 in the final two quarters for a 28–17 win. I stayed till the bitter end, despite the best efforts of a malicious pretzel vendor.

My brother and I found seats in the student section at the very top of the South end zone, in the eastern corner; Jordan was in high school at the time.[3] From our position we could look down onto the stadium concourse and see a pretzel vendor wearing an Alabama sweatshirt. I doubt we would have noticed him if not for the two guys sitting in front of us. We did not appreciate the presence of an Alabama fan doing business in the student section at Jordan-Hare Stadium. The guys in front of us, however, did appreciate the opportunity to throw ice at him.

Perhaps these young men had played this game before; or, maybe they saw something we did not. Either way, after a few minutes of pelting the bama-fan-pretzel-monger, they wisely relocated. So when a police officer ascended the stairs to our row after the culprits' departure, who did he grab? Me. I suspect the pretzel vendor described my hat to the police. It was distinctive: a navy hat, purchased in the 1980s by my uncle, with a simple orange A rather than an interlocking AU. As the officer began leading me away, a few surrounding students attempted to save me by making false reports of distress at the other end of the section. It didn't work. A friend saw me being escorted down the steps, and I enjoyed offering the standard cliché, "This is not what it looks like." We reached the bottom of the steps and proceeded through

---

[3] In 1999, one could still sneak a friend into the student section by simply entering the seating area and then sending one's student ID back out with an individual who was willing to pass it along to the non-student waiting under the stands. In 2000, the University began efforts to curb this practice. The first method was to stamp students' hands as they came in the gate, thus requiring a student to roll the top of his or her hand (finger-printing style) against the top of the non-student's hand to transfer the image. In 2001, they introduced a wristband policy that required the student to successfully remove the wristband—without doing too much damage—and pass it out to the waiting non-student. Nowadays, access to the non-seating areas behind/beneath the student section is controlled, and the student ID is swiped (as a ticket) upon entering the stadium. To my knowledge, this level of control virtually eliminates sneaking in non-students. Of course, non-students can still get into the student section, provided they have the ID of a student who will not attend the game. As of 2013, the last time I sat in the student section was 2009, against West Virginia. Yes, I remained in the stands throughout the rain delay; probably a good one to end on.

the tunnel to the concourse, where the officer handed me off to another officer, who began leading me toward the gate. Suddenly, it hit me; "What?! Are you throwing me out?!"

Throughout the proceedings to this point I had naïvely assumed this misunderstanding would be easily cleared up once I had a chance to explain myself. It never occurred to me that the police might eject an innocent student simply on the word of an Alabama-fan-pretzel-vendor. Once I realized what was going on, I began to talk very quickly. I told the officer that I was not the one who threw the ice. He did not seem to care. I then said something about having a right to face my accuser. Whence came this appeal? The previous school year Matt and I watched two episodes of Law and Order per day on A&E; plus, of course, a third episode Wednesday nights on NBC. I asked for the name of the vendor. The officer told me to wait outside the gate, and that he would bring it to me. I did not believe him. "No! Give me your word that you are going to bring me his name and address; because I will be filing suit after the first of the year." I do not know why I said that. Nonetheless, my New York (that is, Hollywood) legal training actually seemed to be getting me somewhere. I then made an excited, desperate utterance of truth: "I told my little brother I'd be right back." To this appeal the officer responded by saying he was about to turn around, and that when he turned back around, I better be gone, and I better not return to the same seat in the stadium.

The way the game ended, of course, one might argue justice proved unmerciful. I am glad, however, to not have the ignominious distinction of being kicked out of my final game as a student.

A Foundation Built?

Tuberville, unfortunately, did earn the distinction of being the first Auburn coach to lose to Alabama at Jordan-Hare Stadium. The loss finalized the record at 5–6, making Tuberville's first Auburn campaign a losing season.

How are we to evaluate Tuberville's debut season? The coach himself judged the results in relation to what he considered realistic expectations. He prefaced his assessment by saying there can be no satisfaction in a losing season, but he certainly sounded happy regarding the bigger picture.

> Just looking at the groundwork we've done within our weight room, with the redshirt guys we didn't play, with the discipline and the enthusiasm of the players we have, we're a lot farther along than I would have even imagined at this time.[n]

Tuberville was not the only one who thought the program was making progress.

At season's end there were rumors Tuberville would soon be leaving Auburn for Baton Rouge. After returning from a duck-hunting trip to Arkansas, Tuberville claimed some LSU boosters had approached him about the job, but that he told them he was not interested.[o] These boosters must have agreed Auburn had been at the bottom, and that Tuberville was pulling us out.

I do not remember just what I thought about Tuberville after 1999. As noted above, I wanted to fire him after the loss to State. Would I have been upset had he left us for LSU? I don't know. The bottom line for me was that Tuberville was not Pat Dye. Of course, there was nothing he could do in one season to excuse that flaw.

Nonetheless, by the summer of 2000 I was looking forward to the new season with great anticipation. I was far from coming to grips with no longer being an Auburn student. In football season everyone acts, to some degree, as though he or she is a student. I was more than ready to entertain that delusion.

Among the New Faces

Before we move on to 2000, there are two more staff additions in 1999 not mentioned above that are worth noting.

In January 1999 Tuberville hired Kevin Yoxall to be the Tigers' strength and conditioning coach. How badly did we need new direction in this area? Ben Leard recalls the first spring practice with Yoxall.

> The team went in the indoor facility and ran three sprints. There were double-digit guys who quit that day, whether they be walk-ons or scholarship guys. That showed us how far out of shape we were as a football team.[p]

Rob Pate also remembers this workout in his book, A Tiger's Walk. Pate explains that each "sprint" was actually a *gasser*—that is, running from one sideline to the other four consecutive times for a total distance of 208 yards. "We had guys throwing up all over the place. One guy was vomiting blood."[q] Pate goes on to say that before he left Auburn "we could all run three gassers in our sleep without a problem."[r] Obviously, Yoxall's presence made a difference.

Another addition Tuberville made in 1999 was not just a new hire, but a new position. He created Auburn's first ever full-time football chaplaincy. The man he brought in for that role still holds the position today—Chette Williams. According to Williams, Tuberville told him, "I've got my offensive coordinator and my defensive coordinator, and I'm looking for a spiritual coordinator."[s]

In his book, Hard Fighting Soldier, Williams describes one of the differences between his role and that of the previous, part-time position.

Previous Auburn football teams had a local pastor who served as chaplain and on Saturday mornings offered a devotional to a few of the players. Coach Tuberville changed all that. He scheduled my devotional for Friday night before games, after the entire team had finished eating dinner together. He wanted to make sure every player heard the message.[t]

In a later chapter we will note an instance when this adjustment by Tuberville made a remarkable impact on our team.

3

2000

The outlook for 2000 was markedly different from the year before. In August 1999 Tuberville tentatively named a starting quarterback by default. In 2000 we had a proven leader in Ben Leard. Also, we had a new player in the backfield behind Leard.

In 2000 Tuberville welcomed junior college transfer Rudi Johnson to Auburn. Johnson had rushed for 2,224 yards and 31 touchdowns in 1999 at Butler County Community College in Kansas. Rudi's arrival gave Auburn fans hope for once again running the ball effectively.[1] It was easy to imagine Rudi running behind Heath Evans, and Tuberville told us the offense would include some two-back sets. Relative stability in the backfield did not, of course, mean all the Tigers' personnel issues were resolved.

---

[1] Stephen Davis led Auburn in rushing in 1995 with 1,068 yards. The leading rushers for the years 1996–1999 averaged 389 yards.

All the starters—and most of the reserves—from the 1999 defensive line were gone.[2] Other positions lacked depth as well. Tuberville was uneasy about relying on inexperienced players.

> About half of them [the players new to the team in 2000] are going to play this season . . . You really don't want to play that many, but we don't have a choice.[a]

He contrasted our personnel situation to the competition.

> So many teams have a jump on us . . . It's kind of like we're just out of the blocks and everybody else is halfway around the track. We're just trying to play catch-up in a lot of areas.[b]

Tuberville seemed to be making excuses for games not yet lost. He did, however, balance the poor-mouthing with a reminder of his vision for the program; and added a plea for the Auburn Family to do our part. "If you stay positive, we're going to win that national championship a lot sooner than people think."[c] Most people were not thinking about Auburn winning a championship in the summer of 2000. Sports Illustrated ranked the Tigers 55th in their season preview; the summary read simply, "Nation's third-worst rushing attack hopes that juco transfer Rudi Johnson is the answer at tailback."[d] Only the story on the field would tell whether those hopes were well-founded.

Two Key Players: One on the Field, the Other Not Yet

Before we look at how the 2000 season played out, there are two preseason personnel decisions by Tuberville worth mentioning. Firstly, he chose to keep Damon Duval as both his placekicker and

---

[2] Starters Leonardo Carson, Quinton Reese, and Marcus Washington were all selected in the 2000 NFL Draft.

punter. This decision is remarkable given Tuberville's comments about Duval after the 1999 season.

> I think it [Duval's kicking] cost us three games. It could have cost us more than that . . . This [finding a new kicker] is a priority. We're looking at junior college and we're looking at high school players. We'll sign one and we're going to remedy that problem.[e]

It appeared Duval, who took over for Rob Bironas in 1999, would now himself lose the job to a newcomer.[3] True to his word, Tuberville signed highly-touted kicker Philip Yost. When Yost failed to stand out in summer camp, Tuberville said the job was open; ultimately, Duval won it.

Another key personnel decision was made at quarterback. As noted above, the starting job in 2000 clearly belonged to Ben Leard. Nonetheless, a particular freshman garnered considerable attention in preseason practices—a quarterback Auburn fans know well: Jason Campbell. Redshirting Campbell was a no brainer despite his performance in practice. To credit Tuberville for prolonging Campbell's eligibility to 2004 is, therefore, to acknowledge he had established depth at the position. Had Tuberville not signed Allen Tillman in the 1999 class and brought in junior college transfer Daniel Cobb in 2000, who can say how Campbell's availability might have been viewed differently?

---

[3] The situation in 1999 was not really as simple as Duval just winning the job in midseason. Bironas, who was All-SEC in 1998, started the 1999 season poorly and was replaced by Duval. On two occasions, however, Tuberville announced Bironas had won the job back, but after each such announcement Tuberville later suspended Bironas for violation of unspecified team rules. After the second suspension, Tuberville said Bironas was likely gone for good; otherwise, the swapping out might have continued all season. Bironas later transferred to I-AA Georgia Southern. He is currently the kicker for the Tennessee Titans, a job he has held since 2005.

The 2000 Season

The big story from the first game of Tuberville's second season was not that we won, but how we won—running the football. Rudi Johnson carried 27 times for 174 yards and three touchdowns in a 35–21 victory over Wyoming. Johnson's performance was well complemented by Leard's. He threw for 266 yards plus two touchdowns with no interceptions. Yes, it was only Wyoming, but this win certainly inspired more optimism than the previous year's near-calamity against Appalachian State. After getting the first win of the season, the Tigers hit the road. Nonetheless, for Tuberville the second game of 2000 was—in a way—close to home.

Before There Was Tuberville Orange . . .

On September 9, 2000 Tommy Tuberville returned to Oxford, Mississippi to face the team he coached from 1995 through 1998. Tuberville spoke reflectively about revisiting the Magnolia State.

> The game this week is going to be a little emotional for myself and the coaches…We're going back for the first time to a place that is very dear to us. It was an opportunity for me to be a head coach and a head coach in the SEC.[f]

He also acknowledged that some Ole Miss fans might anticipate his homecoming differently.

> I know there'll be some hot tempers in the stands… Hopefully, the security there is good enough to make sure everything is equal on both sides and that the coaches and players can concentrate on the game at hand.[g]

Was there reason for Tuberville to be concerned about security? To understand how the Rebels felt about Tuberville after his time in

Oxford, we have to remember what he did there, and the way that he left.

Tuberville's first head coaching opportunity was not an enviable one. Ole Miss posted a record of 5–6 in 1993. When the NCAA began investigating recruiting violations in July 1994, the school fired head coach Billy Brewer. Defensive coordinator Joe Lee Dunn was named interim head coach, and the Rebels went 4–7 in 1994. In November 1994 the NCAA announced the penalties against the Rebels: four years probation; a two-year post-season ban; a one-year television ban; loss of 12 scholarships in each of the next two years; and, reduced recruiting visits for two years. Reportedly, the NCAA determined that nothing had changed at Ole Miss since they were found guilty of essentially the same violations in 1986, hence the severity of the sanctions.[4] It was into these dire straits that Tuberville stepped when he took over at Ole Miss. What he was able to do despite the circumstances quickly made him an attractive prospect for larger programs.

In his first year at Ole Miss—1995—Tuberville won six games, good enough for the Rebels' first winning season since 1992. He further endeared himself to the fan base by beating Mississippi State. The 1996 season was a slight regression at 5–6, but still respectable given the NCAA probation. In 1997, when the crippling effects of reduced scholarships should have been especially evident, the Rebels won seven regular-season games, earning a bowl game appearance in their first year eligible after the post-season ban. The Rebels again beat Mississippi State; then Marshall in the Motor City Bowl. He was now Tommy Tuberville, miracle worker. After the 1997 season, he was a candidate to be the next head coach at Texas and was offered the head coach position at Arkansas. Just how high was Tuberville's stock at the

---

[4] Billy Brewer had been the head coach since 1983.

time? Some were saying he might be hired to replace Barry Switzer as head coach of the Dallas Cowboys.[h]

While other schools dreamed of what Tuberville could do with their resources, Ole Miss fans wanted to see how many games he could win with their program at full strength. Should they have known Tuberville would soon parlay his success into a higher-profile job? Yes, but college football fans are under no obligation to be logical. So what Tuberville did when he was in Oxford shaped how Ole Miss people viewed him after he left. Before we revisit the way Tuberville left Ole Miss, let's look at one more thing he did in Oxford—something not apparent from the records of wins and losses.

When Tuberville asked the Auburn Family to wear orange on game day, it wasn't the first time he changed the complexion of an SEC stadium. In September 1997 Tuberville wrote an open letter to the Ole Miss students asking them to stop waving Confederate flags at football games.

> I'm asking everyone that supports Ole Miss and the Rebels to use good judgment on what you elect to bring into the stadium, not only on game day, but at every event that you support. It's time to support our teams physically, mentally and morally with enthusiasm and not with symbols.[i]

Tuberville's motivation for removing the flag was pragmatic—he was more concerned with his ability to recruit broadly than with preservation of an Ole Miss tradition. When asked about negative responses to his appeal, Tuberville explained what it was all about.

> I don't want to start attacking any groups. I've told those people that 'I'm not saying your cause is good or bad, but my cause is to win games and what you're doing is at my expense, basically.'[j]

In response to Tuberville's request, the Ole Miss Student Body Association passed a resolution asking their fellow students to stop bringing the flags to games; and the University altered game-day policies so as to prohibit sticks of any kind (including flag sticks) inside the stadium. These formal efforts to keep the flag out initially increased its presence. After all, the students were Rebels. The University held its position, and in time the flag more or less disappeared. So while Tuberville made his mark on the field in Oxford, he all the more left it in the stands. Still, neither winning games nor changing game day is Tuberville's closest, lasting association with Ole Miss.

Jilted Rebels

The Rebels managed to keep their coach despite his popularity in 1997, but it was only a matter of time. When Terry Bowden resigned in October 1998, Tuberville was immediately thought a candidate for the job. Three weeks later, however, he expressed his commitment to Ole Miss. "I'm not involved in the Auburn thing and don't want to be . . . I have a job and look forward to being here a long time."[k] Tuberville later said he had some tough decisions to make regarding his career. Then, apparently having resolved these tough decisions, Tuberville made his famous declaration—the prime example of job-search coach-speak: "They'll have to carry me out of here in a pine box." So when he was announced as Auburn's new head coach just two days after the 1998 Egg Bowl, the Rebels saw Tuberville not just as a deserter, but also as a liar.[5]

When Tuberville returned to Oxford in 2000, Ole Miss had already gained a measure of revenge by beating his Tigers the year before. That game was at Jordan-Hare Stadium. The Rebels more

---

[5] Presumably, Tuberville actually left Oxford in a baby blue Chevy Lumina, as that is what Rob Pate saw him driving in Auburn the weekend after the announcement. (Pate, Rob. *A Tiger's Walk*. Kindle edition: location 1016.)

so wanted to teach Tuberville a lesson in Oxford—as evidenced by record attendance at the game of 52,368.[1] Unfortunately—for those tens of thousands and more hoping to defend the honor of Colonel Reb—Tuberville brought Rudi Johnson with him. Johnson rushed for 165 yards and two touchdowns. The Tigers won 35–27. To Ole Miss, Tuberville was a returning traitor. His players treated him like a returning victor, carrying him to midfield on their shoulders at the end of the game. His first trip to Oxford as an opposing head coach was a success. The next week would bring another first for Tuberville at Auburn.

The third game of the 2000 season was the first time a Tommy-Tuberville-coached Auburn team entered a contest ranked in the top 25. We were no. 24. Our opponent, LSU, was unranked, having beaten only Western Carolina and Houston (as noted above, LSU was 3–8 in 1999). The LSU game was a first for me as well— it was the first game I attended as an Auburn alumnus.

Legends of the Amphitheater

The 2000 LSU game is one of my favorite Auburn football memories, but not on account of the game itself. Tuberville's second season was the first since 1994 that I did not live in walking distance of Jordan-Hare Stadium. So the LSU game would be my first time, as an adult, to travel to an Auburn home game. I had a clear vision of just how I wanted the day to look. How it turned out fulfilled my vision and exceeded my expectations.

The first emphasis of my vision was personnel. I wanted our traveling party to consist of myself, my brother Jordan, and my friends Sam Lasseter and Joshua "Action" Jackson. I knew this combination was potentially volatile. Sam and my brother did not always get along. Also, Jordan does not always tolerate loud people. He had never before met Action, who prior to domestication was rather loud. I accepted the risk. Sam and Jordan accepted the invitation, but Action was initially reticent, complaining of financial shortcomings. I told him I would pay for his ticket and his food; suddenly, it sounded like a fine idea.

My second emphasis was to leave early enough to secure the perfect tailgating spot. Growing up, my family usually tailgated next to the wooded area where Duncan Dr. ended (just past Sasnett Residence Hall).[6] On a few Saturdays, however, when we got to campus early enough, we would park off the road that circled Bibb Graves Amphitheater. That location was the nexus of the Auburn Tailgating Spirit—perhaps the very zenith of all of football tailgating.[7] The Amphitheatre is at the heart of campus. On game day it is a center of diversion where people focus only on tailgating itself; even the game, for a moment, is of minor concern. The location's proximity to the stadium means there is heavy pedestrian traffic; plenty of people watching. The fulfillment of my vision required that we get to campus early enough to park at the Amphitheatre. Sam was a graduate student at Jacksonville State at the time, which is where he met Action, who was a JSU freshman. Jordan and I would be leaving from Gadsden that morning; I mandated that we would get to Jacksonville in time to depart from there by 7:30 am. Kickoff was at 6:30 pm. I was serious about this vision.

The third emphasis of my vision was alcohol; not that I wanted us to have some obscene amount—I just didn't want to run out. I knew all three components had to be in place to accomplish the perfect home-game road trip; I planned accordingly.

---

[6] Currently, Duncan Dr. does not end here, but continues south past the new Forestry and Wildlife Sciences Building and then ends at its intersection with Lem Morrison Dr. / Mell St.

[7] Talking heads frequently espouse the Grove at Oxford as some kind of Eighth Wonder of the SEC. I imagine before it became so densely populated as to resemble a refugee camp, the Grove must have been something like the Amphitheatre.

We stopped in Anniston to remove most of the soft drinks from the cooler (Jordan and I had started the day at our parents' house) and replace them with beer and bottles of Mike's Hard Lemonade. We made it to Auburn early enough to secure the perfect tailgating spot at the Amphitheatre. I was pleased.

What did we do all day? We fulfilled my vision—we did nothing but tailgate and have a good time. I issued a decree that anyone wishing to drink a Mike's Hard Lemonade must precede it with an Icehouse.[8] I figured this rule would slow consumption in general and protect our inventory. It worked; not that we just sat around and drank all day—we also passed a lot of time throwing the football, but not just any football.

Somewhere in our childhood my brother and I heard about some gold standard of a football known as the "1001." We knew if we wanted to own the official football, the all-supreme football of footballs, we had to have a "1001." And it came to pass on Christmas Day, I guess 1988 give or take a year, our Grandmother gave us the "1001"—not a ball like the 1001, not any synthetic-leather duplicate, but the very materialization of the game: from Heisman, to Shug, to Dye—the whole history and essence of the sport was there to be held in our hands. By 2000, this ball was showing its age, and when I was loading the Camry for our epic journey, it occurred to me: *maybe it's time for a new football*. But

---

[8] When I first began reconstructing this day, I was surprised to not remember what type of beer we drank. I guessed maybe it had been Miller Lite, a notion to which my brother in a 2012 interview responded, "You can class it up by saying it was Miller Lite, but it was Icehouse." When I asked Action, he did not remember, only confident that it was "something raunchy." When I told him Jordan's response, Action agreed, recalling that Sam drank Icehouse during his Gamecock tenure. Sam did not remember, but when I told him Jordan's response, he said I had always been considerate of what others preferred to drink—I don't remember this either—and that, yes, he had been a big Icehouse guy at the time. That the beer we had was a kind only Sam would voluntarily drink is consistent with my perceived need to protect the Mike's Hard Lemonade inventory.

the 1001 did make the trip, and at one point in the afternoon a passerby, a young man, called to me, asking me to hit him one time. I did so. He began to throw it back, but then stopped. Something caught his eye. He examined the ball in his hands; a moment of realization visible on his face. He looked up at me and said, "This is a *real* football."

Around noon I sent Action and Jordan uptown with cash and instructions to buy their tickets and everyone's lunch. Sam and I already had tickets, so we sat around and drank while our junior partners walked across campus.[9]

Later in the afternoon Jordan needed a nap; or, as Action put it in a 2012 interview, "Your brother decided to go back to bed." Jordan is 6' 2". He laid down in the backseat of the Camry with his bare feet sticking out the window. Several passersby asked if he was ok. One particular gentleman took notice of Jordan's podiatric vulnerability. This gentleman, who was drinking a beer as he walked—I do not think it was his first of the day—briefly tickled Jordan's feet before his less inebriated wife pulled him away. He explained himself, "Hey, that's feet. You can f— with feet!"

Eventually, it was time for the game. We of course snuck into the student section. The students stand virtually the entire game, which made it easier for Jordan to stretch out on a bleacher and resume his nap. It was just as well—LSU led 10–0 at the end of the first quarter. The exciting stuff came later.

Ultimately, Ben Leard and Rudi Johnson both performed the way they did the first two weeks. The highlight of the game, however, came from a different member of the Auburn offense. LSU scored with 6:45 left in the third quarter to make it Auburn

---

[9] Per Action's memory, Sam and Jordan were the hunter-gatherers, and he and I stayed at the tailgate. I think it is possible two excursions were made.

20, LSU 17. Tim Carter returned the ensuing kickoff 100 yards for a touchdown. Tuberville described the impact of Carter's crowd-igniting sprint: "I thought that was a deciding blow . . . We've been waiting on that. He's been getting close . . . getting close for two years now."[m] Auburn controlled the rest of the game and won 34–17.

My vision of the perfect game-day experience had not even required a win, so to beat LSU and become 3–0 (and already 2–0 in conference) well exceeded my expectations. I am thankful for that day. Not everyone has yet experienced his or her ideal tailgate. Were we to consider my tailgating career in analogy to Tuberville's tenure at Auburn, LSU 2000 was my 2004.

In the weeks following the LSU game we added convincing wins over Northern Illinois and Vanderbilt, after which we were 5–0 and ranked 19th. Things were looking good. Unfortunately, they soon took a turn for the worse.

Lesser Hospitality

Sam somehow got the idea to buy tickets for the Mississippi State game at Starkville. I guess he was riding the high of winning and wanted to see us beat the Bulldogs in person. I wish it had worked out. To the contrary, State did what not one else had been able— they stopped Rudi Johnson, who gained only 26 yards rushing. Actually, State stopped our entire offense; we failed to earn a first down in the first half. One person who could not be stopped that day was the DJ.

As bewildering were the events on the field, even more so was a phenomenon that pervaded the stadium and all the campus. I have never seen a group of people so fired up about "Who Let the Dogs Out." They played it after every single down. After the game, while Sam and I were waiting to get out of the parking field, we found ourselves stuck for a moment beside another vehicle. The driver rolled down his window and yelled at us, "This is for you guys!" He then hit play on his stereo, which blared *Who let the dogs out*! He proceeded to jam out in his car *con mucho gusto*. How is one to respond to such a display, "Congratulations?"

The next week, Florida seemed to score as frequently as the Starkville PA had let the dogs out. The Gators scored five touchdowns in the first half en route to a 38–7 victory. Things did not look as good after two consecutive losses, but Tuberville put the situation into perspective: "We're 5–2 and have a chance to have an excellent season."[n] Starting the next week, the end of the regular season looked a lot like the beginning.

The Road to Atlanta

In the eighth game of the season Auburn played Louisiana Tech for Homecoming. It was not an especially satisfying win: La Tech, who entered the game at 2–5, led 14–7 at the end of the first quarter. Auburn eventually took control, but the Bulldogs cut the lead to 10 with seven minutes left in the game. Fortunately, that was the end of the scoring; we won 38–28. Though a lackluster victory, the game contained a milestone for the offense: on a five-yard run in the third quarter Rudi Johnson eclipsed the 1,000-yard mark for the season. Tuberville spoke highly of Rudi after the game.

> We knew Rudi would get 100-150 yards, but I never expected 249. He just continues to get better. One guy never brings him down. He gets stronger as the game goes on. And he was the difference in the ball game.[o]

The remaining schedule gave reason to hope Rudi would continue getting better. With a record of 6–2, our remaining opponents were Arkansas, Georgia and Alabama.

With these games remaining, Auburn had the same number of SEC losses as everyone else in the West: two. The division was wide open in some regard, but we did not control our own destiny; the loss to Mississippi State meant the Bulldogs had to lose for the Tigers to make it to Atlanta.

Against Arkansas, we managed a 21–14 advantage through three quarters and made two interceptions (by Stanford Simmons and Rodney Crayton) to hang on for a 21–19 win.[10] The Tigers then had their first off week of the season—a much needed rest after playing nine consecutive Saturdays.

We needed all the strength a day of rest could supply in the next game, against Georgia. The Bulldogs led 13–0 until Damon Duval hit a 48-yard field goal as time expired in the first half. We went on to take a 23–13 lead, but Georgia scored ten fourth-quarter points to send the game into overtime. Georgia had the first overtime possession and kicked a field goal. On our possession, Rudi Johnson took over, gaining 24 yards on three carries. Tuberville said after the game, "We should have won it in regular time, but we went to overtime and kept our poise."[p] Georgia, however, must have felt they should have won the game in regulation. They had a solid late-fourth-quarter drive and earned first-and-goal at the Auburn eight with under two minutes left. After an incompletion, and then a completion for no gain, Georgia ran the ball down to the Auburn two, but settled for a game-tying field goal on fourth down. Georgia's kicker, Billy Bennet, made four of four attempts in the game, including one in overtime. Our kicker, Damon Duval, made three of three (from 48, 37 and 49). Duval played a significant role the next week as well.

---

[10] We failed to run out the clock after the second interception. On fourth down, Duval lined up to punt and then tried to kill time in the end zone before stepping out of bounds for a safety, *a la* Mississippi State, 1999. This time, fortunately, only three seconds remained after the safety, and time expired as Arkansas attempted to return the free kick.

Beautiful Tuscaloosa

The final game of the 2000 regular season gave Tuberville a unique opportunity. Having become in 1999 the first Auburn coach to lose to Alabama at Jordan-Hare Stadium, Tuberville now led the Tigers into the first Auburn-Alabama game to be played in Tuscaloosa in the modern era. Though we entered the game with an 8–2 record, and Alabama was 3–7, the Tigers were only favored by one point. I am sure Tuberville would have been happy with a one-point win. That would have been enough to secure a tie for the SEC Western Division championship, necessitating only a loss by Mississippi State to Arkansas for Auburn to represent the division in the SEC championship game.

November 18, 2000 was a beautiful day in Tuscaloosa—41° and raining at kickoff. The game mostly matched what one would expect in such weather. Neither team threw the ball very well: Auburn's Ben Leard completed 10 of 20 attempts with two interceptions; Alabama's Andrew Zow connected on 12 of 29 attempts and threw one interception. The Tigers established control by winning the line of scrimmage. Rudi Johnson carried 37 times for 130 yards. One way the game did not reflect the conditions was their apparent non-effect on Damon Duval. Like the week before, Duval made three kicks on three attempts. He was the game's only scorer: Auburn 9 – Alabama 0.

Tuberville earned his first victory over Alabama, and Auburn avenged its first loss to Alabama at Jordan-Hare by winning the rivalry's first game in Tuscaloosa since 1901. On the same day, in Starkville, Mississippi State lost to Arkansas. Auburn's win over Alabama therefore clinched an appearance in the SEC championship game. Tuberville reflected upon the accomplishment: "It's been a fun day. It's been a fun year. As I told the team, they just earned themselves another game."[q] Most of the fun of the 2000 season, unfortunately, came to an end that day on the wet turf at Tuberville-Deny Stadium.

Problems With, and In, Florida

Arkansas beat LSU the following week, making Auburn the outright Western Division champion. For 2000 there would be no higher championships. We lost to Florida 28–6 in the SEC Championship in a game that looked more or less like the previous meeting in October. Nonetheless, the nine-win regular season earned Auburn a New-Year's-Day bowl appearance, against Michigan in the Citrus Bowl.

The Citrus Bowl was something of a shootout. Ben Leard threw for 394 yards, and the two teams combined for 939 yards of offense. Leard's last touchdown as an Auburn Tiger came with 2:26 left in the game, a 21-yard pass to Deandre Green that cut Michigan's lead to three. We failed to recover the onside kick, and Michigan successfully ran out the clock. The loss dropped Auburn's final record for 2000 to 9–4.

Tuberville's second year as Auburn's head coach may be evaluated simply this way: he won a championship. Yes, it was only an SEC Western Division Championship, but it was still a higher accomplishment than expected. Furthermore, the nine wins in 2000 were more than the total wins in the previous two years combined. The University felt Tuberville had performed well enough that another program might attempt to lure him away. In the week prior to the Georgia game, Tuberville was awarded with a contract extension and a raise.

—The 1001 has seen a lot of abuse since 2000.

4

2001

The first story of the 2000-2001 off-season is the exodus of skill players from Auburn's offense. Ben Leard actually graduated prior to 2000 and played his remaining eligible year as a graduate student. Rudi Johnson, Heath Evans and leading receiver Ronney Daniels all left early for the NFL Draft. Had Johnson and Evans stuck around for 2001, their presence might have eased the quarterback transition. The impact of Johnson's departure, however, extended well beyond the 2001 season.

Who Will Run the Ball?

In early January 2001 the top high school recruit in the state of Alabama was planning to play college football as a Volunteer. While Auburn and Alabama were both on his list, Tennessee was decidedly at the top. When Rudi Johnson declared for the draft, Auburn suddenly had a new selling point. "With Rudi not there, it means I could become the No. 1 guy my freshman year. Auburn is still my second choice but now it has become a close second."[a] Aspiring to be the number-one running back at an SEC school as a true freshman is rather ambitious; but, perhaps not unreasonable when the freshman is Carnell Williams. Cadillac visited Auburn after Johnson's departure was announced, and Tuberville took advantage of the situation.

> They showed me a video of the past, present and future of Auburn football. It showed Bo, Stephen Davis, Rudi Johnson and then they showed a clip of me running the ball. It made me feel like I was important to them now, not when my senior year comes. I didn't get any promises or handouts from them, but I will have the opportunity to be the starting running back this year.[b]

Williams accepted the opportunity. He was not the only high-profile recruit to choose Auburn in 2001. Wide receiver Anthony Mix and defensive tackle Wayne Dickens were also among Tuberville's best class yet. The strong recruiting effort showed Tuberville knew how to carry over the momentum of success. One thing he did not know in 2001 was who would be his next starting quarterback.

Who Will Throw It?

The quarterback competition in the spring and summer of 2001 was wide open. The contenders were: Jeff Klein, who played about half the 1999 season with unremarkable results; junior-college transfer and former Georgia quarterback Daniel Cobb; and redshirt freshman Jason Campbell. Cobb was no. 1 on the depth chart after A-Day, and while Tuberville said the competition was ongoing, he also wanted the starter established sooner rather than later.

> I think the next four months, this position will be up for grabs, but it won't be up long in two-a-days. I'll have a first-team quarterback within a week when we come in for two-a-days. You've got to have somebody to consistently run your offense.[c]

44

In fall camp, however, the coaches consistently postponed naming a starter.

"We'll draw straws."[d] That's how offensive coordinator Noel Mazzone described the quarterback dilemma in mid-August. After the final scrimmage of the summer, the situation was different. Tuberville announced he had found a leader.

> The main thing was to look at the players in the huddle, see if they're listening to the quarterbacks; who's taking control. There's more to it than just going out and throwing the ball. You've got to be a leader, got to run the huddle and you've got to have the confidence of your teammates.[e]

Tuberville's leader was Jason Campbell. With an inexperienced quarterback taking over, and last season's playmakers gone, expectations for 2001 were unsurprisingly low.

In a Birmingham News poll, the 12 SEC sports information directors picked Auburn to finish fifth in the SEC West. Other predictions varied considerably. The Sporting News ranked us a relatively optimistic 36. It only goes down from there. Lindy's put us at 45; Athlon, 63. Kevin Scarbinsky of the Birmingham News described the low expectations as an opportunity for Tuberville.

> When Auburn wins seven or eight games and contends for the SEC West title and reaches a bowl game—without Rudi Johnson and Ben Leard and Ronney Daniels and Heath Evans—the experts won't say they weren't smart. They'll say Tuberville's a genius.[f]

Did Tuberville prove himself a genius in 2001? Let's take a look at the season and decide.

The 2001 Season

The season opener was pleasantly unremarkable—a 31–0 win over Ball State in which our defense allowed only 92 total yards. The second game of the season, against Ole Miss, looked to be just as comfortable a win—we led 27–0 midway through the third quarter; but, a few key completions by Eli Manning (and a few key penalties by the Tigers) made things tight. We held on for a 27–21 win. While Manning had the bigger game in some regards, our quarterback was the more efficient that day, and came away from the game with a 2–0 record as a starter.

With two games under his belt, Jason Campbell appeared to be well adjusted in his new role. Mazzone liked Campbell's progress. "We're pretty much staying on schedule on how I thought we'd add stuff, and right now, I think he's a little bit ahead of schedule in what we've put in our game plan."[g] It was a good thing Campbell was ahead of schedule. We would not be able to rely upon a simplified offense at LSU the way we did against Ball State and Ole Miss. Or, that would have been the case had the two teams played that Saturday; but they did not—nobody did.

Timeout

It is strange now to think the SEC ever considered playing on the Saturday following the September 11, 2001 terrorist attacks. Of course, we cannot require of the decision makers then the insight retrospection provides. On the day of the tragedy, Tuesday, the conference announced that the decision on whether to play would be made by Thursday.[h] Auburn began making bus arrangements in case flying to Baton Rouge on Friday would not be possible. The next day the member institutions actually voted unanimously to play the games as scheduled. SEC Commissioner Roy Kramer said the vote was taken after a consultation with presidential advisers Haley Barbour and Karl Rove. The White House was encouraging people to get back to normalcy, and the SEC presidents and athletic directors obliged.[i] Or, at least I am sure that is how they would prefer their action be remembered. There was also speculation the SEC simply did not want the headache of rescheduling games.[1] It was not until Thursday, after the NFL cancelled their games for Sunday, that the SEC and other leagues decided to take the weekend off. Tuberville's position on the matter was unremarkably compliant. After the conference voted to play, he supported the initiative to move on.[2] After the games were postponed, he said not playing was the right decision.[3] With the LSU game put off, the next team on Auburn's schedule became Syracuse. The Tigers devoted a little extra time to preparing for the Orangemen once the trip to Baton Rouge was postponed, but it would not be enough.

Play Resumes, Somewhat

I do not watch much pro football, but I watched enough in the last ten years to hear Dwight Freeney's name a few hundred times; and, every time I did, I thought about the night he single-handedly shut down our offense in the Carrier Dome. We had no answer for Sweeney's dominance, and Syracuse won 31–14. The Tigers

---

[1] "On Wednesday the SEC, Big 12, Big Ten and others decided to play this week's college football schedule. Their reasons may have more to do with money and rescheduling and travel than whether it's morally right or wrong." Charles Hollis, "Auburn, Bama Should Win Close Games," *Birmingham News* (September 13, 2001): 1-D.

[2] "I think it's probably beneficial for us to go play now. Personally, I don't think that everybody's really been into the game. I don't think everybody's going to be into the game going into this week—fans, players, coaches—because of the tragedy. But, we've got to get on with our lives and go on with it. Our presidents, our athletic directors, made the decision, so let's go play." Charles Goldberg, "SEC to Take the Field - UAB-Pitt Game Reset for Dec. 1; Other State Schools will Play," *Birmingham News* (September 13, 2001): 1-D.

[3] "But, over the long haul, this is the best decision for everybody." Charles Goldberg, "SEC Reverses Field - Auburn-LSU May Now Meet Dec. 1," *Birmingham News* (September 14, 2001): 1-C.

returned from New York, but not yet to Jordan-Hare Stadium—first we had an engagement in Nashville.

The Vanderbilt game was uncomfortably close. The Commodores never led, but tied the game three times and looked as though they might do so a fourth time at the end. Damon Duval hit a 49-yard field goal with 2:58 remaining to give Auburn a 24–21 lead. Vandy responded by driving 52 yards in eight plays before lining up a potential game-tying, 44-yard field goal. They ran a fake for a loss of two yards. Unconvincing as it was, the win gave us a conference record of 2–0, good enough for first place in the west heading into games against Mississippi State and Florida.

I attended the 2001 Mississippi State game with Sam Lasseter. Sam is the real thing. Sometimes frustration can bring the deep feelings of an Auburn man to the surface in a less positive way. What I remember most from Sam's analysis that night is his prophetic exclamation about the efficacy of our offense. After scoring first, Auburn surrendered two field goals plus a touchdown and a two-point conversion to trail 14–7 after three quarters. When we settled for a field goal early in the fourth quarter, making the score 14–10, Sam celebrated facetiously: "Great! Two more of those and we win!" That is exactly what happened. Duval added two more field goals, the final one from 47 yards with only 18 seconds left in the game. We won, 16–14. Duval thus kicked game-winning field goals in consecutive weeks. He was not done yet.

Daniel Cobb vs. Steve Spurrier

I seriously considered not attending the 2001 Florida game, but decided at the last minute to try and get a ticket. I bought one for $15 at the corner of College and Roosevelt from a guy with a handful; he said I was his first sale of the day. The weather—raining and windy—and the point spread—Florida by 21—made for a buyer's market. Closer to the stadium I could have bought one for five dollars, but I didn't care, especially not after sitting down—to this day it is the best view I have had of any sporting event at any venue. That seat was made for watching the game; the rest are just there to make money.

As it turned out, I would have gladly paid $150 to witness the enigma that unfolded that night. A number of phenomena played out in the game that just did not make sense. It all seemed irreconcilable with the reality that we were playing: Florida; coached by Steve Spurrier; and, ranked no. 1 in the nation. It started when the Gators had to settle for a field goal on their first possession—that alone was improvement over our two games with Florida the year before. After the score, Tim Carter returned the kickoff 68 yards to the Florida 34, setting up Duval's first field goal of the game. The surprises continued when Tuberville, after only three possessions—still in the first quarter—pulled our starting quarterback and replaced him Daniel Cobb, the senior who had not been able to win the job over a redshirt freshman. Cobb came into the game and promptly led an 11-play scoring drive that gave us a 10–3 lead.

The strangest sight of the evening came with about four minutes remaining in the third quarter, when Steve Spurrier sent his punt team onto the field on third down. Granted, it was third and 25; nonetheless, the Gators had reasonably safe field position, at their own 38. Steve Spurrier punting on third down—how can one process something so anathema? The Shug-like conservatism backfired. The punter bobbled the snap and then fumbled; he recovered, making it fourth and 43—a more conventional punting situation. One other unexpected dynamic of the game harkened back to the first of the two meetings between the teams in 2000.

After our loss to Florida in October 2000—when the Gators scored touchdowns on their first five possessions—Florida quarterback Rex Grossman joked about the failure of the Auburn defense. "I think the scout team would have at least stopped us one out of five . . . ." The Auburn defense also failed to stop Grossman in the 2000 rematch, but the 2001 game was quite different—we intercepted him four times. The final pick was made by Karlos Dansby with the game tied and 4:28 left to play. The Tigers started the final drive from our 24-yard line.

In the final minutes of the game Daniel Cobb led the Auburn offense through the wind and rain on a march into the legendary. Cobb completed three of three pass attempts on the final drive for thirty yards. Carnell Williams added 14 yards rushing, and the Tigers made it to the Florida 27—easily close enough for kicker Damon Duval, even in the unfavorable conditions. Tuberville knew just how long the drive needed to be because Duval told him. "Damon came to me and told me to get the ball to the 35 and we would win this thing . . . He told me not to worry about the wind."[j] Duval himself handled the wind worrying.

> I started the ball about four or five feet outside of the right upright. It started way outside, but we had a 30 to 40 mph wind, and you can see on the video how it curves inside. I did that on purpose.[k]

It was Duval's third game-winning kick in as many weeks. The win was Auburn's first over a no. 1 ranked team at Jordan-Hare Stadium and gave us a record of 4–0 in conference. If only it had been 5–0.

A Long Way Down

The 2001 Tigers continued to live on the edge and continued to win for one more week, beating La. Tech 48–41 in overtime. After that win, the season began a downward spiral from which it would never fully recover. We lost 42–17 to Arkansas and then beat Georgia 24–17. With the Alabama game and the rescheduled LSU game left to play, we needed only one more win to claim an outright SEC Western Division Championship and a second straight trip to Atlanta. We won neither game. In fact, the Alabama game was one of the more demoralizing defeats of the modern era. Alabama was unranked with a 4–5 record, but whipped us 31–7. I initially had trouble remembering whether I was at this one. Then I remembered—oh yeah, Dad and I bought student IDs from two sisters right before the game. They argued with each other about whether to take our money or attend the game even as we were negotiating the price. We, of course, took sides with the older sister, who was more interested in our cash than in seeing the game. We convinced the younger one to take the deal, and I am sure she has no regrets. The game was an ugly sight—and not the last one of the season.

Pitiful Peaches

After finishing the regular season with losses to Alabama and LSU, we accepted an invitation to play North Carolina in the Chick-fil-A Bowl as a parting gift from relevancy. I initially had no interest in attending the game—"four losses is enough." But, Matt and Sam said they were going, and I had a change of heart. We had a pretty fun trip. There was pedestal joust at the fanfest before the game. Sam knocked me off once; I overpowered him twice.[4] The game itself was decidedly less fun.

Our offense looked bad. Damon Duval ultimately punted nine times. Our inability to move the ball was especially frustrating to Sam, much as it had been earlier in the season when we relied on field goals to beat Mississippi State. Just as Sam spoke prophetically at that game, so did he in the Georgia Dome, albeit regarding a different connotation of *prophecy*. When I remember Sam's verbal attacks against our coaching staff that night, it brings

---

[4] Do the victors write the history, or is it the other way around?

to mind the Latter Prophets of the Old Testament, particularly Amos: boldly speaking an unwelcomed message; harshly critical of those in power; telling the truth with no concern for the consequences. What I remember best is that Sam posed the following question to everyone his voice could reach: "Is this Coach Barfield on the sideline?" We were not sitting among many fans of our own generation. Most of the surrounding Auburn people were closer to my parents' age; in other words, fans who lived through the Barfield era. I noticed one woman in particular looking back at Sam. The expression on her face was easy to read: *what does this kid know about Doug Barfield?* Later in his proclamations Sam called Tuberville "our million-dollar Barfield." This characterization was a little extreme, of course—Barfield compiled a record of 14–18–1 in his first three seasons (1976–1979) while Tuberville was 21–15 at Auburn from 1999–2001. Nonetheless, Sam was right in saying the pitiful performance in Atlanta that night—we lost to the Tarheels 16–10—appeared to be the product of poor coaching. Tuberville himself, in effect, agreed. He accepted the resignations of both offensive coordinator Noel Mazzone and defensive coordinator John Lovett three days after the loss to North Carolina. The need for change was clear in the first days of the New Year, but it would have been unthinkable in mid-October; and that is the story of the 2001 season.

Where are we going?

We won six of the first seven games in 2001, but then lost four of the final five. One might argue the first half, rather than the second, was the aberration, given the four consecutive final-minute (or overtime) wins. Tuberville promoted a big-picture view of the season that focused on the number of wins; not on the dichotomous chronology. "It was a successful season, it wasn't a great season. We just lost a bowl game. A lot of teams are sitting at home."[1] Fair enough? The first half of the season was so good that, even after the second-half collapse, the Tigers were SEC Western Division co-champions; one win shy of another conference championship game appearance. Matt McGee was hesitant to adopt Tuberville's positive assessment. He noted a different trend, pointing out that in Tuberville's first year we lost the final game of the season; in his second we lost the final two; and in his third year we lost the final three games. So at season's end Tuberville was no genius. His first priority for 2002 would be to hire new coordinators who could make him look one.

5

2002

"He should have another year to prove himself, but if he doesn't do so well, there are better people out there." This waning patience was not expressed by an Auburn power broker, but by a fan quoted in the Birmingham news.[a] This fan was not alone. Yes, Tuberville outperformed Doug Barfield in his first three seasons, but other comparisons were not as positive. Pat Dye won 25 games over his first three seasons with an SEC and National Championship in 1983. Terry Bowden won 28 games over his first three seasons, with an SEC and National Championship in 1993.[1] To expect Tuberville to match the early success of Dye or Bowden, of course, would have been unreasonable; and questions about his fitness for the position stemmed not so much from having won only 21 games from 1999–2001, but rather from how his third season ended—losing four of the final five games. There was a reason from his

---

[1] Yes, I realize we did not technically win the SEC championship in 1993. I leave that matter for a Bowden era historian. For an explanation of how I recognize national championships see the chapter titled Tuberville's National Championship.

first three years, however, to hope the next three would be better—a reason that continued to build in the 2001-2002 offseason.

New Talent and New Coaches

"This will be the best recruiting class since we've been here."[b] As good as the 2001 class was, Tuberville said 2002 was better. Once again Auburn signed Mr. Football from the State of Alabama; and again a move from the SEC to the NFL played a role in that recruit's decision. In 2001 Carnell Williams became more interested in Auburn after Rudi Johnson declared for the NFL draft. When Steve Spurrier became the head coach of the Washington Redskins in 2002, Florida lost ground in the recruitment of Hewitt-Trussville quarterback Brandon Cox. Tuberville found players to catch the ball, too.

The receivers who joined the team in 2002 include some of the most recognizable names from the Tuberville era. We received a commitment from Devon Aromashodu and then managed to maintain a commitment from Courtney Taylor despite a late push by Alabama. More suspenseful still was the recruitment of Ben Obomanu, who remained uncommitted until the first week of February. He had entertained offers from LSU, Alabama, and Notre Dame. Aromashodu, Taylor, and Obomanu would certainly have been enough to make an exceptional cohort of receiver signees. To these three Tuberville added Montavis Pitts and Lee Guess. The question of who would throw the ball to the new receivers, however, was one that took months to answer.

Daniel Cobb received a sixth year of eligibility due to medical hardship, thus renewing the quarterback battle between Cobb and Jason Campbell. Cobb decided to use his final year of eligibility only after consulting with Auburn's new offensive coordinator, Bobby Petrino. Cobb wanted to know if he would have a real chance to earn the job he had lost, won, and then lost again in 2001. Petrino assured Cobb that no priority to optimize

Jason Campbell's remaining eligibility would preclude Cobb from having a chance to compete.[c]

The quarterback competition was as tight in 2002 as the year before. Cobb and Campbell were listed as "co-starters" on the spring depth chart.[d] The race continued until August 20, when Cobb was named the starter. Petrino's system required simpler decision making by the quarterback than had Mazzone's. Nonetheless, Tuberville said understanding the system made the difference. "We feel like, mentally, Daniel is a little bit farther ahead."[2e] Auburn's defensive players, too, learned a new system from a new coach in 2002.

Coordinators Noel Mazzone and John Lovett, who both left Auburn after the second-half collapse in 2001, had been with Tuberville since 1995 when he became head coach at Ole Miss. So in 2002 Tuberville faced the challenge of restructuring, of refocusing. He needed coordinators who could translate Auburn's success in recruiting into more wins on the field. To complement the addition of Petrino to coach the offense, Tuberville hired University of Central Florida defensive coordinator Gene Chizik. In Chizik's four seasons at UCF the Golden Knights' defense improved from the 81st best in the country to the 16th.[f] The strong recruiting class and the hiring of Petrino and Chizik helped Auburn fans look forward from the disappointments of 2001. Unfortunately, not all the news from the 2002 offseason was good.

A key member of the 2002 recruiting class was quarterback Brandon Cox. Jason Campbell still had three years of eligibility remaining, but had yet to prove himself a reliable starter; thus signing Cox was a big deal. It appeared, however—at least in

---

[2] Tuberville's statement reminds me of a line from J. Wes Yoder's novel, *Carry My Bones*. One of Yoder's characters is an Auburn fan and explains the 2003 loss to USC this way: "The coaches got a boy under center who gets too confused and I don't got to tell you why."

August 2002—that signing day would be as close as Cox ever came to playing as a Tiger. First, the Auburn coaches redshirted Cox shortly after fall camp began.[g] Next, he missed practice on August 8th due to headaches after a car accident the week before.[h] Then, after practice on Saturday August 11th, Tuberville announced Cox had left the team. He said Cox would hopefully "rejoin the team in the near future," but did not specify when he might return or why he left.[i] Cox's departure made a headline or two, but in mid-August our attention was already focused on the upcoming trip to southern California. How did the growing talent pool and the new coordinators shape expectations for the season?

Ready to Compete?

The SEC sports information directors picked us third in the West, up two spots from their projection for 2001. At SEC media days we were picked fourth, despite being division co-champions the year before and returning key personnel such as Daniel Cobb, Carnell Williams—who missed the last three games of '01 due to injury—and linebackers Karlos Dansby and Dontarrious Thomas. One national publication, however, raised the bar a little for Tuberville's Tigers in 2002. Sports Illustrated ranked us 23rd, citing Williams' running ability and the return of seven starters on defense as reasons Auburn would compete for the Western Division Championship.[j] The season would begin in the West, but not in the SEC.

The 2002 Season

Auburn traveled to Los Angeles for the 2002 season opener against USC. The game was nationally televised on a Monday night. Tuberville relished the spotlight, even if not in a stadium full of orange. He also understood that making the opportunity count required getting a win. "Exposure helps, but winning exposure helps more. To really take advantage of the exposure, you have to play well and win."[k] The game was tied at 14 when Carnell

Williams, who had 97 yards rushing in the first half, was basically overcome by leg cramps. Our defense was on the field for way too much of the second half, and USC scored with 1:26 left in the game to earn a 24–17 win. We appeared to have come a long way since the Chick-fil-A Bowl. This debut performance seemed to hint 2002 could be a good season. A month would pass before there was any doubt.

Four Wins

We overpowered Western Carolina 56–0 and beat Vandy 31–6. Mississippi State put up little resistance; we beat them 42–14. With one third of the season complete, two things appeared to be true: the optimism regarding Carnell Williams' sophomore campaign was well founded; and, Tuberville and Petrino picked the right quarterback. In the two conference games, Cadillac totaled 297 yards on 48 carries. Cobb's stats were not as important as his leadership. After beating Mississippi State, Williams said, "Cobb has established himself as the man."[1] For quarterbacks, however, establishment is a tenuous thing.

The fifth game of the 2002 season gave us a rematch with Syracuse, this time at home. Fortunately, Dwight Freeney had moved on to the NFL. The 2001 game was a lowlight for Jason Campbell. In 2002, Daniel Cobb was ineffective in the first half, and twisted an ankle in the second quarter. When the Tigers took the field to start the second half—down 17–3—Jason Campbell took over under center. After a Carlos Rogers interception gave us the ball at the Syracuse 31, Campbell led the offense on its first touchdown drive of the game. We ultimately won 37–34 in triple overtime. Perhaps now Campbell was the man, though Carnell Williams had a claim to that title himself. Against Syracuse he carried 40 times for 202 yards and two touchdowns. Whoever the man might have been, the Tigers made it to an off week with a 4–1

record. A four-game stretch of conference opponents lay ahead—
two at home and two on the road.

Trouble, at Home and Abroad

Jason Campbell's off-the-bench performance in the win over
Syracuse did not mean Cobb's season was over. Per Petrino, there
was no quarterback controversy: "If Daniel is ready to go, he'll be
the starter."[m] In retrospect, nobody looked ready against Arkansas.

We apparently used the off-week to think too much.
Tuberville described an extensive self-evaluation made possible by
a new computerized film review system.

> By scouting yourself we can tell what works and
> what doesn't. What are we doing on first down? On
> second down? Are we too predictable? Can teams
> guess what we're trying to do? That's what we're
> looking for.[n]

In the end, none of our self-scouting enabled us to stop the run.
Arkansas had three rushers who averaged 11 yards (or better) per
carry.[o] We were down only seven at the half, but eventually quit
keeping up. Campbell came in at the start of the fourth quarter,
down 31–17, but was unable to spark a comeback. We lost 38–17.
It was the first conference loss of the season. The following week
brought another conference match up—at Gainesville.

I watched the 2002 Florida game with Action and another
friend, Neal, at an exceptionally nasty trailer they were renting. We
decided to mute the TV and listen to the Auburn Radio Network
broadcast. Our video was behind our audio. Hearing what happens
before seeing it was weird, but we stayed the course. In hindsight, I
wish I had listened to the radio every game of 2002.

Any hope of winning in Gainesville appeared to have been
crushed in the second quarter when Carnell Williams suffered a

serious injury. We were down 14–0 and our offense had yet to make a first down when Cadillac—the leading rusher in the SEC at the time—was carried off the field on a stretcher. Game over? Not yet. Ronnie Brown came off the bench and, on the first play after Carnell's injury, ran 12 yards for a first down. Later in the drive we gave Brown the ball on fourth and one—he ran 26 yards for a touchdown. The offense then struggled for two quarters while Florida slowly grew their lead. At the start of the fourth quarter we saw another change in the backfield.

Our coaches stuck to their plan of playing Cobb until we were down at least two touchdowns and then bringing in Campbell, who this time inherited a 16-point deficit. The strategy worked against Syracuse but failed against Arkansas. It was good enough to force overtime in Gainesville. Regardless, Brown was the star of the fourth quarter. He rushed for 57 yards and a touchdown, and made a 54-yard receiving touchdown. We converted two-point attempts after both scores, tying the game at 23. We later seemed to have the game in hand after driving to the Florida six with only 30 seconds left to play, but Duval's field goal attempt was blocked. The Gators won 30–23 in overtime. The 2002 season suddenly seemed primed for a disintegration like that of 2001. The schedule offered no break—next up, LSU.

Recovery

When coaches talk about an underdog's chances of pulling off an upset, they often mention the importance of making a quick start. "We've got to catch fire early and make some big plays and get some confidence going." Scoring points is not the only way to set the tone early. "We've got to get some three-and-outs."[p] Gene Chizik knew his players had to start strong for our team to score a mid-season upset over 10th-ranked, once beaten LSU. He got what he wanted. They forced and recovered a fumble on the first play from scrimmage. Many Auburn fans got what they wanted on the ensuing play—Jason Campbell entered the game as our starting quarterback. We failed to convert the turnover into points, but there were more to come. Travaris Robinson, Donnay Young and Karlos Dansby all made first-half interceptions, and we led 17–0 at intermission. The second half was not much different. Dansby added another interception (with a 60-yard return). There was little pressure on Campbell. Ronnie Brown ran for 95 yards, and newly-promoted second-string rusher Tre Smith added 80. The upset was complete: 31–7. The next week's challenge was to avoid becoming an upset victim.

For the ninth game of 2002 the Auburn Tigers visited Oxford, Mississippi to face the Ole Miss Rebels, led by junior quarterback Eli Manning. Manning was on his way to 3,400 yards passing for the season, but the star of this game would be Ronnie Brown, who rushed for 224 yards on 33 carries and three touchdowns. Our defense intercepted Manning three times, the last of which—by Travaris Robinson—came with 1:32 left in the game, allowing the Tigers to hold on for a 31–24 win. Three opponents remained on the 2002 schedule: Louisiana-Monroe, Georgia and Alabama.

The Louisiana-Monroe game served its purpose well. Jason Campbell threw four touchdown passes, and several reserves, on both sides of the ball, acquired valuable playing time in a 52–14 win.

Failure, an Inclusio

I learned how to buy tickets from my Dad. He has better luck some Saturdays than others; so do I. To buy tickets on game day, one needs the right amounts of two things: money and patience. Dad's ticket buying does not usually entail negotiating. It is just about picking and choosing; waiting to encounter the right tickets at the right price; being comfortable walking away from multiple opportunities in faith that a better seat-cost combination can still be found.

On November 16, 2002 I made the very familiar walk from my apartment on North Gay St. toward Jordan-Hare Stadium. I had no ticket, only a little cash, and, it would seem, too much patience. I encountered the first non-scalper seller earlier than usual. He was walking up College Street from the intersection with Glenn. I got his attention and discovered he wanted $50 for his one extra ticket—fifty dollars to see Auburn, on a three-game winning streak, play seventh-ranked Georgia; the South's Oldest Rivalry; both teams still contending for their respective division titles. Fifty dollars. I have since paid more than $50 to watch us play Louisiana-Monroe. This kid was offering me a great deal. I must have been blinded by my tendency to never buy the first ticket. Or, maybe I hadn't been out of bed long enough—my brain was still warming up.

Truthfully, with full cognitive abilities I might have made the same decision. I didn't know how big a game it was. The contextual information noted above was not something I always kept up with in that period of my life. I cared as deeply as I always had about Auburn Football. I went to every game I could, and I lived and died with the success of our team. What I did not care about was Georgia, or how many wins or losses they had or how highly they were ranked. Georgia was not my team—Auburn was; and I was mostly oblivious to anyone else when they were not on the same field as the Tigers.

Once I arrived at the Raiders-of-the-Lost-Ark black market closer to the stadium, I realized my mistake. I do not remember exactly what tickets were going for on campus, but it was much more than $50. Never mind how much I was willing to pay, sellers were asking more than I had in my wallet. I may have seen one ticket for $125, and it was in the upper deck. As kickoff drew near, the reality began to dawn upon me that, for the first time in my life, I was about to definitively fail in an attempt to attend an Auburn Football game. My Dad had never completely struck out. I was about to bring shame to my family. I held out hope that prices might drop after the start of the game. They did not; and soon the sellers disappeared.

In disappointment and disbelief I resorted to my backup plan. I knew there was to be a game-watching party at Auburn Christian Fellowship on Gay St. They must have known of enough non-students connected to the ministry for such a party to make sense.

When I arrived at ACF I found a total of two people there to watch the game: a girl I somewhat knew and a guy who was there to hang out with her. Great—I failed at buying a ticket; my backup plan now consists of being a third wheel.

I decided to not bolt immediately. We made small talk, and one of them asked why I was not at the game. As soon as I said I couldn't get a ticket, the guy stood up and reached for his wallet. "Here you go. Take my ID." What? It soon became clear that it was only the girl, who had already graduated, who did not have a ticket. The guy, on the other hand, was recovering from an "upset stomach," meaning he really wanted to hang out with the girl all day.

I made it to the stadium just in time to realize I was missing something. The crowd erupted as I climbed the stairs, looking for a seat. I turned around but couldn't really tell what was going on. It was the first score of the game, a 53-yard touchdown run by Ronnie Brown with 6:29 to go in the first quarter. It seemed my day was only getting better. In reality, it had peaked.

The game's ending looked more like my day's beginning. We squandered as badly our opportunities to put the game away as

I had my best opportunity to buy a ticket. Jason Campbell ran 21 yards for a touchdown to give us a 21–10 lead with 5:45 left in the third quarter. After that we went three-and-out on our next six possessions. We began our last possession at our 29, with a 21–17 lead and 2:41 left in the game. A first down there may have been enough to win the game. Instead, we gave the ball back to David Greene, who threw a 41-yard completion to Fred Gibson. Four plays later, on fourth-and-fifteen, Greene found Michael Johnson in the back of the end zone for the final score of the game.

As I was walking home a Georgia fan yelled at me from the back of a pick-up. "It's fourth down. We heave it to the end zone. All you gotta do is knock it down. Can you do it? No!" It was a tough loss, and a major obstacle to winning the western division. Our next opponent was the division leader.[3]

Skullduggery

I like to call the 2002 Auburn-Alabama game *Skullduggery*. I do so because the guy who burned my DVD of the broadcast created an intro scene; the audio picks up in the middle of an exchange between the commentators so that the first words one hears after the disc loads is: "as long as it wasn't skullduggery." As the commentator finishes that line, Auburn snaps the ball, and our tailback breaks loose for 51 yards. Alabama entered the game with the no. 1 ranked defense in the country. That they gave up so big a run was surprising. Also surprising was who made the run—Tre Smith. Ronnie Brown rushed for 124 yards the week before against Georgia, but suffered an injury late in the game and had to sit out against Alabama. Brown's absence forced true freshman Smith into active duty. He was joined in the backfield by another true freshman, Cooper Wallace. Throughout the season, whether it was

---

[3] This statement is true in a sense, even if inconsequential—Alabama entered the game with the best conference record in the division but was ineligible to play in the SEC Championship Game due to NCAA probation.

Carnell Williams or Ronnie Brown racking up yardage, fullback Brandon Johnson had been leading the way. Johnson also suffered an injury against Georgia and was replaced in the Alabama game by Wallace, whose normal position was tight end. While Auburn came into the game with a makeshift backfield, Alabama entered the contest ranked ninth and with a five-game winning streak in which they outscored the competition (all conference opponents) by a total of 165–43. Alabama was favored over Auburn by 11 points. Beating the Tide is always most fun when they think there is no chance they can lose.

The fun started in earnest two plays after Smith's long run, when Jason Campbell hit tight end Robert Johnson for a 14-yard touchdown. On our next possession Campbell found Johnson wide open in the end zone to go up 14–0. We concluded our scoring for the day on the following possession with a Damon Duval 40-yard field goal. After that, we just held on. Alabama's only points came after an interception midway through the third quarter: Auburn 17 – Alabama 7.

Tuberville's second win over Alabama was a big one—an upset; the continuation of our dominance in Tuscaloosa; and, it gave us a good enough record for an SEC Western Division co-championship. Tuberville understood the significance of the in-state rivalry.

> Alabama. That's the one we deal with everyday. To win recruiting in our territory, so to speak, that's the one you got to win. I don't look at any of the games like I look at the Alabama game. . . . For us there are three seasons: non-conference, conference, and then there's Alabama. We work hard on them, and if there is a game we put a personal touch on, it's that last one every year.[q]

Tuberville beat Alabama in 2000, but it was in 2002 that he really began putting his personal touch on the rivalry. We will further engage Tuberville's emphasis on the Alabama game in subsequent chapters. For now, we turn our attention to the closing of the 2002 season.

The 2002 Auburn Tigers won four of their last five scheduled games. The strong finish earned an invitation to play on New Year's Day in the Capital One Bowl, against tenth-ranked Penn State. The Nittany Lions' offense featured Heisman Trophy finalist Larry Johnson, who rushed for 2,012 yards in the regular season. Johnson was expected to continue his exceptional year against Auburn, and Penn State was favored by seven points. The Auburn defense, however, stopped Johnson early and often—he rushed for no gain on his first carry; minus two on his second. The Nittany Lions kicked two field goals in the first half and took a 6–0 lead into intermission. They finished their scoring with another field goal in the second half—that would not be enough. Ronnie Brown returned from injury and decidedly overshadowed Penn State's Heisman contender.

Johnson: 20 carries, 72 yards.
Brown: 33 carries, 184 yards, 2 touchdowns

Brown was voted the game's MVP. His performance since Cadillac's injury evidenced the value of his head coach to the Auburn Football program.

The Tigers' success in 2002 displayed Tuberville's executive acumen in at least two ways. Firstly, the coordinator hires produced marked improvement over 2001. In 2002 our offense scored, on average, about seven more points per game, and our defense allowed about seven fewer points per game, than the year before. Secondly, the recruiting success of the previous years was translating into wins on the field. Our depth allowed us to win more games in the second half of the season—with backups at quarterback and running back—than we did in the first half with the starters.

The loss to Arkansas was the only shameful moment of the season. The other three losses were good games against tough teams. By beating Alabama and Penn State we ended the season on a high note; perhaps, too high a note.

6

Defense and Touchdowns

Let's take a moment here between 2002 and 2003 to address some matters that fit in neither the preceding nor following chapters, the first because it's a departure from our method; the second because it is bigger than anything else in this book.

They Say It Wins Championships

In reviewing football history it is all too easy to focus disproportionately on the names that score the points and rack up the yards, to the neglect of the defense. I am guilty of this neglect. In effort to make up for it a little, let us here take a closer look. It makes sense to examine the 2002 defense both because it was Gene Chizik's first of three years as our defensive coordinator and because of the outstanding defensive performances in the biggest wins of the year.

Chizik took over a squad that had no shortage of talent; the question was how he could get the most out of it. Two changes Chizik made to that end were: adjusting our base defense to use three true linebackers; and, moving Karlos Dansby from safety into one of those linebacker spots. Dansby flourished in his new role: "He [Chizik] came in with a new plan, a new game style, and I'm fitting right into his plan . . . ."[a] Chizik's new plan also required more aggressive play from the secondary. Junior Rosegreen, Donnay Young, Carlos Rogers, and Travaris Robinson responded well to Chizik's ideology, and Auburn led the league in interceptions in 2002 with 21. Robinson also made 92 tackles, second only to linebacker Mark Brown. Chizik's adjustments showed he understood how to put his defenders in position to make plays. When the team lost two straight games in mid-season and appeared on the verge of collapse, Chizik proved he could coach his players up.

On Friday night prior to the LSU game, Chizik called a meeting with the defense. According to defensive tackle DeMarco McNeil, the discussion was not about Xs-and-Os. "It was basically a gut check. It got a little personal. I took it a little personally. He just basically challenged us."[b] The defense responded heartily to the challenge, particularly Karlos Dansby. Or, perhaps it is more true to say the rest of the defense responded to a challenge to play the way Dansby had been all season. That's how Tuberville put it after the game: "Karlos Dansby has been our most consistent guy each and every game. Our players rose to his level this week."[c] The defense again played at that high level in the regular season finale against Alabama.

> With all their option and all the things they can potentially give you problems with, we just wanted to line up and know where we were, and who had all those option responsibilities. Then we had to stop that turn-back draw.[d]

Chizik knew his defense had to stop Alabama's running game to give Auburn a chance to win. His plan was to stop the run to set up stopping the pass. "When we got them in some predictable third-down situations, we felt like we could blitz them. The kids executed the plan just the way we designed it."[e] Another strong performance by Travaris Robinson was integral to making the plan work. Robinson's 12 tackles and two pass break-ups earned him SEC Defensive Player of the Week—an award won previously in the season by Karlos Dansby (against LSU) and Reggie Torbor (against Mississippi State). Robinson's fellow defensive back Carlos Rogers made Auburn's only interception of the game. While ball security did not factor largely into the outcome, turnovers on downs did. Alabama attempted to convert seven fourth downs, and our defense stopped them five times. The play of the defense allowed the Tigers to score a major upset and put the team in position to achieve one more upset before closing the book on 2002.

The final performance of the 2002 Auburn Tigers Defense was arguably their finest. The opponent, Penn State, came into the Capital One Bowl on a four-game winning streak, averaging 43 points per game.[1] We held them to nine. The plan was the same as against Alabama: stop the run; force the opponent to throw. Stopping the run, however, would be a much greater challenge against Penn State on account of their feature-back, Larry Johnson. As noted above, the Tigers shut Johnson down. Without his usual production, the Nittany Lions managed only three field goals. Chizik attributed the effectiveness of the defense to its variable quality that maximized the talent. "We don't have great size, but we have great speed and we try to give other people different looks that leave them confused."[f] That confusion led to a late-fourth-quarter interception by Roderick Hood that helped secure the win.

In 2002 we learned that Gene Chizik was cut out to be a defensive coordinator at the highest level of college football. Tuberville's early recruiting success at Auburn set up Chizik with

---

[1] Opponents: Illinois, Virginia, Indiana, Michigan State.

a talent base that he was able to optimize, and for which he effectively game planned in preparation for tough opponents. They say defense wins championships. While the 2002 Auburn defense cannot claim a championship, they prepared the way for a defense that can.

The Greatest Loss of the Tuberville Era

In 2012, ten of Auburn's twelve games were broadcast on network or cable TV. The other two were available on pay-per-view. Generally speaking, anyone who wanted to sit at home and watch the Tigers play could do so. There was a time when it was not so. I remember one Saturday afternoon from that earlier time. It was October 17, 1987. Auburn was playing, but the game was not on TV. My Dad and I spent the day just riding around. I know we went to a car dealership on Meighan Boulveard in Gadsden; we might have gone to the Burger King across the street. We were in and out of his truck all afternoon. All the time we were riding, we watched the game, so to speak, through the eyes of Jim Fyffe. I well remember hearing Fyffe's call on one critical play, though he delivered it so excitedly that I did not really understand what he was saying at the time: "Burger sets up to throw—oh my!— Touchdown Auburn! Touchdown Auburn! Touchdown Auburn! Tillman! Tillman! Tillman!" Jeff Burger's touchdown pass to Lawyer Tillman was the final play of a 91-yard drive that gave Auburn a 14-10 lead with 24 seconds left in the game. Many Auburn fans have memories of hanging on the every word of Jim Fyffe. As noted above, another of my memories is of listening to the radio broadcast of the 2002 Florida game even while watching the game on TV. The reason I wish I had listened to every game on the radio that year is because it was Jim Fyffe's final season.

Fyffe died of a brain aneurysm on May 15, 2003.[g] It is beyond the scope of this work to adequately pay tribute to Fyffe's life and career; nor do I feel I can communicate how deeply the loss was felt by the Auburn Family. Many of us, even while never having met Fyffe, felt a sense of grief just as if we had lost a loved one. Fyffe truly was loved by the Auburn Family. His first season as Auburn's radio announcer was 1981. For anyone who was an Auburn fan in the 1980s—and perhaps especially for those who grew up in that decade—Fyffe is wrapped up in the mythos of those wonderful years as much as Pat Dye or Bo Jackson. To listen to Jim Fyffe was to listen to the very heartbeat of Auburn Football. We would be remiss in our remembering Fyffe's passion for the Tigers to not also recall how exceptionally well he did his job.

The near-indecipherable exuberance of "Tillman! Tillman! Tillman!" was not the rule. To the contrary, Fyffe distinguished himself from other well known play-by-play announcers in that he actually gave the listener everything needed to visualize the action. Give it a try sometime. Mute the TV and attempt to say aloud all the information that Fyffe provided before the snap: where everyone is lined up, who goes in motion where, what the defense is showing; and then tell what is happening, in detail, as quickly as it happens once the play begins. It is not easy, but Fyffe mastered both the art and the science of bringing the game to life.

David Housel said of Fyffe's death, "In a very real sense, the voice of Auburn has been silenced."[h] Indeed, for a moment; but we hear Fyffe's voice still, and his legacy is secure. He is indissolubly attached to all the richness and complexity of Auburn Football from 1981 through 2002.

7

2003

A breakdown of expectations for each of Tuberville's first five seasons at Auburn might look something like this:

1999	Losing season
2000	Possibly a winning season
2001	.500 at best
2002	7-8 wins
2003	National Championship

In 2003 it was that simple—Auburn would win, or at least make a strong run at, a national championship. It is uncharacteristic of Auburn people to get caught up in hype. Perhaps beating Alabama and then Penn State, and having closed the season winning five of the last six games, plus the expected return of Carnell Williams was just too much. I first knew things were getting out of hand when I saw the marquee at Anders Bookstore a few days after the Capital One Bowl. It read something to the effect of "Congrats Tigers! Next Year: New Orleans." New Orleans was the site of the next BCS Championship Game. Talk of winning it all actually started prior to the win over Penn State. Regarding preparations for the Capital One Bowl, fullback Brandon Johnson remarked, "We've all been real serious about it, because we know we have a legit shot at a national championship next year."[a] It's one thing for a player to make such a statement, but even Tuberville fed the early hype. "Hopefully, we can learn from this bowl game and possibly get to one that might mean a little bit more in the near future."[b] The first reason this early-onset enthusiasm should have been tempered was the departure of offensive coordinator Bobby Petrino, who left to become the head coach at Louisville. Tuberville, however, saw no reason why Petrino's absence should disrupt the recent success of the Tigers' offense.

"I'm looking at guys on the staff to keep running the same stuff."[c] In 2002 Petrino revitalized an Auburn offense that had sputtered and then ground to a depressing halt by the end of 2001. The dramatic improvement in 2002 could have been reason to lament Petrino's departure. Tuberville more saw it as reason to keep Petrino's offense, even without keeping Petrino. He wanted the offensive staff already in place, plus a new quarterbacks coach, to run the same offense Petrino installed in 2002. Offensive line coach Hugh Nall, who had never been an offensive coordinator, was promoted to that position, but not given play-calling responsibilities. Tuberville: "Whatever I do, the quarterback coach will normally call the plays, whether he's the coordinator or not."[d] Tuberville hired Steve Ensminger to coach the quarterbacks and call the plays. So the plan was to have two guys run a third, absent guy's offense. What could go wrong? After all, we still had many of the players that made Petrino's offense work in 2002.

Auburn's backfield was a major reason for the high expectations in 2003. Jason Campbell finally secured the quarterback position with his performance down the stretch in 2002. The tailback position seemed overstocked. Carnell Williams, who rushed for 745 yards over 6 ½ games of 2002, was recovered from injury and ready to once again lead the rushing attack; but he was not alone. Also returning was Ronnie Brown, who took over after Williams' injury and finished 2002 with 1,008 yards. Next in line was Tre Smith, who rushed for 126 yards against Alabama in 2002. The newest member of the group was transfer Brandon Jacobs, who rushed for 1,896 yards and 20 touchdowns in 2002 at Coffeyville Community College. Auburn's offensive coaches seemingly had the task of making sure no yards or touchdowns were left on the bench.

The depth at running back fed the hype. The front page of the New York Times' season preview—which ranked Auburn no. 1—featured a photograph of "Auburn's Four Horsemen" striking a pose appropriate to that title. Our running backs were not the only Tigers who had a pre-season photo shoot.

Gene Chizik's defense returned eight starters for 2003, two of whom—Karlos Dansby and Dontarrious Thomas—received nearly as much pre-season attention as the running backs. The linebackers were featured on the cover of ESPN The Magazine's 2003 college football preview. As noted in previous chapters, Tuberville spoke openly about the importance of exposure. In 2003 the program had all the exposure it could stand; and with it came high expectations.

The 2003 Season

I don't remember when I decided 2003 would be the year I attended every game. The decision had nothing to do with the expectations. It was something I wanted to do at least once in my life, and I knew the logistics would never get easier. I was single. My work week was Sunday through Thursday, so I could get into town on Fridays and take in the anticipation. I had friends who were still in school with whom I could party and crash every weekend. Sure, history says I should have put this adventure off just one year. Such is life. Will I ever achieve perfect attendance again? If I do, it can't have much worse a beginning.

Fire on the Launch Pad

We opened the season as four-point favorites against eighth-ranked USC. The game's beginning tells the story well enough. Carnell Williams lost two yards on the first play of the game. On the next play Anthony Mix dropped a pass. Jason Campbell threw an interception on third down. Five plays later USC quarterback Matt Leinart threw a touchdown pass to Mike Williams. This sequence, more or less, repeated all night. USC won 23–0.

It was disappointing to lose. The way we lost was downright depressing. After all the buildup, the ineptitude of our offense—never mind the end zone; we crossed midfield only twice—was sickening. Being shut out was underscored by a sad irony.

Before the game, the mic man (i.e., the one cheerleader everyone can actually hear) told us we would be starting a new Auburn tradition. The idea was to honor the late Jim Fyffe, whose signature call was "Touchdown Auburn!" The mic man explained we would now celebrate touchdowns with a new cheer: upon scoring, the east side of the stadium would yell "touchdown;" the west side would respond, "Auburn!" We practiced this new cheer while awaiting kickoff; and that it is the only time the proposed tradition was ever carried out. We had no occasion for it that Saturday night, and we wondered how long until we would.

Our failure to score against USC raised questions about the offensive play calling; not just why we ran the plays we did—Ronnie Brown and Carnell Williams combined for only 20 carries—but also how the plays were called. Was dividing the roles of offensive coordinator and offensive play caller among two coaches really a practical arrangement? The terrible debut of this system put Tuberville on the defensive.

> I think a lot of people have a misconception how this is going. Hugh is the offensive coordinator, and it is his responsibility. What we ran Saturday night was basically from his communication to Steve in the press box.[e]

Right—what could go wrong? Let's go to Atlanta and get a win.

The second Saturday of the 2003 season was the closest I came to missing a game. In the summer Matt McGee asked whether I would still go to every game if we got blown out in the opener. I told him I would, but when it came time to drive to Ga. Tech, I was certainly feeling under motivated. Jordan got up first that morning, and I declined several of his wake-up calls; eventually suggesting we just stay home. Only after he had given up trying to get me out of bed did I finally rouse and start getting ready. I wonder how closely analogous our decision making that morning was to Nall and Ensminger's play calling.

We made it to the game, but there was not much to see. The offense showed no improvement. Williams and Brown were inconsequential. Campbell was sacked six times by USC. The Yellow Jackets got to him seven times. With 33 seconds left in the half, the 2003 Auburn Tigers finally put points on the board. A 22-yard field goal by John Vaughn both opened and closed our scoring for the day. Tech won 17–3. To start any year 0–2 is disappointing. In 2003 we lost more games the first two weeks than many people thought we would in the whole season. It was time for a gut check.

"It's definitely a pride thing. A lot of people are down right now. A lot of people are disappointed, so now you've got to take the pride and see if you're a man or not."[f] Karlos Dansby and other seniors called a players-only meeting to talk about the team's focus. I wish that meeting had taken place in August. In the third game of the season we beat Vanderbilt 45–7. Johnny Cash died the day before the game. Dad and I enjoyed WSM's non-stop tribute to the Man in Black on our trip to Nashville. Auburn was off the next Saturday, after which we faced the Man in Red.[1]

We beat the Hilltoppers 48–3, bringing our record to 2–2 before a stretch of four consecutive conference games, starting with Tennessee. The Volunteers came to Jordan-Hare ranked seventh in the country, with wins over Florida and South Carolina. For much of the game, however, the Tigers looked to be playing another overmatched opponent. Our running game finally delivered. Williams rushed for 185 yards, and Brown added 65; each scored a touchdown. Our quarterback also played well. Campbell threw for 157 yards with touchdown passes to Ben Obomanu and Cole Bennett. The Tigers led 28–7 early in the fourth quarter when the Tennessee offense came alive. Casey Clausen threw two touchdowns, and the Volunteers were driving for a third when Carlos Rogers intercepted Clausen in the final minute to preserve a 28–21 victory. Putting aside the expectations, our season now seemed downright salvageable. The heart of the schedule lay ahead, with two of the next three games on the road; first stop—Fayetteville.

I decided to fly to Dallas and ride with Matt to the Arkansas game. Matt had only been a transplant Texan for a couple years at the time, but had somehow already developed a distaste for Oklahoma. On the rides to and from Fayetteville we hit a gas station just outside the Sooner state, and Matt let us know we better get whatever we wanted to eat or drink for the next three hours because we sure as hell were not stopping in Oklahoma.

---

[1] That is, Big Red, the mascot for the Western Kentucky University Hilltoppers.

Matt may not have cared for Oklahoma, but he should have felt right at home in Arkansas. After all, it was homecoming.

Defensive end Reggie Torbor took the role of Homecoming guest personally. "Usually you pick somebody you're going to run over for homecoming, and they might have thought that; I don't know. That was just fuel to the fire."[g] The entire Auburn defense seemed to play with a fire inside. Arkansas came into the game ranked seventh and with the league's leading rusher in Cedric Cobbs. The Tigers held Cobbs to only 78 yards, and the Hogs' only big plays were brought back for holding calls.[2]

Trailing 10–3, Arkansas started a drive on our side of the field late in the game. Karlos Dansby sacked Matt Jones on fourth down to crush the Hawgs' last hope. Matt, of course, bought tickets in a home section so we could agitate our neighbors. Every time Arkansas made a first down the stadium announcer would say, "That's another Arkansas Razorback," and the crowd would respond, "First down!" When Dansby rode Jones to the turf, I yelled, "That *was* another Arkansas Razorback," and then Matt and I shouted, "Fourth down!" I usually reserve antagonism for bammers. What can I say? Peer pressure.

The Auburn defense played the role of aggressor again the next week, at home against Mississippi State. Karlos Dansby, Reggie Torbor, Bret Eddins and Kyle Derozan each recorded a sack. Will Herring added an interception. In all, the Tigers made 14 tackles for loss. State's defense was less impressive. Auburn rushed for 405 yards. Carnell Williams scored six touchdowns, and the Tigers won 45–13. A season that seemed lost in August looked much different in late October. After losing the first two, the

---

[2] I have never witnessed so unified a display of collective bitching about officiating as we saw while looking for something to eat after the game. One restaurant even used their "Today's Special" chalkboard to explain that the Razorbacks had been beaten not by the Tigers, but by the referee.

Tigers won five straight and sat atop the division with a league record of 4–0. What could go wrong?

Falling Down the Mountainside

With renewed confidence we traveled to Baton Rouge. I drove to the game with Action, his roommate Brad Gregg, and some guy Brad knew from somewhere, named Andy. Between Birmingham and Baton Rouge Andy told us about 100 stories; every one belonging in a very different sort of paperback.

When we got to the stadium, it was somehow decided that Action and Brad would sit together, and I would sit with Andy. We would use Andy's tickets, which were in an upper deck. Action and Brad would sit in a lower section. The journey to the upper deck at Tiger Stadium was unlike any I had experienced. Instead of walking a coiled ramp, we stepped onto the tallest escalator I have ever seen. Once we reached the top of it, we made a hairpin turn and stepped onto another escalator, equally tall. We finally made it to the upper deck, and when we began climbing the stairs to our seats, Andy said something about having a fear of heights. From the first time he mentioned it, I could tell he was not joking around. I made a variety of arrangements to be able to attend every game in 2003, but somehow forgot to read up on counseling acrophobia. As we continued our climb, Andy became increasingly defeatist.

"I don't think I can do this." He was applying a death grip to the hand rail at every step. I tried to encourage him. Once we took our seats, I thought he might be OK; that once the game got started he would quit thinking about it. We didn't make it that long. He told me that, though he knew it was not rational, he felt if he were to stumble forward even slightly, he would then fall all the way to the field. To be sure, from our seats to the field was quite a distance.

Shortly before kickoff, or at least before the scheduled kickoff time, Andy said he absolutely had to switch seats with Action or Brad. At Jordan-Hare this swap would have been no big deal. At Tiger Stadium, it was not so simple. The upper and lower sections had separate stadium entrances; once inside the stadium, neither was accessible from the other. I had to get Andy cautiously back down the stairs and then ask a stadium employee for help. I called Action, and he had to get an employee in the lower section to help as well. The woman helping us led Andy and me to a spot where the three of us waited for Action and his escort. I was surprised they were willing to accommodate us. This process took half an hour. We had left our seats just a few minutes before kickoff, but, while we waited—under the bleachers—it was clear from the lack of cheering that the game had not started. I could only conjecture that movement between the upper and lower levels at Tiger Stadium warps the time-space continuum. Action and his escort finally appeared. He and I then made the ascent. Not until the next day did I learn kickoff had been delayed a half-hour due to lightning.

It had been a pretty fun trip to that point. I think we ate twice at the Hooters across the street from the hotel. As for the game, I enjoyed it about as much as Andy would have a hot air balloon ride. LSU scored 21 points in the first quarter. We did not score until 6:10 remaining in the fourth quarter; LSU won 31–7.

Heartbreaking is usually a term reserved for games decided by fewer than 24 points. There were two moments in Baton Rouge that night, however, when I felt I had been stabbed in the chest. Both times came after the initial onslaught. On our possession following LSU's third touchdown, our offense put together a 14-play drive, moving the ball into corndog territory. It ended with a missed field goal, but at least we had shown a sign of life. More reason for hope followed: our defense delivered their first three-

and-out of the game, and the Bayou Bengals lined up to punt. I was hoping to see our offense carry over the momentum from the previous drive. Momentum, of course, changes the same way a football bounces—unpredictably.

Sitting in the upper deck provides a different perspective on punts. It is something like watching an airplane overhead. Those who can see the whole field—and then some—better appreciate the yardage that a good punt covers. As the ball soars upward, closer to the upper-deck fans than in any other point in the game, and then falls away again, time passes more slowly. It may pass most slowly for the return man, who must keep his eyes on the ball while the eyes of the entire stadium and TV audience fall upon him. Our return man that night in Louisiana was Tre Smith. God bless Tre Smith. I still think of him, now seven seasons beyond his Auburn career, almost every time an opponent punts. Tre did not successfully field the punt that followed our defense's first stop of the night. The ball ricocheted off him on its way to the ground; LSU recovered. I would not remember this play, except that it recurred before the end of the half. Again our defense made a stop, and again I thought we had a chance at getting into the game, but again Tre knocked it down, like a catcher blocking a bad pitch. LSU again regained possession.

Memory can be as fickle as momentum. Those two muffed punts were not the difference in a 31–7 game. LSU did not score on their possessions following either of them. Nonetheless, those are the plays I remember. After that night, I imagined Smith's days as the return man were over. To the contrary, he continued in the role, off and on, the rest of his Auburn career. Against South Carolina in 2005, Smith returned seven punts. I held my breath every time.

After the unfruitful trip to Louisiana we hosted other Louisianans, beating La.-Monroe 73–7. Tuberville afterwards said our team benefitted in no way from playing the game. Offensive coordinator Hugh Nall expressed a related assessment. "I thought that was one of our worst games, especially up front as far as technique and fundamentals. If we had played somebody better, it would have been a rough day."[h] A game against somebody better was only a week away.

Falling Further

"I am trying to understand . . . The Lord put me in this situation for a reason."[i] How can your heart not break for a young man so distraught over not making a play that he searches his soul—even looks to his maker—for an answer? I feel compassion now, but I cannot say I did at the time. I referred to Ben Obomanu as "Butterfingers Ben" for so long after the 2003 Ole Miss game that I eventually couldn't remember why.

Jason Campbell and the Auburn offense started their final drive of the game at our 19-yard line with 2:39 left to play. Ole Miss led 24–20. Of the 81 yards between us and a win, the Tigers made quick work of all but the last three. Most of it was covered on one play, when Obomanu caught a screen pass and ran 51-yards to the Ole Miss ten. A completion to Jeris McIntyre and a short run by Cadillac got us down to the three.

By the time we played Ole Miss, the 2003 season had already been counted a total bust for a couple months. That assessment, of course, was only relative to the hype. In reality, on November 8 Auburn was still playing for an SEC Western Division championship; and around 5:30 that evening we were just three yards away from keeping that hope alive.

Campbell receives a shotgun snap at the left hash and rolls to his right. An Ole Miss linebacker slips through traffic and gets into the backfield untouched. Campbell, however, calmly keeps moving to the right; his eyes up, searching the end zone. As our quarterback stretches the play, the Ole Miss defenders lose track of Obomanu in the end zone. Campbell nears the sideline; the linebacker is about to hit him; and Carnell Williams is in a tangle with two other pursuing defenders, who have about pushed him into his quarterback. Suddenly a passing lane opens up—a wide passing lane. Campbell is about a yard from the sideline when he throws the ball perfectly to Ben Obomanu. The sophomore receiver is lonely. He has 25 square yards of the end zone to himself. The ball hits him in the hands and falls to the earth.

We ran a similar play on fourth down, and Campbell made another good throw, but an Ole Miss defender was in position and knocked the ball away. Final: Ole Miss 24 – Auburn 20.

If a national championship was ruled out the first week—or certainly the second—an SEC championship was scratched the eleventh. The two games remaining, nonetheless, are always big: Georgia and Alabama.

I have been to Sanford Stadium twice, but I would not really say I have seen a game there. The first time my seat was too low to see much of the field at all; the second time, too high. Some upper decks are better than others. At Georgia, from our high perch we could barely see the people in the lower bowl. The field? Forget it. Most of what we could see was not good. Georgia scored first and steadily built their lead to 19–0. When it appeared we might get into the game, Jason Campbell threw a pass on third-and-goal that was tipped, intercepted and then returned the length of the field. We didn't score until the final five minutes of the game: Bulldogs 26 – Tigers 7. Now on a three-game conference losing streak, we had to beat Alabama to finish the regular season with more wins than losses. Some speculated the stakes for Tuberville were higher than that.

"We plan on being here and going recruiting next week, coaching the bowl game and finish up on a good recruiting year and having a spring practice. That's how you have to look at it."[j] Tuberville may as well have answered questions about his job security with, *If you have to ask . . .* There was plenty of Iron Bowl week discussion about whether Tuberville would—or should—be retained beyond 2003. We did not know at the time that the power brokers had already decided Tuberville's fate—or so they thought. We will look at that matter in detail in the next chapter. For now, there is one more game on the 2003 schedule.

An Inconvenient Win

Alabama came to Jordan-Hare in 2003 with a record of 7–4. I don't remember what I expected, but I know when Carnell Williams ran 80 yards for a touchdown on the first play from scrimmage, I naïvely hoped the rest of the game would follow suit. For one quarter, a blowout seemed possible. We gave up a safety on our second possession, but followed that with a 64-yard touchdown pass from Jason Campbell to Ben Obomanu. On our third possession we drove 72 yards to the Alabama five before settling for a field goal. We led 18–2 after fifteen minutes, but then the scoring went cold for the half.

Alabama returned the second half kickoff 96 yards for a touchdown, getting themselves back in the game. We then went three and out, after which Alabama drove 82 yards for another touchdown, making the score 18–16. John Vaughn kicked another field goal, giving us a 21–16 lead. Then, midway through the fourth quarter, Cadillac scored his second touchdown of the game, and things seemed more comfortable at 28–16. Alabama did, however, score once more—a touchdown with about a minute left. They failed to convert an onside kick, and the Tigers ran out the clock for a 28–23 victory.

With this win Tuberville did something his predecessor, Terry Bowden, never accomplished—beat Alabama two consecutive years. Afterwards, Tuberville mentioned the cloud of uncertainty hanging over the program.

> We fought all week long to fight off frustrations and rumors. This game is tough enough. We poured our heart and soul into this game. I told them to get out there and work hard and everything would take care of itself.[k]

Indeed, everything worked out. What we did not know at the time was that—even before the game—certain Auburn elites had already worked out who would coach the Tigers in 2004; or so they thought.

8

Jetgate

The *Jetgate* scandal has not shown the staying power one might have expected. Yes, ESPN and CBS brought it up constantly during Auburn's remarkable 2004 season, but in time our consistent success from 2004 through 2007 overshadowed the old news. Now, of course, we have a more recent rift between Tuberville and the University—his resignation in 2008—making *Jetgate* obsolete. Its diminished presence in the collective Auburn conscience does not, of course, lessen the ugliness of the affair. I would rather not delve into the details, but to understand the role *Jetgate* played in shaping Tuberville's legacy we must look at how the scandal unfolded. We will first go over the timeline of events and then explain why the coup failed. Additionally, I will share my own personal, if indirect, connection to the 2003 near-firing of Tommy Tuberville.

The Jetgate Timeline

Saturday November 22

Auburn defeats Alabama 28–23, improving our record to 7–5 (5–3 in conference). A loss would have ended our regular season with a three-game losing streak and a record of 2–4 over the second half. Instead, Tuberville has leverage to argue for retention: "This is the game we're supposed to win . . . We went out there and won it. I'm going to go home and sleep real good tonight, I promise you."[a] David Housel is asked whether the win saves Tuberville's job. He responds that President Walker had scheduled a vacation for the upcoming week and that he and Walker will meet with Tuberville the following week.

Sunday

Tuberville says he hasn't been told whether he will be retained. He also says he is "shocked" to know his job is not secure after beating Alabama for a third time in his five seasons at Auburn.[b]

Monday

Walker is asked about Tuberville before leaving town for his vacation. He says he has an "inclination" as to what his decision will be, but that it is not yet definite.[c]

Tuesday

The drama escalates from story to scandal. On Tuesday night Walker releases a statement admitting that he, David Housel, Byron Franklin and Earl McWhorter flew to Louisville, KY the previous Thursday night—two nights prior to the Alabama game— to meet with University of Louisville head football coach Bobby Petrino. Walker says in his statement that the meeting was arranged by a search firm, and that "Coach Petrino has been mentioned as a candidate for the job should it become available. I have made no decision and am considering my options. This visit was a part of that process."[d]

While Tuberville's future remains unsure on Tuesday, one individual's fate is sealed. Alabama cheerleader Christopher Bailey, who transferred to Alabama from Auburn, is relieved of his duties after having admitted to an ESPN sideline reporter (during the Iron Bowl!) that he still had feelings—positive feelings—for Auburn.[e] Bailey's situation is analogous to *Jetgate* in that, after making the mistake of agreeing to the interview, he piled on contempt for himself by revealing his feelings, and yet still might have kept his job had he not gone totally over the ledge of good sense by saying "War Eagle" at the interviewer's prompting.

Wednesday

Walker issues another statement, admitting he erred in judgment when deciding to meet with Petrino. This statement ambles along for 300 words—half apology, half self-justification—before finally conceding, "If Coach Tuberville elects to do so, he will continue as Auburn's head football coach next year. I sincerely hope he chooses to remain at Auburn."[f]

Friday

Louisville Athletics Director Tom Jurich says neither Walker nor Housel has called him to apologize for interviewing Petrino without contacting him first, but that Tuberville "called me to apologize for Auburn's actions." Jurich adds, "I told him that he was the last guy in the world that needs to apologize to anybody. But it showed great class on his part—and further shows just how lucky Auburn is to have that kind of individual."[g]

Saturday November 29

Auburn spokesman John Hachtel says the "search firm" from Walker's first statement was actually an individual working at no cost to the university. He does not identify the individual.[h]

Sunday November 30

Tuberville's assistant coaches hit the recruiting trail, presumably for Auburn. Per NCAA rules, it is the first day such visits are allowed.

Monday November 31

Tuberville meets with Walker and Housel at 10:00 am and then holds a press conference. He had the attention of the Auburn Family—and beyond—in a way that perhaps no one ever had before or has since. He was not about to let the opportunity go to waste. It was his moment, and he was ready.

Tuberville begins by discussing the experience of being Auburn's coach over the last five years. Not surprisingly—at least not in retrospect—he becomes philosophical.

> It's not about a coach, it's not about a football team, it's about Auburn University. I felt the love people had for this school and everything that it stands for, and everything they want in their program. We've tried to do that over the last five years.

Tuberville turns to the present-day, saying the meeting with Walker and Housel went well. Here he brings the suspense to a head. "I'm looking forward to coaching in the bowl game." He leaves the statement and its implications hanging in the silence. He pauses and soon becomes emotional. "It's been a long two weeks." Now the tears are falling; Tuberville's and several reporters'. Another grand pause—he then attempts some levity. "Someone say something; it's too quiet." I said something, but no one was listening to me. He has had his moment; and finally shows his hand: "I'm looking forward to being around here for a long time."[i] The room erupts with applause—hoots and shouts of "War Eagle!" No one is neutral. Tuberville has won over them all.

I watched the press conference from a dentist's chair; left alone while waiting for the gas to kick in. For me, it never takes long. I do not remember what I said to Tuberville that day, but he probably doesn't either.

Why the Coup Failed

Why did the *Jetgate* coup fail? There are many reasons. We will emphasize three.

Firstly, Tuberville beat Alabama. The *Jetgate* crew must have thought we were going to lose. Their plan was to have Tuberville's replacement lined up so they could move quickly after a final disappointing loss in a painfully disappointing season. Auburn was favored, but Housel and co. may have thought Tuberville had lost the confidence of his players, and that the losses to Ole Miss and Georgia would prove indicative of a full implosion. I wonder how Walker and Housel reacted when Carnell Williams ran 80 yards for a touchdown on the first play of the game. Did they "go crazy?" When the clock hit zero, and Tuberville had two consecutive wins over Alabama, the conspirators likely wished they had instead set out to depose Mike Shula.

Because Auburn beat Alabama, the *Jetgaters* had to abandon their original plan of firing Tuberville right after the game. Losing to a 4–7 Alabama team would have been very disappointing. Without the firing window such a loss would have afforded, Housel and Walker had to buy time, which is exactly what they tried to do. They closed ranks on the story that Walker had a vacation planned. Housel attempted to disguise the stalling technique with an appeal to level-headed decision making: "He's going to step back, take a deep breath and let all the emotions calm down. Dr. Walker, Coach Tuberville and I will get together some time after that."[j] Buying time was the only thing Walker and Housel could do. Perhaps they thought a week would be long enough for everyone to start thinking less about Tuberville beating Alabama, and more about him losing five games instead of winning a national championship. As it happened, we had something else to think about long before Walker's "vacation" concluded. That brings us to the second reason the coup failed.

The second critical problem for the conspirators was they failed to keep their secret meeting with Petrino secret. Rumors of rendezvous with Petrino only became a real story when public flight records of a Colonial Bank plane flying to Louisville were discovered. This revelation was the support for the rumors—not their instigation. One or more of the passengers on Lowder's plane simply did not keep the itinerary to himself.

Before moving on to our third reason, let us consider another explanation. This assessment—by Tom Arenberg in the November 30, 2003 Birmingham News—works in conjunction with Tuberville's assailants failing to keep their excursion secret.

> The revelation of a clandestine meeting with another coach—while Tuberville remained under contract and clueless—might not have been enough to save him, either, had the timing been ever so slightly different. That graceless move only cost Auburn a chance at Bobby Petrino. The gaffe, and Tuberville's saving grace, was that the trip took place before the Iron Bowl. Had Auburn's cabal hopped the plane one minute after the final play, all of last week's events would have turned out different.[k]

The timing of the trip and its lack of secrecy were major errors in any case, but because we beat Alabama, their implications are compounded. If Tuberville had lost to Shula and finished the season 6–6, the meeting with Petrino would have been less scandalous. Losing to Alabama would have also tempered the outrage in response to when the trip took place.

Even with Tuberville beating Alabama, had the conspirators failed at one of these points rather than both, their plan might have carried forward. As suggested by Arenberg, if the meeting had been after the Alabama game, its revelation would not have been so damaging. Or, if the conspirators had simply kept the trip to Louisville a secret through the last week of November, by then Walker and Housel could have already fired Tuberville. The eventual discovery of when Petrino was interviewed still would have brought strong criticism against the conspirators, but Tuberville would already be out; the coup would have been successful.

The third reason the coup failed is the most important for our purpose of better understanding the Tuberville era. At the conclusion of the Alabama game, a different contest began: a nine-day public relations war in which Tuberville and the conspirators battled for the support of the Auburn People, the media and the general public. President Walker spoke for the conspirators. Tuberville spoke for himself. From their statements over this nine-day period it is clear that Tuberville possessed a better understanding of the values of the Auburn Family than did Walker. This superior understanding is why Tuberville's career at Auburn lasted another five years beyond November 2003, and Walker's was finished in a matter of weeks.

Why the People Chose Tuberville

The difference in how Tuberville and Walker understood the priorities of the Auburn People is easy to demonstrate. We can also show how Tuberville appealed to the Auburn Family. In the critical nine-day period, he communicated through the media his appreciation for the Auburn Spirit to the Auburn Family. His first statement was made Saturday on the field. The following week, there developed a widespread sentiment that to be a real Auburn fan entailed supporting Tuberville. This sentiment was encouraged in the media. Stan White, analyst for Auburn football radio broadcasts, said:

> I would think it would make the university look a lot better if the president came out, or David Housel, and said, 'We're giving a vote of confidence for our coach.' Just say he's going to stand behind him.[1]

In a Huntsville Times article titled *Tuberville Has Done All that Auburn's Asked of Him*, John Pruett expressed his assessment of Walker and Housel this way: "In the name of common sense, what can they be thinking?" These statements were made before the revelation of the trip to Louisville. Tuberville actually began his appeal to the Auburn people before the game. He made a teary eyed Tiger Walk, and in a pregame interview said the win-loss record didn't tell the whole story.

> When you're walking down Tiger Walk and you see the people's faces about how much they want to win this game, it's emotional. It's not just emotional for the players. The coaches get into it as much as anybody else. We pour our heart and soul into this game. I know we haven't played a great season, and we've lost some games. We've played a tough schedule, and our guys have played hard every

snap, every game for four quarters, win or lose. I'm proud of every dang one of them, and I know our fans are.[m]

After the game, Tuberville dedicated the win to the fans—or, at least to some of them. "This is for the fans. This is for the people who back us every day and stayed with this football team."[n]

Walker and Housel said nothing new on Sunday. Their conspiracy had suffered a major setback, and they were scrambling to figure out plan B. Tuberville continued to rally his troops—and recruit new ones. He said he was "shocked" to learn his job was in jeopardy even after beating Alabama.[o] He was telling the Auburn people they should be shocked; that they should find Walker and Housel's behavior and speech shocking. Many of us did.

On Monday, Walked left for his vacation, but managed to sound incompetent before leaving town. When asked whether prolonging the uncertainty could hurt Auburn's football program, he responded, "Any time there's indecision that's a concern."[p] Housel retooled his earlier statement, saying, "Dr. Walker will make the call, and he is an engineer by profession. He likes to get all of the possible solutions and then make a decision. He's not going to be rushed into anything."[q] There was no need for Tuberville to say anything by this point. He had already won over most everyone. His opponents seemed hell bent on losing the confidence of the Auburn people.

Walker confirmed his disconnect with reality in his statement Tuesday night. Tuberville had already won the loyalty of the Auburn Family, especially its most vocal members, and yet Walker thought he was still holding court. "Coach Petrino has been mentioned as a candidate for the job should it become available. I have made no decision and am considering my options. This visit was a part of that process."[r]

Walker's Tuesday statement showed he was out of touch with the Auburn Family, but it was what he said Wednesday that fully revealed the difference in priorities. The statement begins:

> Auburn University has an established tradition of excellence in both its academic and athletic programs. Recently, I have grown concerned that the football program has been falling short of my expectations for its success.

Again, Walker shows his delusion—nobody cares whether the football program meets *his* expectations. Later in the statement he acknowledges Tuberville's popularity and success, but then says:

> I continue to have high expectations for all of Auburn's athletic teams, including football. Throughout the year, I expressed those expectations to the athletic director who relayed them to the football coaching staff. I want to be clear. I expect Auburn to compete consistently for the SEC Championship and to be highly ranked nationally on a regular basis. We have not achieved these goals and that has been, and continues to be, my paramount concern.

Only after the above self-justification does Walker say he hopes Tuberville will remain as coach. Walker's priorities show his fundamental misunderstanding. Anyone who's been to Jordan-Hare Stadium and heard Auburn people chanting "It's great to be an Auburn Tiger" after losing a game knows that, for the Auburn Family, winning is not everything. Pat Dye said it this way: "Winning is not the main thing. Paying the price to be able to win is what matters."[5] For Auburn people, "paying the price" is deeply connected to the Auburn Spirit—"I believe in work, hard work." We want the football team to represent the Auburn Spirit well. We want to be able to look at the football program and say "I believe in Auburn and love it!"

Walker's mistake is that he thought the Auburn people would back him because he had winning as his top priority. At another institution, he might have been right. Auburn is different. After his meeting with Walker, Tuberville displayed his better understanding of the Auburn people.

> I hadn't been here a week and I knew of the love that the people had for this school and everything that it stands for and everything that they want to put in their program. We've tried to do that for them over the last five years.[t]

This insight guided Tuberville's comments throughout the ordeal. Walker may have been answering to the most powerful individuals, but Tuberville appealed to the love of Auburn that makes the school's supporters not just fans, but the Auburn Family—and that is how Tuberville won the power struggle known as *Jetgate*.

et tu, Housel?

David Housel's involvement in the failed coup was difficult for Auburn people to accept. Alternatively, without Housel the scandal loses something of its depth. When Housel boarded the plane, so did Auburn. I wonder if he had time that night to think about a previous flight. Consider his comments from the day Tuberville was announced as Auburn's head coach in 1998.

> I knew he was the man for Auburn when we talked on that plane flying over here. You can measure an Auburn man two ways. One is by the degree he holds. One is by the values he shares, the values he believes in. I think it is far more important to get an

Auburn man in terms of the values that he holds dear, and I think we have done that in Tommy Tuberville.[u]

Housel's reinstatement to Auburn iconic status is virtually complete. His perception as Auburn's chief football historian is unquestioned. The press box at Jordan-Hare Stadium was named in his honor in 2005. *Jetgate* continues to follow him around a little, as it must; enough so that he was asked about it in a 2012 interview with Auburn Magazine.

> I was part of a process that went awry. The (university) president, Dr. (William) Walker, decided that we needed to look in different directions and was eager to go forward. The cart got put before the horse, and the cart fell in the ditch. What more can you say?
>
> There was a long time where Auburn didn't love me, but I never stopped loving Auburn. And I know there are still people out there who are angry and upset, but the only thing a person can do is the best you can do when you have to do it.
>
> I'm kind of like Colin Powell in his 'weapons of mass destruction' speech at the United Nations. I wish it hadn't happened, but it did. You can't change history, but neither can you let history hold you back. But I do think about it.[v]

Whatever love the Auburn People withdrew from Housel, they in turn gave to Tuberville. The sensationalism of the scandal was matched by the enthusiasm of Tuberville's supporters during the nine-day war. The University was bombarded by emails, calls and letters expressing loyalty to—and confidence in—Coach Tuberville. His victory over the conspirators became a victory for the people. This shared triumph heightened the bond between Tuberville and the Auburn Family and increased the Auburn Family's emotional investment in our coach.

Before we begin our best efforts to leave *Jetgate* behind, I have—as the reader has come to expect—a couple stories to tell.

Who is John Mengelt?

When researching the *Jetgate* scandal one expects to encounter certain names: David Housel, William Walker, Bobby Lowder, Earl McWhorter, Byron Franklin, etc. One name I did not expect to come across was John Mengelt. Who is John Mengelt and what is his connection—or alleged connection—to *Jetgate*? Before we answer these questions, allow me to tell my John Mengelt story. To tell my John Mengelt story requires, of course, that I first tell my Dad's John Mengelt story.

Dad's John Mengelt Story

It was the summer of 1970. Dad was working for Texaco and sharing an apartment with a co-op student named Ernesto C. Zuniga. One Friday the two engineers decided to drive from Morgan City, Louisiana to Houston to catch a baseball game at the Astro Dome. Somewhere along I-10 a four-door Lincoln pulled alongside Dad and Ernesto, who were riding in my grandmother's 1965 Comet Caliente. The occupants of the Lincoln rolled down their windows, yelling at Dad and motioning for him to pull over. Dad began to comply, and when Ernesto protested, Dad explained they were yelling "War Eagle" in response to an Auburn decal in the back window of the Comet. Once everyone exited the vehicles on the side of the interstate, the Lincoln guys offered Dad and Ernesto beer from a cooler in the backseat. One of the guys introduced himself, expecting Dad to recognize his name.

Here I must disclose a point of historiographical concern. Dad does not remember what the guy who thought himself a celebrity said his name was. Years after the fact, Dad researched Auburn Basketball archives and, putting together other details of the story that will be presented below, concluded the gentleman must have been John Mengelt, who played basketball for Auburn from 1968 to 1971. For the moment, we will refer to the individual in question as Mengelt; later, we will address the historical difficulties of that conclusion.[1]

Dad is an Auburn graduate and an Auburn Football fan. He has never followed Auburn basketball closely at all; not even when he was a student. He did not know who Mengelt was. One might argue such unawareness would compare to me not knowing who Chris Porter is. Mengelt was a two time All-American at Auburn. On Valentine's Day, 1970—six months or so prior to the encounter on I-10—Mengelt scored 60 points in a 121–78 victory over Alabama. That performance is still the all-time most points scored by an Auburn player in a single game.

Mengelt had apparently told his traveling companions that everyone from Auburn knew who he was. He saw the decal in the back of Dad's car and thought he had an opportunity to prove his fame. When Dad failed to provide such proof, Mengelt's buddies mocked his claims of celebrity status. Dad thinks he remembers that these buddies were Mengelt's teammates on a professional team in Houston.

This detail creates a considerable challenge to the identification of Mengelt as the player in question. Firstly, Mengelt had not yet finished his Auburn career in the summer of 1970. Furthermore, Mengelt enjoyed a successful NBA career, but never played for Houston. I was not aware of these inconsistencies when

---

[1] My John Mengelt story, in fact, includes Mengelt, regardless of whether the guy Dad encountered was actually him.

I attempted to corroborate the story in 2010, which brings us to my John Mengelt story.

My John Mengelt Story

Like my Dad, I am an Auburn graduate and an Auburn Football fan. To say I am an Auburn Basketball fan requires qualification. Do I want our basketball team to win? Of course! I hope we win every time they take the court. I feel this way about every Auburn sports team. "I believe in Auburn and love it!" With regards to actually supporting the basketball team, however, I am a fair-weather fan. Did I show up two hours prior to tip-off during the incredible 1998-1999 season (my final season as a student)? Yes, as soon as it became clear that we had a good team, I was at every game. My attendance prior to that season had been infrequent and socially motivated.

While I am not a committed fan of Auburn basketball, I do feel a strong connection to the venue in which the Tigers played from 1969-2010, Beard-Eaves Memorial Coliseum. When I was a student the Coliseum concourse was a popular indoor running/walking track. Sam and I logged many miles on that concrete.

When I heard that the 2009-2010 season would be the last played in Beard-Eaves, I had a desire to see one last game there. The final Beard-Eaves game was on a Wednesday night, so Sarah and I drove down for the next-to-last game, against LSU on Saturday February 27, 2010. As part of the Beard-Eaves-era-coming-to-a-close festivities, the University honored all Auburn Basketball Lettermen who were able to attend the game. They all lined up down the center of the court, each stepping out and waving when his name was called. I was not purposefully paying attention to this ceremony, but I happened to hear Mengelt's name and noticed the gentleman who stepped out in response. Later in the game I saw Mengelt walking up the aisle near where we were sitting. I realized I had an opportunity to potentially corroborate Dad's story. Here is how our exchange began: "Are you John Mengelt?"

"Yes."
"You know how everybody's Dad has stories?"
"Oh, no."
"Well, my Dad tells a story about you."
"Were we drinkin'?"

To this point, Menglet sounds like our guy. I told the story, and basically ended it by saying, "Dad says your buddies gave you a hard time because he didn't know who you were." Mengelt responded, "They should've given me a hard time." With that, he patted me on the shoulder and walked away. He said nothing to confirm or deny his presence on the side of the interstate on that summer day in 1970.

I now suspect the individual Dad met that day was actually Carl Shetler, who played for Auburn from 1968-1970. Shetler was an assistant coach for the McNeese State University basketball team from 1970-1974. McNeese State is in Lake Charles, Louisiana; I-10 passes through Lake Charles. If I ever see Shetler at an Auburn basketball game, I'll ask him.

What does John Mengelt have to do with *Jetgate*? When President Walker admitted on the Tuesday night following the Alabama game that he met with Bobby Petrino, he said the meeting was arranged by a search firm. Journalist Phillip Marshall later reported that the "search firm" was actually John Mengelt, who owns a search firm called Breckenridge Partners.[w] An Associated Press article[x] published after Marshall's story reported that Mengelt would not confirm or deny setting up the meeting— the same result I got when questioning Mengelt!

9

Before What Happens Next

As Auburn historians we cannot help but approach 2004 with a sense of awe. The 2004 season is not just another year. It is special; distinguished in the whole course of Auburn football history, let alone in the Tuberville era. The 2003 season—as we have seen—was just the opposite; unclean in every way. Between the two stands something of a liminal space; keeping separate, as they always must be, the sacred and profane. In this buffer zone there is both good and bad, but neither to the extremes found on either side. These events touch both seasons, but do not belong solely to one or the other. We will not cover these events in great detail, but we must take notice in preparation to celebrate 2004 properly.

Other Trouble

After Tuberville agrees to reinstatement, a period of relative calm ensues—it lasts one week. On December 9, 2003 the Southern Association of Colleges and Schools—Auburn University's accrediting body—placed Auburn on probation. This action by SACS was one step short of withdrawing the school's accreditation and everything that goes with it, such as students' eligibility for federal assistance. SACS investigated Auburn in response to a complaint filed in 2001 by a group of students, faculty and alumni.[a] In August 2001 the University sued SACS, alleging the accrediting body was not following its own guidelines in the investigation. The lawsuit was successful, at least in one regard. SACS and the University agreed to accept a third party, independent investigator, appointed by the federal court, to take over review of the complaint. The investigator, Richard Y. Bradley, ultimately submitted a report to SACS, and then SACS placed Auburn on probation—not because of the report's contents, but because Auburn had embarrassed the accrediting agency by calling them out on not playing by their own rules. Bradley's report actually concludes that Auburn was in compliance with the accreditation criteria pertinent to the complaints raised by the student/faculty/alumni group.[b] But, because the complaint alleged that the board of trustees micro-managed university affairs, it was easy for SACS to appear justified in placing Auburn on probation in the aftermath of *Jetgate*. The probation announcement prompted more calls for President Walker and the trustees to resign.[c] As 2003 neared its end, the job security tables had turned.

On December 30, 2003 Tuberville said he planned to keep his staff employed at Auburn. "We've had enough ups and downs... I could reorganize some things. As of right now, it looks basically the way we've had it, but I could reorganize some things and move some people around."[d] Having already defeated his opponents on the public-relations battlefield, Tuberville ran up the score with this act of civility. His assistants would not be the only ones staying for another year; but before we discuss that matter, there is actually one more Auburn football game in 2003.

Not Bluegrass, but Country

Nashville is about 530 miles from New Orleans, but the separation is much, much further between the BCS Championship Game and the Music City Bowl. Tuberville, of course, emphasized the bigger picture, with a certain optimistic spin. "The high expectations were obviously over-reacted to, but we did regroup and by regrouping we were able to get to this bowl game."[e] Our opponent in Nashville was the Wisconsin Badgers. After a back-and-forth game, the final minutes played out the way we once hoped the whole season would go. Jason Campbell led the offense on a 87-yard drive capped by a Ronnie Brown touchdown. On the Badgers' ensuing possession, Karlos Dansby hit Wisconsin quarterback Jim Sorgi, forcing a fumble and setting up a short touchdown run by Carnell Williams. The Tigers won 28–14. The much-hyped 2003 season that started infamously with two consecutive losses finished beneath the *Jetgate* headlines with two consecutive wins.

The Music City Bowl was not our biggest post-season win of 2003. That came two weeks into 2004 when Carnell Williams, Ronnie Brown and Carlos Rogers all announced they would remain at Auburn for their final season of eligibility. All three announced their decisions to stay at the same press conference, one day before the NFL deadline to petition for early entry. Tuberville called it "the best recruiting day we've had in awhile."[f] Each player described a difficult decision process. Williams mentioned a desire to overcome the disappointment of 2003.

> As a team, we've still got some unfinished business. With the guys we've got coming back, and the young guys we've got coming—and I heard recruiting is going good—things are looking up.[g]

While Tuberville, his assistants, and the trio of Williams, Brown and Rogers were all staying, there was one individual who was going.

Trouble for the Troublemakers

When the *Jetgate* conspirators' coup backfired, Tuberville became the most popular man on campus, and the conspirators themselves the most despised. None of the midnight flyers initially obliged the public demands for their resignations; nor did they indicate any plans to do so. When the SACS probation was announced, Walker found himself doubly embattled, but the president held his ground, at least until he faced the governor. Alabama Governor Bob Riley met with Walker on January 14, 2004 to discuss the state of the University. Two days later, Walker resigned. Housel, on the other hand, continued to hang on, even as the Alumni Association continued telling him to resign. The group's spokesman, Ralph Jordan, Jr., weighed the severity of the offense against Housel's Auburn pedigree.

> I feel like the people involved in that ill-advised trip to Louisville should step down voluntarily . . . In David's case, it's particularly sad and regrettable . . . . If he chooses to stay on, I wish him well. But I don't see how the people who work for him can have confidence in him."[h]

While the governor fired the president, and the alumni association wanted to fire the athletics director, Tuberville had already said he was firing nobody, but he did make some changes.

Restructuring

Tuberville began reshaping the staff by moving Hugh Nall from offensive coordinator back to offensive line. He then reassigned defensive backs coach Phillip Lolley to Director of High School Relations; Lolley's coaching duties were transferred to defensive coordinator Gene Chizik. Tuberville moved quarterbacks coach—and 2003 play caller—Steve Ensminger to tight ends. The quarterbacks became the responsibility of the new offensive coordinator; and that bring us to the most significant adjustment to Tuberville's staff for 2004.

Two weeks before the start of spring practice Tuberville hired Indiana offensive coordinator Al Borges. Borges had been at Indiana two seasons. In 2002 the Hoosiers won three games, lost nine and their offense ranked 69th nationally. In 2003 they won two, lost ten and averaged 322 yards per game—98th-best nationally. Tuberville explained the selection of Borges not in terms of his results at Indiana, but with regards to what he could hopefully do with Carnell Williams and Ronnie Brown.

> We've got to get them in the game and he had a great plan for that. I thought, through this whole deal, 'How we can get both those guys on the field?' Utilize the talent. That is what coordinators are for—getting your best players on the field the most and utilizing them.[i]

As planned, Borges was also assigned to coaching quarterbacks; so his relationship with Jason Campbell would be equally critical to the Tigers' offensive success. That relationship began well. "He's strict just like Coach Petrino. He talked about how strict he is about the way he wants stuff done in his offense. I think that will bring the best out in me. Things happen for a reason."[j] Even with the rearrangement of Tuberville's staff complete, there are two more career changes in the 2003-2004 offseason.

On March 16, 2004 David Housel finally announced his departure. Rather than resigning immediately as did Walker, Housel scheduled a January 2005 retirement. He said he had not been forced out, but also spoke somewhat candidly about the

Jetgate connection. Housel said he had previously planned to retire in 2006, but that "When I started looking at 2006, I had no idea I would be going to Louisville in November of 2003."[k] Housel's exit had at least the formal appearance of being his idea. That luxury was not afforded another member of the Auburn Family—one who had nothing to do with *Jetgate*.

I noted in the introduction the role of The Auburn Football Review with Coach Pat Dye in my upbringing. It took us inside Auburn football. It brought Pat Dye into our living room. He did not come alone. Dye told his players after the 1989 Alabama game, "I ain't smart enough to tell you how I feel about you." Whenever he was not smart enough to tell us what he wanted to on Sunday afternoon, he had help from Phil Snow. Dye, of course, was the star of the show, but Snow was always there, setting the course with his comments and questions to the coach. Snow clearly loved Auburn football the way we did; so he was as welcome in our living room as Dye.

Snow's contribution to the Auburn experience has been underappreciated. Because the playbacks was such a big part of how I learned the connection between Auburn football and the values of the Auburn Family, to me Snow holds a place of significance comparable to that of Jim Fyffe. After the 2003 season—a year when that connection was momentarily severed—the Auburn Network decided to replace Snow with the same man who replaced Fyffe, Rod Bramblett. Their decision is defensible. Snow belonged to the old guard (he had already retired from his primary job as sports director for WSFA TV in Montgomery); the Auburn Network made a business decision to consolidate roles. The regrettable part is that Snow learned of his removal from the 2004 Football Media Guide. Auburn Network President Mike Hubbard failed to tell Snow of the decision before it was made public. [1]

The end of Phil Snow's tenure as host of the Auburn Football Review is a fitting conclusion to our review of the liminal space between 2003 and 2004 because of its analogous relationship to *Jetgate*—a questionable idea, horribly executed. As the 2004 season begins, the program is still staggering a little from the burden of *Jetgate*, largely due to media fascination and the SACS probation, but also because it shook the foundations of the Auburn Family. We were hurt; and we were still getting our feet when it came time to play football again. Fortunately, though the talking heads kept the broken record playing, for those of us who actually care about Auburn Football, the events on the field in 2004 quickly relegated everything from 2003 to ancient history. And now, dear readers, we have properly dealt with the matters that stand between the vileness of 2003 and the celebration of 2004. We can wash our hands of a moment that brought Auburn to the bottom and look ahead to a day when the Tigers are on top.

10

2004

The expectations for 2004 were lower than the year before, but the drop off would have been greater had Carnell Williams and Ronnie Brown left early for the NFL. As it was, Auburn had two returning 1000-yard rushers and an experienced quarterback. Though Carlos Rogers also delayed his departure, defensive coordinator Gene Chizik was scrambling to make the 2004 personnel fit his scheme. Nonetheless, the overall talent picture was good enough to garner some preseason respect. The voters at SEC Media Days picked Auburn to finish second in the western division. In their estimation, however, it was a long way to the top. Eighty-eight attendees voted in the poll: 61 predicted Georgia would claim the SEC championship; 19 picked LSU; one picked Auburn.[a] Second in the West was a consensus prediction for Auburn in 2004. The Birmingham News and Sports Illustrated also picked Auburn to finish behind LSU.[b] So for the year after the year when Auburn was supposed to do something special, the expectation was respectable mediocrity—an ok season, but not a great one; a good team, but not as good as LSU. Before we re-experience how reality exceeded those expectations, there is a development beneath the surface in 2004 that deserves our attention: a player who has been waiting for his moment; who will wait just one season more.

Brandon Cox became an Auburn Tiger on signing day in 2002, but left the team before the season began. When Cox left in August, Tuberville said he would hopefully rejoin the team sometime in the future. Sometime turned out to be December 2002 when the Tigers started practice for the Capital One Bowl. We learned at that time that Cox lives with a neuromuscular disorder called Myasthenia Gravis. Moreover, he was in a car accident in the summer of 2002 and suffered a concussion, which led to some health problems related to MG.[c] After sitting out 2002, Cox was redshirted in 2003—another year of waiting. In 2004, Jason Campbell was our no. 1 QB, but Brandon Cox was getting closer, moving from fifth to second on the depth chart. By the end of fall camp, Cox had shown Borges he was ready to play: "We have found that when he gets into scrimmages there is very little drop-off, if any at all sometimes. I have no reservations about putting Brandon Cox into a football game."[d]

Why bother talking about Brandon Cox in the lead up to the 2004 season? As we approach one of Auburn's best seasons ever, we are also approaching one of the best four-year runs in Auburn football history. Brandon Cox is an integral part of those latter three years. Furthermore, he is representative of the foundational work that took place before 2004 to make the Golden Age of Tuberville possible. There were setbacks and delays, but there was also perseverance and preparation.

The 2004 Season

The 2004 season opener against Louisiana-Monroe was pleasantly undramatic. Jason Campbell threw touchdown passes to Carnell Williams and Devon Aromashodu. Brandon Cox and Ronnie Brown each ran for a touchdown. Our defense recorded their first shutout since 2002: AU 31 – ULM 0.

The next week the Tigers scored earlier and more often against Mississippi State. The Bulldogs did not score until the final two minutes of the game. Auburn 43 – State 14. Points would be much harder to come by the following week.

The First Test

For the second time in four years, the Auburn-LSU game week was wait-and-see: not regarding how the match up would play out, but whether it would be played at all. In 2001 the game was postponed, as were all games scheduled for September 15. In 2004 the problem was Hurricane Ivan. On Tuesday Auburn cancelled classes for the rest of the week and announced the decision on whether to play the game would be made Friday.[1] After a week of uncertainty and speculation—everyone on the internet knew someone who knew someone who knew for sure the game would be postponed—Saturday September 18, 2004 turned out to be a pretty day. LSU likely wishes Ivan had headed straight for the Plain and pushed the contest back to November—that scenario worked out for them in 2001. The 2004 season, of course, belonged to Tigers of a different stripe.

Both offenses started strong. LSU opened the game driving 80 yards on 14 plays. They scored a touchdown but missed the extra point. Auburn responded with a 14-play drive that ended with a field goal. LSU kicked a field goal on their second possession, taking a 9–3 lead; with that kick, the scoring was done until the final two minutes of the fourth quarter.

---

[1] At least one member of Auburn's coaching staff was willing to play, rain or shine—defensive coordinator Gene Chizik: "I can coach in a tornado, a hurricane, a blizzard, Alaska—they're all the same to me." CHARLES GOLDBERG. "WITH MUDDERS ON TEAM, RAIN'S NO PAIN FOR CHIZIK." *Birmingham News (AL)* 16 Sep. 2004, Sports: 8-C. *NewsBank.* Web. 7 May. 2013.

Over the course of the game each team punted six times. The Auburn offense struggled after their opening drive, but our defense made big plays to shut down LSU, especially in the second half. LSU made a first down early in the third quarter, but then defensive end Stanley McClover forced a fumble, and Auburn recovered. The Bayou Bengals put together an eight-play drive on their next possession before defensive end Bret Eddins sacked Marcus Randall for a loss of ten yards on third down. LSU later went three-and-out to conclude the third quarter, but Carnell Williams muffed the punt, and the Corndogs started anew at about midfield.[2] LSU took advantage and made two first downs, but then tried a reverse, which defensive back Junior Rosegreen stopped for a loss. LSU appeared to be driving on their next possession, but Antarrious Williams stopped LSU running back Justin Vincent for a two-yard loss, after which JaMarcus Russell threw an incompletion on third-and-ten. It was then time for the Auburn Tigers to make something happen—no ifs, ands or muffs.

The next twelve plays comprise a drive that is difficult to overstate in importance. It is where *the season after Jetgate* becomes something else. It starts with great field position, at our 40-yard line. On second down Ronnie Brown turns up field on a toss sweep. He shoots the gap between blocks by offensive tackle Marcus McNeal and tight end Cooper Wallace. He then gets a pancake block from offensive tackle Troy Reddick. He negotiates the remaining traffic and stiff arms a defender before finally going down after a 20-yard gain. Brown gains another six yards on the next play. Then Carnell Williams and Jason Campbell add short runs to get another first down. The Tigers struggle, however, on the next series. Williams is stopped for a loss on first down, after which Campbell throws two incompletions, bringing up fourth-

---

[2] I did not remember this play, but the record books say it happened. If Tre Smith had been the return man, I certainly would not have forgotten the muff that could have ruined 2004.

and-twelve. Auburn calls timeout to make sure we have the right play called for the game's critical down. Here's what happens when the offense retakes the field.

Campbell takes the snap, drops straight back, then rolls to his right. He fires the ball downfield toward the near sideline just before one LSU defender hits him in the chest and another in the back (a third pass rusher is closing at arm's length). The coverage on Courtney Taylor is good, but Taylor's route is perfect. He comes back to Campbell's pass, leaps to make the catch and comes down in the arms of the defender. The play gains 14 yards. Borges later says of Campbell: "The throw he made—under that kind of pressure, [with] that kind of location, was a first-round-draft-pick type play."

After the fourth-down conversion, Carnell Williams lost three yards on a toss sweep. On the next play Anthony Mix fumbled after catching a short pass from Campbell, but Auburn recovered. LSU failed doubly on the next play. They did not pressure Campbell, but still left Taylor open in the end zone. Tuberville raises his arms expectantly once Campbell releases the ball. When Taylor catches it, Tuberville pulls off his headset and leaps along the sideline. Everyone goes into hug mode; but the game is not over.

We missed the extra point, which for a moment was devastating. A new rule, however, saved the day. The NCAA decreed prior to the 2004 season that jumping over the line of scrimmage and landing on an opposing player is a personal foul. On this critical extra point, LSU's regular kick-block-high-jump specialist was on the sideline due to injury. His replacement jumped too far forward and landed on our snapper, redshirt freshman Pete Compton. The penalty gave us another chance at the PAT, and John Vaughn made the kick to give Auburn a 10–9 lead with 1:14 left in the game. LSU coach Nick Saban did not argue the call, only the outcome. "I'm not criticizing the officials, but it's a cheap penalty to end up losing a game on."[e] To say that play decided the game neglects the remaining minute, in which LSU drove 43 yards on seven plays, to our 44-yard line. On third-and-one, JaMarcus Russel finds an open receiver near our 30-yard line, but the ball gets through his hands and is intercepted by Junior Rosegreen. From the video it appears that if Early Doucet had held on to the ball, he might have run between our two safeties on his way to the end zone. Instead, Rosegreen wisely wraps it up and goes to the ground.

We knew beating fifth-ranked and defending BCS Champion LSU was big. The question remaining was: how big? I was immediately enamored with the fourth-down conversion. After the game I asked Matt McGee if Courtney Taylor had made one of the biggest catches in Auburn football history. He replied presciently: "No, not unless we go on to finish the season undefeated." Speaking of comments made after the game, Tuberville said something interesting to the players in the locker room. "I knew all week long y'all was focused and ready to play."[f] In a week when whether to play or not was up in the air until Friday, and the opponent—should the game be played—was the defending BCS Champion (who beat us 31–7 the previous year), our team was ready. If this week could not break their focus, what could?

After beating LSU, Auburn jumped from 14 to 9th in the AP poll. It was our first non-preseason top ten ranking of the Tuberville era. The Tigers played like a top ten team against The Citadel, winning 33–3. More telling was the discrepancy in total offense: 593–169. The next game promised to be less comfortable, both because of the opponent and the location: Tennessee at

Neyland Stadium. We would soon learn, of course, that this team could play comfortably anywhere.

After The Citadel, the bulk of the conference schedule lay ahead. Prior to the fifth game of the season, Doug Segrest of the Birmingham News made an interesting observation: "Beat Tennessee . . . and Auburn is no longer the national disappointment of 2003. It is a legitimate national contender in 2004."[g] Before the trip to Knoxville, Segrest's comment might have seemed sensational speculation resting on a significant contingency. By halftime, the country was on notice—Auburn was in the hunt for a national championship.

Voluntary Houndslaughter

On Auburn's first possession of the game the Tiger offense drove 55 yards on nine plays. The payoff provided one of the more picturesque moments of 2004. Ronnie Brown lowered his shoulder and knocked defensive back Jason Allen on his butt. Allen's helmet rolled along the turf as Brown lunged into the end zone. The Tigers never looked back. At the half we led 31–3.

Tennessee's problem was that their leading receiver was Junior Rosegreen. Ok—technically C. J. Fayton was the leading Vols receiver, but Rosegreen caught just as many Tennessee passes: two interceptions in each half. Rosegreen's performance barely surpassed his personal expectations. "I was telling everybody I was going to get three. When I got two, they were like, 'man, you can get another one.' When I got that [third] one, they were like, 'I think you're going to get another one.'"[h] In all, Auburn took the ball away from Tennessee six times. Auburn 34 – Tennessee 10. The win solidified the Tigers' status as national title contenders. Their identity was firming up in another regard as well.

In the chapter on 1999 we mentioned that Tuberville hired Auburn's first ever full-time football chaplain, Chette Williams.

The impact of Bro. Chette's work with our players over the past five years became visible in a certain way at Knoxville in 2004. Remember seeing our players coming out of the tunnel in 2004. Instead of running, they locked arms and walked—almost marched—onto the field, with Tuberville in the middle of the front row. They didn't do that prior to the fifth game of the season.

The first time our players ever hooked up to come onto the field was against Tennessee. Chette Williams tells the story in his book, Hard Fighting Soldier.[i] For the team devotional the night before, Williams spoke to the players about how Roman soldiers hooked themselves together before going into battle. "That's what you've got to do. You have to hook up with your teammate and protect him while you fight side by side." It was at this devotional meeting that the players first sang "Hard Fighting Soldier" together.[3] Carrying forward the chemistry of Friday night, someone yelled "Hey, let's hook up" before the team took the field on Saturday. The Friday night singin' and the Saturday hookin' up became standard practice the rest of the season. The Auburn players were believing in themselves; in what they could do if they fought together. Not everyone outside the locker room was on board yet.

Beating Tennessee lifted the Tigers to no. 6 in the AP poll, and yet talk of Auburn even competing for a national championship still took on obligatory tempering. Such is the media bias in the state of Alabama. Kevin Scarbinsky of the Birmingham News responded to the blowout in Knoxville with a column titled, "Dare Auburn Dream of a National Title?" His concluding thought was this:

---

[3] Per Williams, sophomore tight end Kyle Derozan taught the song to many of his teammates the preceding Wednesday night at an FCA (Fellowship of Christian Athletes) meeting.

> It's still a long way to Atlanta, and never mind Miami. But if you can get out of here, there's a chance you can get there. If you can dominate here, you have a shot to celebrate there. Crazier things have happened.[j]

At 5–0 with two wins over top ten teams—and one of those on the road—plus another SEC road win (also a blowout), the possibility of Auburn playing for a national championship was "crazy." Consider the source. Consider the audience.

The following week Auburn overwhelmed Louisiana Tech., 52–7. A couple of superlatives from this game deserve mention. Firstly, Campbell's 87-yard touchdown throw to Silas Daniels set a new record for the longest pass play in Auburn football history.[4] Also, Carlos Rogers' 53-yard interception return for a touchdown was his only score in 50 games played for Auburn—a well deserved trip to the end zone for a player who made 181 total tackles as a Tiger. In the next game of the 2004 season, players more accustomed to the end zone scored the touchdowns—all five of them.

Harmless Hawgs

The Tigers, now ranked fourth after losses by Georgia and Texas, opened the scoring against Arkansas in entertaining fashion.[5] On the third play of the game, Campbell takes the snap at the Auburn 33; he pitches to Carnell Williams, who hands the ball to Courtney Taylor, apparently running a reverse. Taylor, however, tosses the

---

[4] This record stood until 2009, when Chris Todd completed a 93-yard touchdown pass to Terrell Zachery, also against La. Tech. That record was broken in 2010 by a 94-yard touchdown pass from Cam Newton to Emory Blake against Louisiana-Monroe.

[5] Georgia had been no. 3, but lost at home to no. 17 Tennessee. Fifth ranked Texas lost at no. 2 Oklahoma.

ball back to Campbell, who then unloads downfield to Devon Aromashodu. Campbell actually underthrows his receiver a little, allowing two Arkansas defensive backs to catch up. One of them grabs our receiver's jersey inside the five, but Aromshodu fights forward and drags the defender into the end zone with him. We never relinquished the lead. The Tigers led 30–0 with four minutes left to play in the half. The Razorbacks did manage a touchdown before the half, plus one each in the third and fourth quarters, but never presented any real threat. The offensive effectiveness was matched by defensive aggressiveness. Carlos Rogers, Travis Williams, Kevin Sears, Montavis Pitts and Stanley McClover each made a tackle for a loss. Auburn 38 – Arkansas 20.

Staying Focused

With the win over Arkansas, Auburn had beaten its four opponents since LSU by a cumulative score of 157–40. The Tigers played on seven consecutive Saturdays, and would go two more before getting a week off. One might have wondered when the Tigers would have a letdown. It would not be against Kentucky.

We dominated the Wildcats. Auburn led 21–0 after the first quarter. The defense gave up only 110 yards total offense. Third-string defensive end Quentin Groves made four sacks.

Auburn 42 – Kentucky 10. This stretch of the season is a little boring in a way; the Tigers cannot find a decent challenge on the schedule. The next week would be no different—even on the road, at Oxford.

Actually, Ole Miss appeared to present a challenge early on. They shut us out in the first quarter, and almost the whole first half, but the Tigers drove 99 yards on eight plays and scored on a Jason Campbell quarterback sneak with 26 seconds left in the second quarter. The second half went more to plan. Courtney Taylor, Ronnie Brown and Carnell Williams all found the end zone. Campbell added another one-yard touchdown run, and the

Tigers won 35–14. By beating Ole Miss—and improving to 6–0 in the SEC—the Tigers clinched the western division championship prior to October's end. While one post-season appointment was now secure, another was undetermined.

Auburn earned an appearance in the SEC championship game on the field of play. The question in November 2004 was whether winning every game on the schedule, plus the SEC championship game, would be enough to garner a BCS championship game appearance. This question was no less ridiculous then than it would be now. The only difference is that, while everyone understood the superiority of the SEC in 2004, only in more recent years has it become fashionable on a national level to concede and even celebrate the higher level of competition in the SEC. Ridiculous as it was, the politics of college football were heavy in the air as Auburn prepared to finish the regular season with games against Georgia and at Alabama. When asked about the brewing BCS controversy, Tuberville suggested the national champion be determined by a four-team playoff, an idea finally scheduled to be implemented in 2014.[k] The pollsters' refusal to vote objectively was frustrating to the fans, but, according to Tuberville, the players maintained focus.

> They've handled it well. I haven't heard one player even mention it in the training room or around anywhere. It's mostly talk in the newspapers and TV, which is fine. That's what it's all about, but we're still a long ways away from having any talk about that that really means anything.[l]

There was, however, at least one player who mentioned it after the Georgia game. "We're ready to jump somebody." Carnell Williams understood what should have been the implication of Auburn's performance against the Dawgs.[m] Tuberville used different words, but expressed the same sentiment. "One thing I'll say, I'd hate to play us. I know the people will be fair when they vote."[n] What could Auburn have done against Georgia that would have been enough? Before we answer that question, let us look at what Auburn did.

Whipping the Dawgs

Georgia opened the game with an 11-play drive, making it to the Auburn 19 before missing a field goal. The Bulldogs would not get that close to the end zone again until the final five minutes of the game. The Tigers were quicker and more productive on their first drive, moving the ball 80 yards on eight plays. Carnell Williams carried six times, including the final yard into the end zone. Auburn 7 – Georgia 0

Georgia punted on their next two possessions, as did Auburn—or at least attempted to. The second punt was blocked, and Georgia would have gotten the ball at the Auburn 27 if not for a personal foul. Georgia got those yards back on a David Greene pass to Reggie Brown, but when Greene tried to find Brown in the end zone two plays later, Carlos Rogers intervened—INT; Georgia's last real threat of the first half was turned away.

After the turnover the Auburn offense returned to form with a nine-play, 80-yard drive that concluded in sensational fashion. On second-and-nine at the Georgia 29, Campbell pitches the ball to Williams, who runs to his right. Williams runs a few yards beyond the right hash before he pulls up and throws the ball downfield to wide-open Anthony Mix, who easily makes it to the end zone. Williams' sell on the play is impressive. He holds the ball in both hands for a few steps after taking the pitch, and then tucks it in his right arm, down on his hip. Only at the last moment, with Georgia defenders closing in, does he bring the ball up and throw it in one motion. Williams described his execution: "That's what all the great quarterbacks do. They wait to the last minute."[o]

Borges later said he had called a toss sweep on the previous play to see how the Georgia defenders behaved.

> It's when you call it. That one, fortunately, was dialed at the right time. But, he made a great play; he made a hell of a throw. And Anthony Mix showed great patience to kind of sift his way through the garbage and get to the spot he needed to be.[p]

Williams' throw to Mix made it Auburn 14, Georgia 0. Georgia did nothing with their next possession. Stanley McClover sacked David Greene on third down for a loss of ten. Carnell Williams returned the ensuing punt nine yards to the Georgia 38. Auburn's final drive stalled, but not before Campbell hit Cooper Wallace for a 22-yard gain. John Vaughn hit a 32-yard field goal to conclude the first-half scoring. Auburn 17 – Georgia 0

The second half provided more back-and-forth punting, but it also included a play of some notoriety. On a third-and-two play at the Auburn 28 David Greene throws a short pass to Reggie Brown, who jumps to catch the ball. Just as Brown's feet return to the turf, Junior Rosegreen knocks his head off. Ten years ago I thought this play was awesome. I'm older now. If a player were to make this hit in 2013, he would be ejected. We cannot, of course, judge Rosegreen by today's standard. In 2004 there was nothing of the talk about helmet-to-helmet contact that we have now. That language, however, was already in the rulebook. The critical determination by the officials was that Rosegreen did not intentionally hit Brown with his own head.[q] We can forgive them for not seeing such intent in real time; but the video evidence is conclusive. Brown remained motionless upon hitting the ground. He was apparently knocked unconscious, and the game ceased while trainers attended to him. Rosegreen made some interesting comments afterwards. "They were talking trash and I took it personally. I was happy he got up. It ain't personal. It's just business. We wanted to play a physical game and hit them in the mouth. Fred Gibson was talking trash. I really wanted to get Fred Gibson, but Reggie was the one I got."[1]

After an Auburn punt Georgia went three-and-out, despite gaining nine yards on first down. Carnell Williams returned the ensuing punt 40 yards, all the way to the Georgia 31. The Tigers gained a first down on the ground. Then on third down at the Georgia 15 Campbell has time to wait for Ronnie Brown to run a wheel route from the backfield. Campbell delivers the ball perfectly over a Georgia defender, and Brown reaches up to make an impressive catch over his head in the end zone. Auburn 24 – Georgia 0

With Auburn now holding a solid lead, each team drives but then punts, eating up much of the fourth quarter. Georgia finally gets on the board when David Greene throws a touchdown pass to Leonard Pope on a fourth-and-five play with 2:13 left in the game. The Bulldogs go for two but fail. Final: Auburn 24 – Georgia 6

Having looked at what the Tigers did, let us return to the question of what they could have done to jump Oklahoma in the polls. The answer is simple: nothing. Georgia began the year ranked third in the AP poll (with five first place votes). They remained number three until losing their fifth game of the season. The Bulldogs won their next three, crept back up to eighth and came to Auburn with an 8–1 record. Auburn beat them 24–6. The voters who persisted to rank Auburn the third-best team in the country after the Georgia win were not voting USC first and Oklahoma second; they were voting themselves first, first and first. The AP voters overwhelmingly placed USC and Oklahoma at no.

one and two, respectively, in the preseason poll.[6] They desperately wanted—for once—to be right; so they made those two teams irreproachable for anything other than a loss. We will return to the matter of voter bias (in favor of their own opinion) momentarily. For now, there are two more games to enjoy.

10–0. Not only did the Tigers maintain focus after clinching the division title, they soundly outplayed Georgia and improved to a record of 10–0, a feat only two previous Auburn teams (1957 and 1993) accomplished.[7] Now the challenge was to complete the perfect regular season. To do so, we had to beat Alabama at Tuscaloosa.

Takin' It Easy

The Birmingham News solicited Iron Bowl prognostications for their *Sound Off* feature the week of the game. I was happy to oblige, and delighted that they published my projection.[8]

> UAT, already intimidated by Auburn's prowess, will become further discouraged by the Tigers' quick start. The Cadillac and Ronnie Brown will each gain in excess of 200 all-purpose yards in a third victory at Tuberville-Denny Stadium. Auburn 45 Alabama 10

That is not quite how the game turned out; though it could have— perhaps should have—been, as we will see.

Alabama opened the game with an impressive drive, moving the ball all the way to the Auburn 14, but then backed up

---

[6] USC received 48 first place votes and Oklahoma received eleven.

[7] Prior to 2004, seven other Auburn teams (1972, 1974, 1983, 1986, 1988, 1989 and 1997) had won ten or more games, but each suffered a loss before getting the tenth win. Since 2004, two more Auburn teams, 2006 (11-2) and 2010 (14-0), have won ten or more games; only the latter achieved 10-0.

16 yards when Alabama quarterback Spencer Pennington tipped a shotgun snap over his own head and retreated to gather it up. The Tide settled for a field goal.

Neither team scored the rest of the first quarter. Alabama drove to the Auburn five, but then threw an interception. Early in the second quarter the Tide defense created a great opportunity. Alabama's Anthony Madison intercepted Campbell and made a good return, down to the Auburn six, giving the Tide first-and-goal. The Tiger defense, however, needed even less ground than that to defend the end zone. Alabama ran Kenneth Darby right at our D on first, second and third down; each time Bret Eddins, Will Herring, Jay Ratliff, Tommy Jackson et al. stopped him for little or no gain. Alabama settled for another field goal.

We turned the ball over on the ensuing possession, but Alabama punted it back. Then the Auburn offense came alive for the first time of the day. Starting at our own 16, Campbell completed passes of 16 and 22 yards to Ben Obomanu and Courtney Taylor, respectively. Cadillac added two nine-yard runs, and Ronnie Brown added a nine-yard run of his own. The drive ultimately stalled at the Alabama five, setting up a short field goal attempt by John Vaughn on the last play of the first half. It appeared we would at least get on the board before intermission, but Vaughn's attempt struck the left upright. I watched it oscillate for several minutes, surprised by how long it continued to wobble, and found myself in a trance of sorts that took me back to 1998.

Auburn was concluding a train wreck of a season in the 1998 Iron Bowl, but somehow led 17–0 in the first quarter. Alabama then scored a couple touchdowns, and was poised to take the lead right before the half, but threw an interception in the Auburn end zone. They ultimately won 31–17. As the flux capacitor—uh, I mean the goal posts—finally settled down, I thought this game would be like that one. Although we missed an opportunity to score before the half, the stronger team would take over in the final two quarters. My premonition was confirmed by the so-called Million Dollar Band, who chose for their halftime performance selections from West Side Story. The announcer noted that the musical opened on Broadway in 1957. Even the Alabama band knew we were going to win the national championship.

While I was undergoing hypnosis in the stands, the Auburn coaches were talking gut check in the locker room. Borges found it a teachable moment.

> I told the offense that championships aren't about beating Louisiana Tech 52–7, or being ahead 30–0 at halftime. Championships are about when you're sputtering, and the crowd is on the other side, you pick yourself up and make a comeback.[t]

The offense heard Borges' wisdom and continued their momentum from the first half. On the first possession of the third quarter the Tiger offense drove eighty yards. Carnell capped the drive with a five-yard touchdown run. Vaughn hit the extra point, and the Tigers would not trail again the rest of the game.

Alabama punts again, and then Auburn puts together another solid drive. This one culminates with a 32-yard throw from Campbell to Taylor. Campbell rolls to his left, but then turns his shoulders and delivers the ball downfield. Taylor catches it as he crosses the goal line in a space between the sideline and three Alabama defenders.

Alabama attempts to convert a fourth-and-one on their next possession, but Montavis Pitts and Karibi Dede stopped Kenneth Darby for no gain.

Auburn converted a fourth-and-one at the Alabama seven on the next possession, and two plays later Ronnie Brown scored our third touchdown of the game. At this point it seemed we could turn it on and pull away; even if too late to make my prediction of 45 points. Regardless, we didn't score as many points as we could have.

> We knew we were going to win if we halfway played. But how do you coach this game, the biggest game in the state, knowing if you lay it on the line . . . you might not have anything left for the SEC championship game? I told our coaches going into that 2004 game with Alabama, we're not going to downplay it, but I don't want them jumping around too much. We're going to win this game, but I want to go into the SEC championship game against Tennessee knowing we have everything locked and loaded.[u]

Had Tuberville notified me of this plan, I could have adjusted my prediction for the Birmingham News accordingly. I think it's clear from the above we could have beaten them as badly as we wanted.

Alabama scored a late touchdown, cutting the lead to eight, but failed to recover the onside kick: Auburn 21 – Alabama 13

By beating Alabama, the 2004 Tigers became only the second Auburn team to go 11-0.

The SEC championship game was not as lopsided as the Auburn-Tennessee game in October, but the Tigers' superiority was still clear. We scored first. Tennessee never led. They did tie the game at 21 with six minutes left in the third quarter, but from there we outscored them 17–7 and won the game 38–28. Our offense made more mistakes in this game than in most, but they also made more plays than did the Vols. The BCS distraction persisted, but two things were certain: for the first time since 1993, Auburn was the SEC champion; and, the 2004 Auburn Tigers were 12–0.[8]

The day after the 2004 SEC championship game is difficult to remember and impossible to accept. The injustice had been brewing, and its inevitability apparent, for weeks, but December 5, 2004 was the day it became official—the champion of the best conference in college football was undefeated, but they would not be allowed to play in the game that determined the supposed "national champion." We will take another look at this *traveshamockery* in the next chapter. For now, there is one more game for the 2004 Auburn Tigers to play—the Sugar Bowl.

One More Game

The Virginia Tech Hokies lost two of their first four games in 2004, but finished the regular season with seven consecutive wins. Their conference record of 7–1 made them ACC Champions and earned them an invitation to play Auburn in the Sugar Bowl.

Auburn moved the ball effectively in the early going. Campbell completed a 35-yard pass to Cooper Wallace on the Tigers' first offensive play. We made it to first-and-goal on each of our first two possessions, but each time scored only three points. The score remained 6–0 for much of the first half. Midway through the second quarter the Hokies tried to convert fourth-and-goal at our one, but their fullback dropped a pass in the end zone. The Tigers then drove 92 yards on twelve plays, but still did not get into the end zone. John Vaughn hit his third field goal of the game, and we led 9–0 at the half. On the first possession of the second half our offense again covered most of the field—half of it on one play when Campbell threw deep to Anthony Mix for a 53-yard

---

[8] Auburn did not play in the 1993 SEC championship game, but we beat both the teams that did, and lost to no one.

gain. This threat did not end with a field goal. Three plays after the big gain Campbell hit Devon Aromashodu for the game's first touchdown, making the score 16–0. It is a good thing we scored here. Of our next five possessions, two ended on turnovers, and the other three were three-and-outs. Fortunately, our defense stayed solid, for the most part. The Hokies scored their first points with 6:58 left in the game. After a failed two-point conversion the score was 16–6.

Derrick Graves made an interception on the Hokies' next possession, and with 3:32 left to play it looked like we could close things out. Instead of finishing strong, however, we almost preserved the victory away. After the interception our offense took over at the Tech 39. We then ran for one yard, two yards and minus one yard. Kody Bliss punted the ball into the end zone, thus giving Tech the ball just 17 yards down the field. On the next play our secondary left a receiver wide open, and the Hokies made things uncomfortably close with an 80-yard touchdown. Fortunately, Cooper Wallace recovered the onside kick, and we finally ran out the clock. Auburn 16 – Virginia Tech 13

There it is. Auburn's 2004 perfect season. It provides a great deal to take in, to digest; even opportunity to philosophize. We will take it all head on in the next chapter. But first, the rest of January 3, 2005 . . .

New Orleans

After the game was my first—and to date only—time to do Bourbon Street. I enjoyed all the obligatory tourist activities: had a hand grenade, drank beer from plastic bottles and nearly provoked an NFL linebacker to homicide. It was early in the evening, yet I was not watching where I was going—likely turned around talking to somebody, when I bumped into some guy; actually put my shoulder into him at full, jovial, we-just-won-it-all-but-didn't gait. I might have said "excuse me" or something; I don't remember. I thought we were in a crowd—a street-party crowd—and that this kind of thing was no big deal. I went along my way a few steps before Action asked if I realized who I just slammed into. It was Karlos Dansby. How do I respond to this revelation, by showing contrition and begging forgiveness? Not exactly. The first thing that comes to my mind is his performance on my fantasy football team. Yes, I played in a league that year that scored individual defensive statistics. I drafted Dansby, and he had done well. I turn around, and Dansby is staring at me. Undeterred, I yell at him something to the effect of, "You hooked me up in fantasy football." Dansby's silent response is difficult to put into words. He looked me in the eye; his countenance betraying some mix of mild amusement with contemplation of lifting me from the ground by my neck and choking me to death with one hand. War Eagle, Karlos!

I saw Ronnie Brown later in the evening. That encounter was a little more refined. I was outside Action's hotel, getting a cab for the ride back to mine. The running back suddenly bopped out of the lobby, apparently headed back out into the night. "War Eagle, Ronnie." He, too, seemed a little annoyed, but obliged the proper response as he kept walking. It was 3:00 am. I was tired and ready for bed. Brown looked like he could play another 60 minutes.

11

Tuberville's National Championship

Championships are won on the field. Anything else is a joke. The BCS is a joke. The winner of the BCS championship game is determined on the field, but the participants are not. Who gets to play is determined by opinion. Two teams are selected by people; by observers who are only human, who cannot be totally objective. We all bring prejudices and preconceptions to our evaluations of which football team is better than another. Unfortunately, the opinions of a select few determine who plays for the supposed national championship.

Everyone plays a number of games against scheduled opponents. Some teams play a conference championship game, the contestants of which are determined by performance on the field. Others do not; and then there is a vote.

There will be no actual national champion in Division I college football until the participants of the championship game are determined by competition. The upcoming four-team playoff simply extends the opportunity to the top-four voted teams rather than the top two. When all the participants in a playoff are determined on the field, the selection of teams for the championship game will be free of prejudicial influence, and we will then crown a true national champion.

If there is no such thing as a national champion, why bother with the controversy of 2004? We talk about a national champion in the context of the system we currently have. The construct of a national champion is so talked about that the idea is real in a sense. It is a real thing insomuch as people believe it is. If people are going to recognize a national champion according to some criteria, I want Auburn to receive that recognition when deserving. That is why I care about the injustice of 2004, and that is why we will engage it once more in our reflection on the 2004 season.

In the previous chapter I allege that the pollsters who did not vote Auburn ahead of Oklahoma were not judging the teams fairly, but rather protecting the notion that they had correctly picked the two best teams before the season began. We will now look at an example.

Accountability

In the week leading up to the SEC championship game, it was widely expected that Auburn could do nothing to jump into the top two. That being the case, my friend Matt McGee decided to reach out to some AP voters, to encourage them to cast their ballots based on performance. At least one voter responded. Here is Matt's email to Jim Carty, who at the time wrote for The Ann Arbor News.

Dear Mr. Carty,

My name is Matt McGee, and I should let you know up front that I'm an Auburn graduate. I want you to know that I'm grateful for your service to the sport of college football through your journalism and your participation in the AP poll. College football is the greatest sport in the world, and media members such as yourself have played a vital part in helping the sport become what it is today.

My purpose in this email is to ask you to please consider voting for Auburn as the #1 team in the nation (if Auburn should beat Tennessee) after all the games have been played this weekend. I understand that you have a very difficult decision in trying to decide between three deserving teams. I would greatly appreciate it if you would thoughtfully consider the points I make below.

Tony Barnhart is one of your fellow voters in the AP poll. Please take the time to read this article that he recently wrote:[1]

The article is a couple of weeks old, but Barnhart's points are still relevant.

Please also consider the following points before casting your vote:

- Auburn has had only one game this year (LSU) in which the outcome of the game was realistically in doubt at the start of the fourth quarter. Both USC (Virginia Tech, Stanford, Cal, OregonState) and Oklahoma (Texas, Kansas St., Oklahoma St., Texas A&M) have had multiple such games. To their credit they won all these games, but the fact that they have struggled against bad (Stanford, Kansas St.) and mediocre (Oregon St., Ok. St., A&M) teams is something that should be considered.

- Auburn has the #1 scoring defense in the nation.

---

[1] Here Matt's email contains a link to a column titled, "There's a good case for Auburn being ranked No. 1." As of May 17, 2013, the link is still good: http://www.newscoast.com/apps/pbcs.dll/article?AID=/20041116/NEWS/41116 0588/-1/INDEX.

- Contrary to what some people have been saying, the SEC is not "down" this year. The SEC has four teams in the current BCS top 15 (3 teams in the top 11). No other conference has more than two teams in the top 15.

- Auburn's much-maligned out-of-conference schedule (Louisiana Tech, Louisiana-Monroe, the Citadel) is not much different from Oklahoma's (Houston, Oregon and Bowling Green). For teams as good as Auburn and Oklahoma are, is there really a big difference in playing against the #50 ranked team and playing against the #100 ranked team? The bottom line is that Auburn and Oklahoma both played three non-conference games against teams who had no realistic chance of winning. USC did play one game (Virginia Tech) against a non-conference opponent with a realistic chance of winning, but this is more than offset by the totality of USC's schedule.

- Isn't the overall schedule (as opposed to merely the non-conference schedule) what's really important anyway? If Auburn beats Tennessee on Saturday, Auburn will have four wins (LSU, Tennessee, Georgia, Tennessee) over teams who have won nine or more games. This is more than USC and Oklahoma combined. Auburn is the only one of the three schools to have a win over a nine win school (Tennessee) in the opponent's stadium.

- Finally, if you have not seen tape of the Auburn wins against Tennessee and Georgia, I ask you to please make an effort to watch these games.

Thank you very much for considering Auburn!

Sincerely,

Matt McGee

The reader can judge both the basis for, and the respectful tone, of Matt's request. Here is Jim Carty's response.

> Matt,
>
> I don't know what you do for a living, but if I came to your job and suggested that you couldn't do your own research and I could tell you how to do the job better, would you find that inherently insulting and condescending?
> Let me ask you some questions:
>
> Have you seen every team in the AP Top 25 at least twice this season?
> Have you talked to coaches in each of the major conferences?
> Do you have friends who are coaches or former coaches who will give you private, honest evaluations of teams?
> Do you spend 40 to 60 hours of your week covering college football?
> If you can't answer yes to each of those questions, why do you think you can possibly give advice to someone who does each of those things?
> It's our job, Matt. Think of the amount of time you put into your own job, the passion I assume you have for it, and the expertise you've developed at it over the years.
> Then ask yourself how you'd feel if dozens of people started sending you e-mail how to do that job.
> Your [sic] not helping your team, you're just annoying people.
>
> Jim Carty
> Sports Columnist, The Ann Arbor News

Does it sound like Matt hit a raw nerve? Notice that Carty does not engage McGee's points. He does not even mention them; because he cannot refute them. Instead, he attempts to establish his superiority as an analyst. He finds it "insulting and condescending" that someone would challenge the notion that for once he finally picked the two best teams in August. Matt makes his argument on what the teams have done. Carty responds by puffing up what he has done. Perhaps we should consider that Carty must have possessed the ability to do competent research and analysis. After all, he later earned a law degree from the University of Toledo. McGee also later earned a law degree; from Duke.

Matt, and others who wrote their congressmen, understood then what is universally known now—the superiority of the SEC. Unfortunately, they were speaking wisdom to deaf ears. The voters got what they wanted. We went, instead, to the Sugar Bowl and won. That reality is in the past. The question that remains is: what do we do with 2004 now?

What It Meant and What It Means

One Auburn football historian answers this question by lobbying the University to officially claim 2004 as a national championship. Michael Skotnicki, author of *Auburn's Unclaimed National Championships*, studied the history of how national championships have been awarded in college football and then devised his own criteria.[2] He identifies seven Auburn teams in addition to 1957 and 2010 that meet his standard. Skotnicki argues that the players from these Auburn teams earned the recognition due national champions, and that they should be acknowledged as such at least by their own school.

I do not agree with Skotnicki—or at least not with his proposal that the University should officially claim additional national championships. His argument is compelling, especially since he frames it as an appeal for recognition of the players. My

---

[2] Skotnicki's standard is that the team in question must have been either undefeated or a conference champion (or both), in addition to being named national champion by at least one recognized selector.

contention is that I do not believe in claiming championships *ex eventu*. Skotnicki cautions that we should not let the liberality of our rival in this area dictate how we respect our own history. His point is well made, and I must admit some trespass against that admonition. All the same, my position is that championships are won on the field; not at the keyboard. Allow me to qualify this argument. While I do not advocate the University making such claims after the fact, what fans do is another matter. As a fan, I do claim 2004 as a national championship. As a historian, I recognize Auburn has the best claim to the national championship for 2004. We will explore both of those perspectives momentarily. First, let us consider someone else's.

"We dang did it"

The debated legitimacy of claiming national championships *ex eventu* is of no concern to Tommy Tuberville because he claimed 2004 in the moment. When Tuberville spoke to the 10,000 people who attended a celebration of the 2004 season at Tommer's Corner in January 2005, he clearly stated his evaluation of the season's success. "Six years ago December when I took the job here one of the last things I said in the press conference is, 'We will win a national championship here at Auburn.' And we dang did it last week."[a] Tuberville's declaration is in part why this chapter is titled Tuberville's National Championship. Auburn did not—and does not—claim it, but Tuberville did. He was not alone.

I attended the Perfect Season celebration; and, as noted above, I was at the Sugar Bowl to watch Auburn beat Virginia Tech. I must admit I found the victory somewhat anticlimactic. It was one more win in a season that should have earned us a spot in the BCS championship game, but did not. I was still a little hung up on that. I still am now. I cannot say I walked out of the Super Dome loudly declaring Auburn the National Champions. Had that

141

been my attitude, perhaps I would have said something like, "Karlos, don't you wish y'all played this good last year?" So while I did not instantly claim 2004 as a national championship, I did do something at the Perfect Season celebration that showed where my heart was. At a table in front of Anders Bookstore I purchased a print of the front page of the January 5, 2005 special edition of The Eufala Tribune. The Tribune conducted a poll of its staff writers. Auburn received all six first place votes. Tribune sports editor Patrick Johnston explained his vote this way: "Auburn is the only team in the nation this year to defeat four Top 10 teams [LSU, Tennessee, Georgia, and Virginia Tech]."[b] While Johnston's reasoning is logical, I viewed this national championship—awarded by a newspaper I had never heard of—much like our rivals must have seen it. Nonetheless, I handed over five dollars and took home my souvenir. Not long after I made the decision to keep the print rolled up and in a tube. I decided to delay framing and displaying it for ten years. My feeling was that after a decade we would all feel differently about the question of whether Auburn was national champion in 2004. We have almost made it to ten years; already there is reason to see 2004 in a new light.

2004, Then and Now

In June 2010 the NCAA ordered USC to vacate all victories from 2004 due to the ineligibility of Reggie Bush. USC's appeal of the NCAA sanctions was denied in May 2011, and two weeks later the BCS Board of Managers voted to vacate USC's championship.[c] In response to this move by the BCS, Tommy Tuberville, already two years removed from his tenure at Auburn, called for a new vote.

> We never complained when they went by the process the last time, and they should go by the process this time. If they were ineligible, I think they should have a revote and let people vote on it and decide who they think was the best team that

142

year. If everybody thinks it was Oklahoma, that's fine. If everybody thinks it was Auburn, that's fine.[d]

So Tuberville claimed a national championship in January 2005 and lobbied for wider recognition of that national championship in June 2011. His assertiveness in claiming the 2004 national championship and his lasting commitment to that claim serve as a model for the fans' philosophy.

Above I attempt to legitimate my claim as a fan to the 2004 national championship by saying I came close to claiming it in the moment. The reality, of course, is that any Auburn fan can claim 2004 as a national championship—and it matters not when he or she first does so. Regarding the fans' claim, the crux is that the fans of no other team can say anything to refute the claim. That is all that is needed —if even that—in the arena of fandom. We have now discussed the perspectives of the University, Tuberville and the fan. Finally, we look at the question from the perspective of the historian.

What History Tells Us

The Auburn Tigers have the best argument for the national championship in 2004. USC is out of the discussion. They were ineligible. We are left with the question of who has the better argument between Oklahoma and Auburn. These are the two teams that should have played in the BCS championship game. USC should have been left out because they did not play in a conference championship game as did Auburn and Oklahoma. The Sooners and the Tigers both played an extra game, the opponent for which was determined by performance. In other words, both teams earned the opportunity to play against an opponent that had also won enough games to earn a championship game appearance. The Pac-10 did not have a championship game in 2004. One may argue that deficiency is not USC's fault. Of course, it is. USC shares the blame equally with all the Pac-10 member institutions for not yet having followed the course of contemporary football and expanded to establish a championship game. Auburn and Oklahoma both won, in essence, playoff games. USC did not. So, back to the question at hand: who has the better argument between Auburn and Oklahoma?

Auburn has the better argument because the Tigers beat the champion of another BCS conference—Virginia Tech in the Sugar Bowl. Oklahoma's 2004 season does not include that accomplishment. We do not hold Oklahoma's one loss against them—it was against an ineligible team. It is not fair that Oklahoma did not have the opportunity to beat an eligible champion of another BCS conference. The playing field is not level. We can only work with the facts. The evidence supports Auburn.

After beating Alabama in 1987, Coach Dye told his players, "You are the Champions of the best football conference in America." Tuberville, of course, could have told his players the same thing after beating Tennessee at the Georgia Dome. Moreover, the 2004 Tigers did even more: they won the SEC without a loss; they then beat the ACC champion in the Sugar Bowl. The recognition was not complete, but the performance was—superlative in a way that Auburn fans had never before seen. Jason Campbell made a couple of noteworthy comments on the 2004 team's accomplishments. The reader may have seen the first one; it was on the cover of the Sports Illustrated commemorative issue: "We're 13–0. I don't care what anybody says. We're National Champions." He was right, and I think a lot more of us understand now how right he was. Campbell also said, "We're national champions in our hearts."[e] Given the way the 2004 team played, that is an enviable place to be champions.

12

2005

How does a program follow up perfection? That was the question facing the Auburn Tigers in 2005. Tuberville knew the accomplishments of 2004 were something special. "If we had all 18 of these guys coming back, it would still be almost impossible to do what we did this year."[a] Auburn's contribution to the 2005 NFL draft was unprecedented. Ronnie Brown, Carnell Williams, Carlos Rogers and Jason Campbell were all selected in the first round. Those players set an example regarding the potential benefits of staying in school; an example followed in 2005 by offensive tackle Marcus McNeill and wide receiver Anthony Mix. Mix originally decided to skip his senior year, but then had an epiphany. "I couldn't leave Auburn. I was trying to take the easy way out. But I was riding around one day and it just hit me I wanted to stay another year."[b] While McNeill and Mix decided staying was the best decision for their career aspirations, one member of the coaching staff decided otherwise.

Defensive coordinator Gene Chizik interviewed for multiple jobs after the 2004 season. His popularity was no surprise.

Auburn's 2004 defense was initially thought to be understaffed and undersized. Chizik adjusted his approach accordingly, placing greater emphasis on technique, and fielded the no. 1 scoring defense in the country. Coach Chizik left Auburn to become the defensive coordinator at Texas. I took offense. It seemed strange that anyone would leave Auburn for the same position at a school in a lesser conference. Chizik explained his move only by saying he felt going to Texas would ultimately get him closer to his goal of being a head coach.[c1] Fortunately, this change in the coaching staff just two weeks prior to signing day made no apparent impact on the recruiting class.

"It's not surprising we had another great recruiting year."[d] Tuberville's matter-of-fact assessment of the 2005 class makes sense following an undefeated season. Nonetheless, we may note his chosen definition of "great." "We weren't looking for numbers this year. We were looking for quality because next year will be a great year in the state."[e] Tuberville was not looking for a quarterback in 2005. He still had one from 2002.

The quarterback race in 2005 was never wide open. Tuberville called Cox the heir apparent prior to spring practice. By July, it was official. "The job is his. It's not even close. We've got two young guys behind him, and they're hoping he doesn't get hurt. They don't need to play right now."[f] The tailback position was less settled. Tre Smith was no. 1, but Tuberville said South Carolina transfer Kenny Irons would be "kind of a co-starter."[g] Regardless, no one expected Auburn's 2005 backfield to even approach the greatness of Campbell, Williams and Brown. Speaking of expectations, what were people saying Auburn would do in 2005?

---

[1] Chizik became the head coach at Iowa State in 2007.

No one expected Auburn to make another run at the national championship, but, neither did they expect any dramatic drop off. The SEC sports information directors voted Auburn second in the western division.[h] Sports Illustrated ranked Auburn 13th in their 2005 college football preview.[i] So the expectations were still for a solid team; for Auburn to be a contender in the SEC. The season would open, however, with an opponent from the ACC.

The 2005 Season

We knew Auburn would lose again someday. We did not think it would be against Georgia Tech in the 2005 season opener. Given that we turned the ball over five times, and failed to score in the second half, it's surprising we lost by only nine points, 23–14. It was Brandon Cox's first game as our starting quarterback. He looked good—at moments. In the second quarter he was 8 of 12, with one interception, but also two touchdowns. Unfortunately, Cox threw three other interceptions in the game, ruining his debut. It is the running game, however, that has generated so much debate concerning the 2005 season opener.

Tre Smith was our leading rusher. His numbers do not look remarkably bad at first glance: 55 yards on 13 carries for an average of 4.2 yards per carry. Anyone who saw the game knows that Smith's performance looked much worse. Closer scrutiny of the statistics is revealing. When we remove his two longest carries—21 yards and 13 yards—the average over the remaining 11 carries drops to 1.9. The controversy arises from an otherwise innocuous play midway through the fourth quarter. On first and five, we for some reason decided to give Kenny Irons his first carry of the game. He ran for six yards and looked strong doing so. Tech's lead was six points at the time. Did we then turn the game over to Irons? No; we followed the first down with a false start and then called a pass play, resulting in another interception. Irons' first carry proved to be his last of the game.

The question that many message board pundits have posed over the years is why Irons was not the feature back the entire game. Tuberville's answer was that Irons did not know his blocking assignments for pass protection sufficiently. The reader can deduce the *non sequitur* of this explanation. Furthermore, there was no indication of this supposed problem before the game. To the contrary, Borges described the running back personnel this way:

> It will be a little more by committee than it was a year ago, but we've got three guys who are pretty even there. In this instance, you're looking at three backs [Smith, Irons and Carl Stewart] who know the offense pretty well.[j]

Moreover, Smith missed two weeks of fall camp due to surgery on his appendix. Why did our coaches not get Irons ready for all aspects of the game during those two weeks? Why did we ask our first-game starting quarterback to throw 44 times against Tech? How badly would we have beaten the Yellowjackets had we run Irons early and often? Such questions produce only consternation. Thankfully, the season turns upward the next week.

After the Wreck

The Mississippi State Bulldogs are the salamanders of the Tuberville era. Just as a stream's salamander population indicates ecological conditions, so is our whipping State—or failure to do so—indicative of the season's success. From 2002 through 2006, we beat State each year by at least 28 points. Over that same five-year stretch we averaged 10 wins per season. In the remaining five years of the Tuberville era (1999–2001 and 2007–2008) we lost to State three times and in the other two contests beat them by a combined score of 19–16. The average number of wins over those five seasons is only seven. So, how did we fare against State in 2005?

Brandon Cox threw two touchdown passes—the same number as against Tech—but against the Bulldogs he threw zero interceptions. After the game Cox said he was determined to not throw into coverage. This strategy led to Cox running the ball seven times, prompting this comment from Al Borges: "If Brandon ran through a car wash he'd drown. He has a good feel about when to run, but we don't encourage him to run."[k] Kenny Irons did get the most carries (13), though three other tailbacks (Smith, Stewart and Brad Lester) also contributed. The most impressive performance of the game was by the defense, holding State to 207 total yards. Nine different Tigers recorded tackles for loss. In 2005 we beat State 28–0. Looks like a decent season awaits.

Over the next two weeks Auburn improved to 3–1 with easy wins over Ball State (63–3) and Western Kentucky (37–14). Seven regular season games remain, all of them against SEC opponents.

The all-conference final stretch began at home against South Carolina. It was first year Gamecock coach Steve Spurrier's first visit to Jordan-Hare since the incredibly exciting 2001 Florida game. This game was not that close. Everything worked. According to Tuberville, "It was obviously one of our best days of the year, execution wise."[l] Auburn dominated the Gamecocks the entire game, leading 31–0 at the half and winning by a final score of 48–7. Brad Lester rushed for 53 yards on 13 carries with two touchdowns; good enough to take the starting tailback job from Kenny Irons, who had previously taken the job from Tre Smith. Lester's first start would be at Arkansas.

Lester got the first seven carries against the Hogs but then suffered a groin pull. Kenny Irons was more than capable in relief. With Marcus McNeill et al. winning the line of scrimmage, Irons rushed for 182 yards on 33 carries. Arkansas led 10–6 at the half, but then the Tiger offense took over. Brandon Cox threw touchdown passes to Ben Obomanu, Cooper Wallace and Tre Smith. Smith also had a rushing touchdown, and Auburn beat Arkansas 34–17.

After five wins . . .

On October 22, 2005 the Auburn Tigers took a 5–1 record (3–0 in conference) to Baton Rouge for a clash with 4–1 LSU. Tuberville's first big win as Auburn's coach had been at Tiger Stadium—a surprising 41–7 blowout. The Bengal Tigers' river den would never again be so hospitable. There are five things that every Auburn fan remembers from the 2005 LSU game, and every one of them came off the foot of John Vaughn. That being the case, this game may be one of the most misremembered in the Tuberville era; that is, the five missed field goals do not, of course, tell the whole story. Nonetheless, a missed field goal is how the story begins.

Auburn opened the game with a 13-play, 52-yard drive that ended with Vaughn's first miss of the night. From the replay, the ball in flight looks as though it will stay just inside the right upright, but it keeps pushing right, from barely good to barely bad. That is basically the story of the game. Before we move on, let us begin sharing the blame. The reader may remember this missed kick, but who remembers the two plays that preceded it? Third down was an incompletion. On second down we gave up a sack. Without the loss on second down the field goal would have been 37 yards instead of 41. What difference does four yards make? Coming into the game, Vaughn was seven for seven on field goals shorter than 40 yards. He was 0–2 from beyond 40 yards. The reader might retort: that is one sack; Vaughn missed five kicks. Very well, let us continue.

After the miss, our defense gave up one first down but then forced LSU to punt. Unfortunately, our ensuing possession did nothing. Kody Bliss then delivered a low punt to Skylar Green, who returned it for a touchdown.

After the touchdown, the two teams traded punts. Auburn then made some big plays, but the drive broke down at the LSU 10. Vaughn came on to make his only successful field goal of the game. The Tigers and Tigers went back and forth the rest of the half with no more scoring. LSU led at the break, 7–3.

T. J. Jackson and the Auburn defense shut down LSU on the first possession of the second half, and after the punt we had the ball at our 41. The offense drove down to LSU's 25 before moving back 14 yards on a sack/intentional grounding play. The drive ended with Vaughn missing a 54-yard attempt. This one is on Tuberville. Trying a kick from that far was a bad decision. We remember five misses, but so far both are after the offense gave up a sack, and one resulted from a poor coaching decision.

Our defense forced another three-and-out. On the first play after the LSU punt, Kenny Irons ran through the line of scrimmage, broke tackles at the second level and broke away for a 74-yard touchdown to take the first Auburn lead of the game, 10–7.

LSU answered with a solid drive and retook the lead 14–10. We punted, and then both teams missed field goals. Vaughn's third miss—from 37 yards—actually might have been the most demoralizing. We drove from our twenty to our opponents' twenty, but came away with zero points.

Our defense—featuring Wayne Dickens—made yet another three-and-out stop. LSU punted, and then our offense put together their best drive of the game. They covered 82 yards on 12 plays and then had fourth-and-goal at the LSU five. Tuberville decides to go for it. The result was a beautiful play. Anthony Mix is in the slot. He spars with a defender as he makes his way to the end zone. Cox drops back, and as a blitzing linebacker careens toward Brandon's chest, he lofts the ball to the back of the end zone, over two LSU defenders. Mix goes up for the ball and comes down with it for the touchdown. Auburn leads 17–14. That play, and drive, had the stuff of 2004. I wish it had been the last play of the night.

Our defense had played a very good game and, as noted above, regularly shut down LSU drives before they started. At the end of regulation, unfortunately, Tuberville and his staff outcoached themselves.

> We decided to defend and see if he could throw the ball downfield in between gaps and make plays. Usually, when you play that zone, you're going to get an interception. But they must have worked on it during the week. They weren't going to turn that ball over.[m]

Jamarcus Russell only completed two passes on the ensuing drive, but one of them was for 31 yards. LSU hit a 44-yard field goal to tie the game.

Our offense responded with an equally productive drive, which gave John Vaughn the opportunity to kick from 49 yards for the win. Vaughn's fourth miss sent the game to overtime. This one is not really on Vaughn because we tried a longer field goal than we otherwise would have due to being out of time (on third down with two seconds remaining).

In overtime LSU hit a 30-yard field goal. On our possession, Kenny Irons gained two yards, and then Cox threw two incompletions. Vaughn comes on to kick from 39. He hits the ball well from the left hash. Viewing the kick from behind, the ball is on a path toward the goal post, but it does not get right enough quickly enough. Vaughn's final kick of the game strikes the left upright and ricochets down and out. To say Vaughn falls to his knees does not capture it. He rocks forward, doubling over so that the top of his helmet hits the ground before his knees do. He cannot believe it. A long night comes to an unmerciful end, as does a 13-game conference win streak. There is a lot of football left to be played on the 2005 schedule, but the implications of this loss at Baton Rouge—already ominous—become clear at the end of the season and, obviously, haunt Auburn fans still. For now let us see whether the Tigers can pick themselves up from the turf.

After Baton Rouge

Ole Miss was a comfortable rebound opponent after Vaughn's nightmare. The Rebels limped into Jordan-Hare with a 3–4 record. The Tigers outclassed them, and Vaughn made two kicks on two attempts: Auburn 27 – Ole Miss 3. After beating Ole Miss the Tigers returned to the road; so did I.

It must have been 2003 when I got the idea to attend a game at every SEC school. As noted above, that was the year I decided to go to every game, home and away. Once I had gone to the trouble of travelling to Fayetteville, I figured I may as well go everywhere else. My travel log as an Auburn fan is relatively brief, but it did not start in 2003.

My first road game—other than Legion Field—was in 1994. Dad planned a family trip to Oxford for the season opener. I think he just welcomed an excuse to drive the Natchez Trace Parkway. Having won every game the year before, and with high expectations for the new season, we were not the only ones who thought the trip a good idea. In fact, there were so many Auburn fans at the game, it felt like we were part of some touring exhibition rather than visitors; like we had beneficently brought the Auburn experience—at least some taste of it—to the people of Oxford for their enrichment; so gracious were we.

The next season, 1995, was my freshman year at Auburn and my only season as a member of the Auburn University Marching Band. I traveled with the band to Baton Rouge and to Athens. The only other away game—again, besides Birmingham—that I attended during my student days was at Starkville. So at the conclusion of 2003 I had been to games at seven of the twelve conference schools and was hoping to complete the circuit soon. If not for this goal, I doubt it would have ever occurred to me to go to Lexington in 2005.

The Queen and the Commodore

I departed Birmingham on Friday and picked up Action in Fort Payne. Action knows people all over the conference. He can usually find tickets, and often a place to crash. On this occasion, he made arrangements for us to stay at an apartment occupied by four Kentucky co-eds. Sounded like a good idea to me; maybe too good. . .

As soon as we arrived, something seemed amiss. One of the girls greeted us in the parking lot; or rather, she made an attempt to head us off. She was sort of saying the things a host is supposed to say, but was making no effort to sound convincing. Truth somehow came through in the lazy deception of her discourse. She had offered lodging to Action, without expecting him to take advantage, and, without having told her roommates. Action kept talking to her like a vagrant who's already been told no, and we eventually made it up the stairs and into the apartment.

The girls were getting ready for an evening out. This process easily overflowed their bathrooms; even their bedrooms. They were using the whole damn apartment to primp. Action and I sat on the couch—the operation happening all around us—but we were being ignored. Actively. Soon we were told the dress code for whatever establishment the ladies were to visit that evening. We had packed only for a football game. There was something about black shoes. We were not given license to lounge at their apartment while they were out. After six hours on the road, and less than one on the couch, we were suddenly on the street.

Action said he could find us another place to stay. I had faith. We knocked around town for a couple hours while he made phone calls. We stepped into a coffee shop, and I played David Gray's Babylon while the house folksinger took a break. Action kept calling people, and kept getting nowhere. Finally, he decided to try a long shot. At this point our fortune changed, and we headed across town to a different apartment, but still one occupied by girls; and even one girl of some distinction. I was a little taken aback when Action explained we were on our way to a sleepover with the Homecoming Queen.[2]

The Homecoming Queen is not always the prettiest girl on campus—this one was; her roommate was second. Our welcome at their place was warm, at least by comparison, even if the hospitality wasn't so much Southern as it was sympathetic. What else could Action have done? He told them the truth. Our plight provided us passage to the living room, where Action spent Friday night on the couch and I on the love seat. My legs hung off one

---

[2] She was not the 2005 UK Homecoming Queen, but at the time a very recent regnant.

end, and I pseudo-slept fitfully through the night, my mind half-working claims the whole time.[3]

The game was unremarkable, like most between Auburn and Kentucky. The absurdity of it all was well captured in our kicking off from the 50-yard line after the Kentucky coaching staff earned two personal fouls for complaining about a no-call on a touchdown reception by Prechae Rodriguez.[4] We ultimately won the game 49–27.

Unlike the lodging disarrangement, Action's plans for our social outing Saturday night proved reliable. We were invited to a party hosted by some UK athletics personnel. Action told me repeatedly throughout the day that David Hobbs would be at this party. I recognized the name, but did not remember who Hobbs was. I think Action asked me if I knew who he was, and I told him I did, not wanting to admit my ignorance and caring too little to hear Action's explanation of why I should know who this individual was.

I spotted Hobbs as soon as we walked in the door. "Who's that guy? I think I recognize him from TV." Action retorted that he had been telling me David Hobbs would be at the party. I still needed reminding. Hobbs was the head basketball coach at Alabama from 1992 through 1998, meaning he coached against Auburn twice a season during most of my time as a student.

Whoever hosted the party must have not wanted the guests watching TV all night. If there was a decent-sized TV in the living room, it was not on. I soon found myself in a huddle around a

---

[3] I was working as a claims adjuster at the time. I was depressed and stressed out.

[4] Rodriguez went out of bounds before making the catch, but the officials ruled he had been pushed out by a Kentucky defender, in which case he could legally be the first to touch the ball after returning to the field of play. The Kentucky coaches disagreed.

small set in the kitchen. Hobbs, too, was in the huddle. What was on? Vanderbilt giving Florida a good game on Saturday night in the Swamp. Hobbs was a lot of fun watching football. He was pulling for Vandy—why, I do not know; maybe he just likes the underdog. Vanderbilt is always an underdog to Florida.

Our little group took sides with Hobbs against the Gators. He was drinking beer and basically coaching the game from the kitchen. For a moment, it was like we were football-watching buddies. Hobbs kept saying the refs were screwing Vandy. They were, but the Commodores overcame several questionable calls on a late-fourth-quarter drive. Jay Cutler hit Earl Bennett on a six-yard touchdown pass, seemingly sending the game to overtime. There was a little drama, however, before any extra play could begin. Immediately upon scoring, Vanderbilt coach Bobby Johnson signaled for timeout. When he did, the refs threw a flag for excessive celebration. Now Hobbs was really ticked. The replay showed Bennett's modest celebratory dance, which was clearly directed at his teammates and quickly absorbed by the embrace of a Vanderbilt lineman. The ESPN commentators lamented the refs' abuse of power, but not as loudly as did Hobbs. The 15-yard penalty not only *kabashed* Johnson's plan to go for two, but also forced the Vandy kicker to make a 35-yard extra point to tie the game. The kick was perfect, and I was glad to have our game-watching party extended.

It lasted as long as we could have hoped. Both teams scored touchdowns in the first overtime, but after Florida scored another TD in the second OT, Cutler threw an interception, ending the game. Afterwards, Hobbs seemed more interested in socializing with the grownups. Oh well, we'll always have Gainesville.

Our royal accommodations had not been promised for Saturday night. Fortunately, Action got us back in. I stole the couch when he went to the bathroom. The next week the Tigers would be looking to steal another conference win on the road.

Recovered

On November 12, 2005, Auburn travelled to Athens to play the 7–1, 9th ranked Georgia Bulldogs. The Deep South's Oldest Rivalry pitted strength against strength. Auburn ranked first among SEC teams in total offense and third in total defense. Georgia was second in both total offense and total defense. John Vaughn's statistics, however, were more interesting to John Kaltefleiter of the Athens Banner-Herald, who interviewed our kicker the week of the game and asked him several questions about Baton Rouge. It seems the reporter was trying to get inside Vaughn's head. The story is even titled, "On a road to recovery." Vaughn finally told his would-be psychoanalyst, "I make a game-winner against Alabama or Georgia, it will all be over. That's why I came to Auburn, to play in these two games."[n] Vaughn was not the only Tiger amped up for the Georgia game.

Kenny Irons ran early and often against the Bulldogs. He carried six times on the opening drive, including a 30-yard touchdown. Irons ultimately carried 37 times for 179 yards. Despite his dominant performance, the Tigers led by only one point going into the final quarter of play.

Georgia opened the fourth-quarter scoring with a six-yard touchdown run by Thomas Brown. The score gave Georgia a 27–21 lead.

Auburn responded with an 80-yard drive and appeared poised to retake the lead, but Irons fumbled at the Georgia eleven, and the Bulldogs recovered. Two plays later, Kevin Sears knocked the ball loose from a Georgia receiver, and linebacker Karibi Dede returned the fumble 15 yards for the lone touchdown of his Auburn career, making the score Auburn 28 – Georgia 27.

At about this point in the game Vaughn's holder, Andrew Motley, predicted a final score of Auburn 31 – Georgia 30.[o] The Bulldogs fulfilled their side of Motley's prophecy with a Brandon Coutu field goal with 3:25 left to play. Then came the Tigers' final chance.

Brandon Cox and the Auburn offense took over at our 20 yard line, trailing Georgia 30–28. Cox completed a pass to Ben Obomanu, and Irons ran for a first down, but then the Bulldogs' defense tightened up. Auburn faced fourth-and-ten from our own 34 with 2:05 remaining. Cox picked up a low shotgun-snap, dropped back, and then stepped forward to hit Devin Aromashodu, who was open over the middle at about the Georgia 35. Aromashodu eluded a would-be tackler, pulled away, and made it to the end zone—but not with the ball. Paul Oliver was the Georgia defender who let Aromashodu get open, but he never gave up on the play and caught our receiver just in time to punch the ball loose around the three yard line. Courtney Taylor jumped on it in the end zone, but, by rule the fumble could not be advanced, and the ball was placed at the 3 yard line. Georgia stopped Irons on three consecutive downs, and then we ran the clock down to eight seconds.

On comes John Vaughn. He missed five kicks against LSU. Against Georgia he made four extra points. This one field goal attempt against the Bulldogs was the same distance as an extra point, and Vaughn made it look just as easy—right down the middle; no need to accept a roughing-the-kicker-penalty. After his final attempt against LSU, Vaughn's head hit the turf in utter despair. He knocked his noggin after this kick, too; but, no matter. "They knocked my legs up from under me, but as I was falling I saw it go through."[p] Final (just as Motley predicted): Auburn 31 – Georgia 30.

The win gave Auburn a 6–1 record in SEC play with one conference opponent left. LSU also had one SEC loss, but still had two conference games to play. The western division was still on the line, as was Tuberville's streak of three consecutive wins over Alabama.

The 2005 Alabama game was a special day for the Auburn Family. Let's first look at what happened in the game, and then we will come back to the larger significance.

Number Four

We have seen in our review of the Tuberville decade that sometimes a bad result on the first play of the game ultimately proves ominous. That is certainly the case for this game—well, at least for the Crimson Tide. Alabama quarterback Brodie Croyle drops back to pass. Immediately after the snap, defensive tackle Wayne Dickens is double-teamed; but then both the linemen blocking him appear to have the same thought—*this guy is already being blocked; I need to block somebody else*. One of the linemen turns to his right, to double-team someone else. The other turns to his left and finds nobody there. Dickens is free to run between them, and straight to Croyle—sack no. 1. Sack no. 2 came just two plays later. After Alabama punted, the Auburn offense moved quickly, and Brandon Cox hit Obomanu in the end zone for the first score of the game. This sequence—more or less—repeats twice, and Auburn led 21–0 at the end of the first quarter. Things slowed down from there. The Tigers added one more touchdown in the second quarter on a five-yard pass from Cox to Cole Bennett. We did not score at all in the second half, but the defense continued hitting Croyle. If the term *sack* comes from the quarterback hitting the ground like a sack of potatoes, our defense looked like Idahoans loading a truck.

Eleven. That is the mythical and simultaneously factual number that tells the story of the 2005 Alabama game. No bumper-sticker-covered wall in Auburn is complete without "Honk If You Sacked Brodie." Here is the breakdown on who got him, and how many times:

Stanley McClover	3 ½
Antarrious Williams	1 ½
Travis Williams	1 ½
Quentin Groves	1 ½
T. J. Jackson	1 ½
Marquies Gunn	½
Wayne Dickens	1

In the end, Auburn won 28–18, extending the streak of wins over Alabama to four consecutive years. We will consider the Streak, and this game's place in it, in a later chapter. For now, we turn our attention to a different historical significance of the 2005 Alabama game, one of pertinence to every single Auburn home game played ever since.

In the Arena, On the Field

On September 16, 2005 the Auburn University Board of Trustees passed a resolution to name the field at Jordan-Hare Stadium, "Pat Dye Field." When I heard the dedication would take place the day of the Alabama game, I knew I had to be there. What I did not know yet was that when the day came, Action would arrange for me to step onto the field for a brief moment before going up into the student section. Stepping onto the playing surface on the day it was named Pat Dye Field was a big deal for me. In light of the inseparableness between Pat Dye and Auburn Football in my life, the naming of the field in his honor seemed too perfect to be reality. It makes official for all the Auburn Family this same connection between Dye and our program. That is not to say everyone recognizes, or even perceives, such a connection—and that is ok; not everyone came to be an Auburn fan at the same time, or in the same way, that I did. Nonetheless, the naming of the field makes the connection official and permanent. Any game played at Jordan-Hare Stadium is now also played on Pat Dye Field.

If

Beating bama completed Auburn's regular season with a conference record of 7–1. If Arkansas could beat LSU the following week, we would be western division champions and play for a second consecutive SEC Championship. The game was at Baton Rouge, and LSU was favored by more than two touchdowns. They won by two points. Arkansas got as close as the LSU 34 in the final two minutes, but took a sack and then threw an interception on a desperate fourth-and-eighteen play. From 1999–2005 Tuberville's record against LSU was 4–3. Two of the three losses cost him trips to Atlanta, and in 2005 losing to LSU ultimately brought about a rather forgettable trip to Orlando.

Despite being ranked seventh in the final regular season AP poll, Auburn did not receive an at-large BCS bid, but settled instead for an invitation back to the Capital One Bowl to play Wisconsin, whom the Tigers beat in the 2003 Music City Bowl. Perhaps the team simply could not get up for another game that was not a big game. Whatever the reason, the Capital One Bowl was by no means a suitable encore to the 2005 season. The defense gave up 548 yards. The offense did not reach the end zone until the fourth quarter. Tuberville described the 24–10 loss in simple terms.

> I'll take the blame. We weren't ready to play. We weren't in synch. We never got anything going. We can look at our defense the first half, but offensively, we couldn't make a first down, and that's not like us.[q]

The 2005 campaign ended in disappointing fashion, somewhat like it began. In between there was only one hiccup. How can we lament a season with a conference record of 7–1? So close. Furthermore, we were one missed field goal away from two consecutive seasons without a conference loss. So close. So close.

13

2006

The 2006 season was a rematch: Auburn vs. expectations. In 2005 the big question was how Auburn would replace the superlative backfield of Jason Campbell, Carnell Williams and Ronnie Brown. The answer carried over to 2006. Auburn returned quarterback Brandon Cox, who threw for over 2,400 yards in 2005, and SEC leading rusher Kenny Irons. Behind Irons was proven tailback Brad Lester. Also, though four years removed from *Skullduggery*, Tre Smith was still on the team due to sitting out 2004 as a medical redshirt. Questions remained at virtually every position other than the backfield, but the consensus was that Auburn had enough talent and experience to have a strong team—very strong. At SEC media days the Tigers received 73 first place votes; second was Florida, with only 11.[a] The high esteem was not limited to the South. The Tigers appeared in the initial 2006 AP poll at no. 4.

In 2003 expectations got the better of the Auburn Tigers. In 2006 we had another shot against our intangible nemesis. After the AP poll was released, Tuberville joked about the short memory of his players. "I thought they learned their lesson from last time, but obviously they haven't."[b] The players may not have learned their lesson, but I think most everyone else did. The Auburn Family was optimistic; the media respectful. But, the 2006 preseason lacked the sensational quality that put 2003 over the top. In 2006 there was no hype. Nonetheless, from no. 4 it is not far to the top, but it's a long way down. The high wire act began, as did the previous season, at home against a non-SEC—but BCS conference—opponent.

The 2006 Season

Kenny Irons stole the show in Auburn's season opener against Washington State. The Cougars' defensive coordinator, Rob Akey, put it this way: "He has my Heisman vote."[c] Irons ran for 183 yards on 20 carries. He was not the only Tiger to have a big day. Will Herring, in his first game after moving from safety to linebacker, ran for 42 yards on a fake punt (on fourth-and-14 at the Auburn 16). Herring added an interception in the fourth quarter. Kicker John Vaughn hit four of five field goal attempts, including a career-long 52-yarder. In all, the Tigers were too much for the Cougars. There was no hyperbolic implosion to begin the 2006 campaign. Instead, the Tigers gave a performance consistent with the expectations: Auburn 40 – Washington State 14. The score would have been even more lopsided if not for a momentary letdown by the defense. They corrected that mistake the next week.

The Auburn defense dominated Mississippi State at Starkville in the second game of 2006. The Bulldogs managed only 161 yards of total offense. Karibi Dede led the Tigers' D with six tackles, followed by Merrill Johnson and Craig Stevens, with five each. The Bulldogs crossed midfield only once in the first half; that drive was ended by a David Irons interception. As for the Bulldogs' defense, their plan was to stop the Auburn running game, so the Tigers took to the air. Brandon Cox completed 18 of 24 attempts for 249 yards and two touchdowns. Half of Cox's completions were to Courtney Taylor, who posted 103 receiving yards. Given our defensive performance, Taylor's production alone would have been enough. Auburn 34 – State 0. The preseason is over.

The Big Game

Before there were games of the century once or twice a year, there was 2006 Auburn vs. LSU—no. 3 vs. no. 6. Having beaten Alabama four consecutive years, the Tigers' biggest game in the prime of the Tuberville era was LSU. The Bayou Bengals provided the closest call during Auburn's 2004 run and delivered our only conference defeat in 2005, denying us the chance to play for consecutive SEC championships. The importance of beating LSU was lost on no one in 2006; and certainly not on Tuberville.

> We've been planning for this game since January. We've talked to people about LSU. We watched film all summer. We've been making subtle preparations for this game all along.[d]

In the early going, all the preparation seemed to be paying no dividends; at least not for the offense. Over our first four possessions, six of our twelve plays went for no gain or a loss. But, the next time we got the ball, we found the right mix of run-and-pass and drove 61 yards to the LSU nine. There the progress stalled, and John Vaughn came on to attempt a 26-yard field goal. Vaughn's kick struck the left upright—the exact result of his last attempt against LSU. I do not believe in Voodoo, but I'm glad that kick was Vaughn's only attempt of the game.

Our drive seemed to wake up the LSU offense. They made the most of the remaining time, and Colt David hit a 42-yard field goal as the second quarter expired.

Our offense carried momentum into the second half. After a stop by our defense, we drove 75 yards on 12 plays—featuring eight carries by Kenny Irons—to the end zone. Cox snuck in on 3rd-and-goal from the one, giving Auburn a 7–3 lead. After the touchdown, both defenses asserted themselves.

The teams traded punts twice; then the LSU offense got moving. After driving 50 yards to our 31, Les Miles went for it on fourth-and-eight. Jamarcus Russell threw deep down the middle to Early Doucet, but the ball was knocked away on an impressive, diving effort by Eric Brock. Auburn defender Zach Gilbert is initially flagged for pass interference, but the penalty is waved off because Brock tipped the ball. It was Brock's outstanding play—not the contact by Gilbert—that prevented the pass from being caught. Regardless, we went three-and-out on the ensuing possession, and LSU got another chance.

LSU began their final drive of the game at their own 20 with only 1:11 left to play. Jamarcus Russell did the same thing on this drive that he did on LSU's final regulation possession against Auburn in 2005—he repeatedly found open receivers for big gains. The Bayou Bengals drove to our 24, but time was running out. On the last play of the game, Russell threw to Craig Davis, who caught the ball at our four but was immediately met with a solid hit from Eric Brock. Davis goes straight to the ground and stays there. He knows his team needs one more play, and they don't have it: Auburn 7 – LSU 3. Thus far, we look to have the upper hand in our rematch against expectations. LSU was only the third game of the season, but the win moved Auburn up to no. 2 and created discussion about the Tigers ultimately playing to be no. 1. Fortunately, an undermanned opponent waited the following week, one we likely could have beaten even without proper focus.

Our offense started slowly against Buffalo. The first score came near the end of the first quarter. John Vaughn kicked a 46-

yard field goal as the first half expired for just a 10–0 lead. Things got going in the second half. Freshman Ben Tate took over in the fourth quarter, rushing for 114 yards and two touchdowns on just seven carries. Auburn 38 – Buffalo 7.

A Close Call in Carolina

At 4–0, and still ranked no. 2, the 2006 Tigers traveled to Columbia, SC to face Steve Spurrier and the unranked, 3–1 Gamecocks. This game is best remembered for the success of Tuberville's second half strategy. South Carolina scored ten points in the first half, and likely would have scored more if not for two turnovers. Because of the Gamecocks' effectiveness moving the ball, Tuberville decided the only way to win was to not let them have it. The Auburn offense did their part to execute this plan, opening the second half with a 17-play drive that consumed 8:38 from the game clock and concluded with a 24-yard field goal by Vaughn. What happened next turned the game on its head.

Auburn running backs/special teams coach Eddie Gran noticed something in his film study for the South Carolina game: a blocker on the Gamecocks' kick-return unit had a bad habit of turning his back on the ball immediately upon kickoff. Tuberville decided to exploit this negligence. Kick off specialist Matt Clark did his best to imitate his normal alignment and approach. He had never before attempted an onside kick in a game situation.[e] Clark sold the bait and then chipped the ball to the overeager blocker's blindside. Tre Smith got to the free ball first but dropped it. Fortunately, Jerraud Powers stepped in to make the recovery. The keep-away continued.

Brandon Cox and the Auburn offense returned to the field. The Tigers used up the remainder of the third quarter driving down to the South Carolina 1. Auburn maintained possession for the entire third quarter. On the first play of the fourth quarter, Kenny

Irons scored a touchdown on fourth-and-goal. It would be the Tigers' last score of the day; and it was just enough. The Gamecocks scored once they finally got the ball in the second half, cutting our lead to seven. They would only get one more possession in the game, on which they drove to the Auburn five, but defensive back Patrick Lee broke up Syvelle Newton's pass on fourth down to settle the matter: Auburn 24 – South Carolina 17. We were glad to escape Columbia with a win; and glad to be headed home. In retrospect, we should have stayed on the road.

The Fall

Auburn historians Van Allen Plexico and John Ringer refer to a "Hawg Hex." They detail how losses to Arkansas have proved critically damaging to numerous Auburn football seasons.[f] On three such occasions prior to 2006 (1995, 2001 and 2002), losses to Arkansas prevented Auburn from playing in the SEC championship game. In each of those three games the Tigers were favored. In no season is the Hawg Hex more depressing than in 2006. Auburn was ranked no. 2 in the country. Arkansas was unranked and came to Jordan-Hare as a two-touchdown underdog. They could have been two-touchdown favorites and still covered. Arkansas running back Darren McFadden ran for 145 yards. Felix Jones added 104 rushing yards of his own. The Hogs won 27–10. Borges lamented the offensive letdown: "We were pathetic, the second half particularly."[g] Muschamp also summarized the loss succinctly: "When you give up 280 yards rushing, you don't deserve to win."[h] The needed adjustments on both sides of the ball had to be made immediately. The next week brought another conference opponent to Jordan-Hare: undefeated Florida.

The Other Big Game

The Auburn Tigers got their first taste of Tebowmania in 2006. When the Gators came to Auburn in mid-season, Tebow had thrown only 14 passes and rushed for just 228 yards. Nonetheless, in the eyes of Gator fans, first-string quarterback Chris Leak was playing second fiddle.[i] Leak was the starting quarterback; Tebow was the feature (and future) QB. After Auburn's loss to Arkansas, the Gators moved up to no. 2. Would our team get up for this big game after blowing a potential championship run the week before?

The Auburn offense looked especially sharp on our first two possessions. Neither, however, resulted in a touchdown. A sack stalled the first drive, and we settled for a field goal. On the second, we fumbled at the Florida three. The Gators led 10–3 at the time, but on the next play committed a holding infraction in their own end zone, resulting in a safety. Florida's next possession was much more effective, concluding with Tebow's first snap of the game—a 16-yard touchdown run. His devotees likely thought he was just getting warmed up, but the second half held surprises for both sides.

John Vaughn added two more field goals in the second quarter; and the Gators led 17–11 at the break. The Tigers' offense did not reach the end zone in the first half. They would not in the second half either; but Auburn scored touchdowns nonetheless, by lesser conventional means.

Early in the third quarter Florida punter Eric Wilbur dropped a deep snap. After picking it up, he still attempted to punt the ball even as he was being tackled by Tristan Davis. Jerraud Powers blocked the punt. Tre Smith recovered and took it to the end zone, doing something akin to a front flip as he crossed the goal line. The extra point gave Auburn an 18–17 lead. We would not trail again. Our defense stifled the Gators' offense throughout the second half, and our offense moved the ball well enough to limit Florida's time of possession. John Vaughn added another field goal in the final minute. On the final play of the game Patrick

171

Lee returned a fumbled lateral for a touchdown. Auburn 27 – Florida 17.

Beating Florida sharpened the sting of losing to Arkansas. We had won both our big games—against LSU and the Gators. The loss to the Hogs nullified those big wins, at least with regards to the ultimate prize. It wasted our otherwise nearness to perfection. To be sure, I enjoyed the Florida win. The entire Auburn Family enjoyed it. Furthermore, the first BCS rankings were released the following day. Auburn was no. 5. Maybe high aspirations were still in reach.

The Climb

The next opponent was Tulane. The Tigers started slowly but eventually pulled away, winning 38–13. Ben Tate rushed for 156 yards. By playing in the game Tate lost the opportunity for a medical redshirt; he had missed the previous three games due to an ankle injury. Tuberville described the decision as necessity: "We need him. Kenny [Irons] is banged up and Brad's [Lester] going to be hobbling."[j] With only four games remaining on the schedule after Tulane—and one of those against Arkansas State—the decision to play Tate indicates Tuberville was thinking 2006 might still hold a BCS championship possibility. Take your shot when you get it; use all the ammo you have. No one knows what the next year brings. The Tulane game was, of course, Tate's tune-up for a modified version of Amen Corner that started with a trip to Oxford.

The Rebels were considerably less gracious host than for our last visit in 2004 when we won 35–14. Ole Miss scored the first points of each half, and scored a fourth-quarter touchdown to tie the game at 17. As did their fellow Mississippians earlier in the season, the Rebels stacked the line of scrimmage, intending to shut down our rushing attack. Again, our offense obliged and relied on the passing game. Brandon Cox threw for 253 yards and one

172

touchdown. Despite the Ole Miss defensive strategy, Kenny Irons still rushed for 106 yards. Brad Lester scored a touchdown, and John Vaughn hit three of three field goal attempts. On the drive that led to Vaughn's final kick, Tuberville went for it on fourth down at the Ole Miss 23 so as to eat up more clock and leave the Rebels with as little time as possible. On fourth-and-one Carl Stewart gained six yards, keeping the drive alive. Like the onside kick against South Carolina, going for it was the right move; and the keep-away strategy worked. Vaughn split the uprights with just 35 seconds to go: Auburn 23 – Ole Miss 17.

One last placeholder remained on the 2006 schedule before the final two games against Georgia and Alabama. The Tigers beat Arkansas State 27–0. The defensive performance was superb. The offense was not as sharp. Borges pointed out the obvious reason for concern. "We kept the game close—well, not close, but more interesting than it should have been—because we did a poor job of taking care of the ball."[k] The Indians[1] did not make us pay for the turnovers. Our next opponent would.

The Second Fall

In 2006 the Deep South's Oldest Rivalry was played in a very different context than the year before. In 2005 the Auburn-Georgia game pitted no. 15 vs. no. 9. The game was televised by ESPN and kicked off at 6:30. In 2006 no. 5 Auburn hosted unranked, 6–4 Georgia for a J-P game that kicked off at 11:30 am.[2] Tuberville said the early kick did not matter. No Auburn fan has believed that ever since.

> I think whenever you play this game or next week's game, it doesn't make a whole lot of difference . . .

---

[1] Arkansas State shape shifted into Red Wolves in 2008.

[2] Jefferson-Pilot "breakfast club" Sports.

> Our guys are excited, no matter when we play
> Georgia. Georgia and Alabama are two games you
> just look forward to, no matter what time it is or
> where it's at.[1]

Looking forward is one thing; playing well is another. On this day, only the Bulldogs did the latter.

In the two weeks leading up to the game, Georgia lost at home against Florida, and then at Kentucky. Someone must have told them they were not "man enough" to beat Auburn, as they obviously showed up believing they had something to prove. Tuberville said afterwards, "They came here today on a mission, and they got it done—at the expense of us."[m] The Bulldogs scored by a variety of means in the first half: a field goal, two rushing touchdowns, a passing touchdown and an interception return for touchdown. They led 30–7 at intermission. There was little to see in the second half. At day's end Brandon Cox had completed as many passes (four) to the other team as he had to his own: Georgia 37 – Auburn 15.

The loss to Georgia was difficult to process. For the second time in 2006 we failed to show up at home against a team we were expected to beat. The corrosion of our shot at playing for a BCS championship that began against Arkansas was now complete and irreversible. The question to the 2006 Auburn Tigers was now this: hang it up and pack it in, or finish strong?

To ask whether the Tigers would finish strong raises another question: would another trip to Tuscaloosa mean the time for the thumb had come? We will talk more about the Streak, and this game's significance therein, in the next chapter. At this point we will focus primarily on the game itself.

The Thumb

The story of the 2006 Iron Bowl is straightforward. The Auburn defense gave our offense opportunities, and the offense capitalized. Alabama scored on their first possession of the game, but on both their third and fourth possessions, Quentin Groves hit Alabama quarterback John Parker Wilson, both times causing a fumble. Both times the Auburn defense recovered; and both times the Tiger offense turned the short field into a touchdown.

The Tide offense eventually answered, scoring touchdowns on their last possession of the first half, and on their first possession of the second half. Trailing 15–14, the Tigers then moved the ball from our own 11 to our 42, allowing Kody Bliss to punt the ball to the Alabama 11, where it was fair caught. The Tiger defense shut down the ensuing Alabama series, and after the punt, our offense took over at our 46-yard line.

On this drive Auburn running back Carl Stewart makes his claim for MVP. On first down, Stewart slips out of the backfield undetected on an end-around-play-action pass. He runs a wheel route and finds himself alone along the sideline. The play gains 37 yards. Two plays later, Cox floats the ball to the end zone. The coverage is tight, but Prechae Rodriguez reacts perfectly to the underthrow; and hangs on to the ball despite the defender's swatting. The touchdown puts us up by five; so we go for two. Cox pitches to Carl Stewart, who runs to his right but then suddenly pulls the ball up and throws it to Lee Guess in the end zone for a successful conversion. Stewart's execution of the half-back pass looks remarkably like that of Carnell Williams from the 2004 Georgia game. Of course, the wheel route run for big yardage by Stewart to start the drive was a play that featured Ronnie Brown in 2004. A tailback conjuring Ronnie Brown and Carnell Williams on the same drive—a touchdown drive against Alabama? Maybe Carl

Stewart was underutilized. Stewart's two-point pass to Guess proved to be the final score of the game, though the outcome was not settled until David Irons intercepted Wilson with 33 seconds left: Auburn 22 – Alabama 15.

As the bama fans slumped down the stairs to exit Tuberville-Deny Stadium, their disappointment hung heavy in the air. For my friend Sam Lasseter, it was literally tangible. We bought student-guest tickets outside the stadium earlier in the day. Once inside, we worked through the crowded student section and accidentally found seats in an area that seemed to be mostly guests—not other Auburn fans, just older-than-students Alabama fans. We were in no hurry to leave when the game ended, and when we saw some of our players on the field holding up five fingers, we did the same. I don't know how long we had been holding this pose when Sam suddenly flew past me. I didn't understand what was going on. I looked to my left and saw a man yanking his wife back into the aisle. She had given Sam a pretty good shove from behind, and she's fortunate he caught himself after a couple of rows, rather than falling and rolling down the emptied bleachers.

Five in a row. We are almost to our chapter on the Streak. But, for just a moment, let us consider this statement by Tuberville on the implications of both the Streak and the sustained dominance at Tuberville-Deny Stadium. "Four straight at your rival's place is huge. These seniors never lost to their in-state rival. They can stick out their chests for a long, long time." Indeed, I imagine they still are. They should be.

11–2

Beating Alabama completed our regular season with a record of 10–2. We accepted a bid to play in the Cotton Bowl against Nebraska, who had lost to Oklahoma in the Big 12 championship game. The Tigers were determined to avoid repeating last season's bowl-let-down, but at the outset it looked like we might sleepwalk through yet another pre-noon kickoff. Nebraska opened the game with a 15-play, 80-yard drive for a touchdown. Fortunately, on the Cornhuskers' next possession we implemented the same formula that produced the win against Alabama: the defense gave the offense a short—this time very short—field. Karibi Dede, Ph.D. intercepted Zac Taylor and brought the return all the way to the Nebraska nine. Two plays later Cox found Carl Stewart, who took it in for the score.

The Cornhuskers tried a fake punt on their next possession. They snapped the ball directly to fullback Dane Todd, who then intended to pitch the ball to a teammate on the reverse, but Patrick Trahan hit Todd at the critical moment, forcing a fumble. Sometimes-running-back-sometimes-defensive-back Tristan Davis recovered at the Nebraska 14, and, again, Carl Stewart ultimately scored. Tigers lead 14–7.

Nebraska answered immediately with a 72-yard touchdown drive to tie the game. Every possession—by either team—for the rest of the first half ended with a punt. Most of the possessions in the second half ended with a punt. One exception was a 10-play, 55-yard drive by Auburn in the 3rd quarter that concluded with a John Vaughn field goal. That was the last score of the game. Final: Auburn 17 – Nebraska 14.

The Auburn Tigers' final record was 11–2. As Ben Bartley of The War Eagle Reader puts it: "The 2006 team won 11 games through luck and grit and confidence borrowed from the previous two seasons."[n] Bartley's assessment well summarizes what our review has shown—that the record far from tells the story of this remarkable team. A cursory examination of 2006 might lead one to emphasize either the eleven wins or the two losses. Here is another reflection that avoids such oversimplification.

Plexico and Ringer note that Terry Bowden deemed Auburn's 1994 game against Florida as the Tigers' "Super Bowl."[o] Keeping that in mind, let us recall the following statements made by Tuberville prior to the 2006 LSU game.

> We've been planning for this game since January. We've talked to people about LSU. We watched film all summer. We've been making subtle preparations for this game all along.[p]

When Tuberville was asked after the Mississippi State game (one week before LSU) when he started thinking about the next week, he replied, "About 14–0 in the first half."[q] Offensive guard Tim Duckworth also commented on the next game immediately after beating State. "This is our championship game, and that's how we'll play."[r]

Auburn beat no. 1 Florida in 1994 at Gainesville. We won the Super Bowl but later in the season tied Georgia and lost to Alabama. In 2006 we beat LSU. We won "our championship game." We won the other big game, too—against Tebow and the no. 2 ranked Gators. But, we lost two other games—both when we were double-digit favorites; both at home; both kicked off before noon.

In discussing Tuberville's national championship we noted that though the recognition in 2004 was not complete, the performance was. While the latter cannot be said of the 2006 campaign, we can say this: The 2006 BCS champion was Florida, who beat Ohio State 41–14 in the championship game. Only one team beat the Gators in 2006—the Auburn Tigers.

14

The Streak

Yes, I know we have only covered through the 2006 season, and another win remains before the Streak is complete. I want to stop and engage the Streak here—where it is still alive; where the last full year is bookended with wins over Alabama.

Why does beating Alabama matter? When I think about this question, I'm reminded of Judges' description of the partial conquest, e.g. "But the people of Benjamin did not drive out the Jebusites who lived in Jerusalem, so the Jebusites have lived with the people of Benjamin in Jerusalem to this day. (Judg 1:21, ESV)" Beating Alabama matters because we live with them; that is, many Auburn fans work, attend church or school, or even share a home with Alabama fans. We see them every day. We hear them every day—their incessant liturgy of self-worship and indulgent delusion. That is why beating Alabama matters—beating them sharpens the ineptitude of their rhetoric, making it more amusing, and thus more tolerable—that, and because they are a divisional opponent. The subject of this chapter, of course, is a question beyond just why beating Alabama matters.

Why does beating Alabama six consecutive seasons matter? The answers to this question are the same ones presented above. One might argue, however, that beating Alabama from 2002–2007 does not really matter, because the team we needed to beat the most in that stretch was LSU. But, again, most of us do not live in Louisiana. The Streak did matter—and still does. Anyone who lived through it understands this reality. Why was the impact so significant? Let us step back a few years further.

The Power Struggle

On November 27, 1982 Bo went over the top, and Auburn beat Alabama for the first time since the incredible Punt Bama Punt victory of 1972. Ending a nine-year drought against our in-state rival is reason enough to assign great importance to Pat Dye's first win over Alabama. If we look at the entire history of the rivalry, the significance is even greater.

Between the first year the two teams played (1893) and the last year prior to the 41-year cessation (1907), Auburn holds a 7–4 advantage (there was one tie). The stretch from the renewal of the rivalry up to 1982 looks much different. Of the games played from 1948 through 1981, Alabama won 24, and Auburn only 10. If we further narrow the range, and look at the seasons between Auburn's five-game winning streak (1954–1958) and 1982, Alabama's advantage is 19 games to Auburn's four. In other words, over the 23 years leading up to 1982, Auburn beat Alabama only four times. Fortunately, in 1981 Auburn hired a man who had the vision, knowhow and determination to make the Tigers competitive again. The field at Jordan-Hare Stadium now bears his name—Pat Dye. A year later, that vision became reality. Bo Over the Top is not just about breaking Alabama's nine-year string of Iron Bowl wins. Its larger significance is that it created the fulcrum on which the balance of power tilted. If we look at the rivalry starting in 1982, Auburn leads the series 17–14. Seven of those wins are Tuberville's; and six of them comprise a Streak, without which we would not hold the series lead in the modern era.

The Foundation

The Streak begins in 2002—the game known by some as *Skullduggery*, in which true freshman Tre Smith rushed for 126 yards, and Jason Campbell looked like the Jason Campbell of 2004. We did not know then that a Streak had begun; but, maybe we should have known something was going on. Beating Alabama is always most fun when they think there is no chance they can lose. In 2002, they came into the Iron Bowl 9–2, having won their last five games, and ranked 9th in the AP poll. They were 11-point favorites and believed 2002 would be the year they spoiled Auburn's perfect record in Tuscaloosa. When the Tigers came out on top, perhaps we should have known the game possessed more awesomeness than can be contained in one win—perhaps we should have known it was the beginning of something bigger. In reality, Tuberville would beat Alabama two more times before we could really see what was happening.

Each of the next two wins over Alabama was overshadowed in its own way. The 2003 victory was quickly absorbed into the *Jetgate* scandal. In 2004, beating Alabama was a foregone conclusion, a subplot in the bigger stories of an undefeated season and the BCS controversy. These off-the-field matters diverted attention from the consecutive wins. In 2005, however, the spotlight shone directly on a new phenomenon.

It's Alive

The 2005 win over Alabama is when the Streak actually comes into existence; when four consecutive victories undergo a synergistic transformation into something with a life of its own. The catalyst for this genesis was largely Tuberville infusing his personality into the rivalry. In a previous chapter we noted

Tuberville's emphasis on beating Alabama. It bears repeating here. "For us there are three seasons: non-conference, conference, and then there's Alabama. We work hard on them, and if there is a game we put a personal touch on, it's that last one every year."[a] When we beat Alabama for a fourth consecutive year, Tuberville wanted to celebrate the payoff of all that work, and he made a gesture that demonstrated his personal touch—he held four fingers up in the air. It was a simple thing, and, in retrospect it seems an obvious thing to do. It did not seem as much so at the time— especially not to Alabama fans. Consider this reaction by Tom Miller of Vestavia Hills, printed in the Sound Off section of the Birmingham News.

> First, I have to congratulate the Auburn Tigers on their convincing victory over the Alabama Crimson Tide. But as the game was winding down, Coach Tuberville held up his hand, extended four fingers and began waving at the fans, signifying four wins in a row. Never have I seen an SEC coach show so little class.
>
> I never saw Coach Jordan, Coach Bryant, Coach Vaught or Coach McLendon do that in their eras. I never saw Coach Dye, Coach Bowden, Coach Perkins, Coach Curry, Coach Stallings, Coach DuBose, Coach Saban, Coach Holtz or, heck, even Coach Fulmer or Spurrier do it. And I've certainly never seen Coach Shula do it. Hey, Tommy, do yourself a big favor and just go out to midfield, shake hands like a good sport should and then go celebrate with your players in the locker room. Save the classlessness on TV for the pro leagues.[b]

Mr. Miller correctly identifies the genius of Tuberville's gesture. He broke from conventional coach behavior, doing something no other head coach had, and thereby got under his opponents' skin in a way no one else had. Or, at least, that was the effect; even if not Tuberville's intent. He held up four fingers not for Alabama fans, but for Auburn fans. "So we're pretty proud that we've won four in a row. That's not pointing anything at their team. It's a pretty good accomplishment for us knowing where we started in 1999."[c] As for the keyword in Mr. Miller's critique, *class* is an idea that is only important to Alabama fans when they are losing. They claim to know how to lose with class and they expect others to win with class, but when they are winning, it is suddenly unimportant. As Ken Tucker of Birmingham pointed out in a response to Tuberville's critics, "So, holding up four fingers is taunting the losing team and showing no class? Then what is singing 'we just beat the hell out of you' at a team you just defeated?"[d]

When Tuberville stepped off of Pat Dye Field on the day when he matched Dye's longest run of consecutive wins over Alabama, he was not yet done celebrating. He was later photographed in Orlando—prior to the Capital One Bowl— wearing a Fear the Thumb t-shirt. He casually explained himself: "I understand it's created some talk back at home. Hey, that's what rivalries are all about."[e] Tuberville's confidence to inject his own personality and his own ideas about what a rivalry should be into the Auburn/Alabama dynamic shaped the Streak's impact on the Auburn Family. In 2005, we were not celebrating beating Alabama, but celebrating beating them again, and again, and again; and our braggin'-rights head-cheerleader was our head coach. The influence of his cheerleading carried over to the next season.

Infiltration

Tommy Tuberville had something in common with Mike Shula in 2006—he was in Alabama's locker room. There were posters of him holding up four fingers, and others displaying his "Fear the Thumb" fashion statement.[f] His infiltration went even deeper than that. Tuberville, or at least his success against the Tide, was in the Alabama players' heads. Alabama receiver D. J. Hall put it this way: "You say 'Thumb,' and everyone's attitude changes."[g] One thing that did not change in 2006 was Tuberville's record at Tuscaloosa. In fact, by beating Alabama again in 2006, Tuberville became the first coach from any visiting school to win four consecutive times at Tuberville-Deny Stadium.[1] Regarding this distinction, Kevin Scarbinsky made an interesting point:

> Tom Thumb just may be the greatest Iron Bowl
> coach in history. Paul Bryant won nine of these
> games in a row with Alabama, but the Bear never
> had to set foot in the Loveliest Village for a single
> one of them.[h]

The following season, Tuberville captured another Iron Bowl superlative.

A Fan's Game

Before 2006, the only Auburn coach to beat Alabama in five consecutive games was Ralph Jordan. In 2007, Tuberville moved one spot ahead of even "Shug," but appropriately shared the credit:

> To do this six times in a row is an accomplishment
> for the players, and the coaches have a little
> something do with it. This is truly a player's game

---

[1] Phil Fulmer won four consecutive road games against Alabama, but the first two (1995 and 1997) were at Legion Field.

and, in turn, a fan's game—they really get into it
and get the players motivated.[i]

Indeed, the Alabama game is a fan's game. As mentioned above, while the players and coaches may prepare for it all year long, we are the ones who live with it—good or bad—all year long. For six fun years, the livin' was easy.

From 2002 through 2007, the culture of the State of Alabama was altered. What happened during the streak was that the bammers' rhetoric of superiority, which has rung hollow ever since the day Pat Dye was hired, finally lost its last hint of meaningfulness, even to those spewing it. Yes, they kept reciting it—their religion requires as much; but, for a moment, they didn't believe it. Their eyes revealed that they, themselves could finally hear "we have Paul Bryant as our father" echoing without substance inside their heads.

Now we have looked more closely at each of the three major historical components of the Tuberville decade. We will look at all three together in the conclusion. For now, of course, there are two more seasons, plus the closing of the Tuberville corpus, to examine.

15

2007

As we leave 2006 behind—with its near-miss substance but overall positive quality—we approach the end of the drama. The 2006 season was Tuberville's last really good year at Auburn. Yes, I include 2007 in the Golden Age of Tuberville; the reasons why will be shown in this chapter. Nonetheless, 2007 does not fully belong on the same list as 2004–2006. The 2004 season was perfect; and 2005 and 2006 both possess some quality of near-perfection; but, 2007 is a step down. We begin to see some unraveling, which should be expected because the remarkable record over 2004–2006 was virtually impossible to sustain. That is enough foreshadowing by way of philosophizing. Let us look at the situation leading up to 2007.

The 2004 seniors may have been the highest profile group of exiting players, but the 2006 exodus was the largest. Kenny Irons, Courtney Taylor and four starters from the offensive line were among 21 seniors who had to be replaced in 2007. Also gone was kicker John Vaughn, along with our punter and kickoff specialist. The defense said goodbye to leading tackler Will

Herring, cornerback David Irons, who led the team in pass break-ups, and player/coach Karibi Dede. Fortunately, defensive end Quentin Groves—projected as a 4th or 5th-round draft pick—decided to play another year as a Tiger. Tuberville saw no cause for panic in the personnel turnover.

> We have a lot of good potential with our redshirt freshmen and sophomores. We'll sit down in the next weeks, put up our depth chart for 2007 and make sure we got the guys at the right position. We'll make some changes. If we're short at defensive end, we'll put somebody over there. If we're short at offensive tackle, we'll look at finding somebody there.[a]

Tuberville was also looking to find talent, of course, in the 2007 recruiting class. By all accounts, he did.

In 2007 Tuberville and his staff continued their string of successful recruiting years. The 2007 class was ranked 7th nationally by Rivals.com and 6th by Scout.com.[b] The signees included names now very familiar to Auburn fans: linebacker Josh Bynes, defensive end Antoine Carter and defensive end Nick Fairley.[c] The two names that most impacted the ratings of the class were Kodi Burns and Lee Ziemba, both of whom were thought potential contributors as true freshman. As the summer neared fall, Tuberville said nine true freshman might play in 2007. How would the departure of so much experience, and the influx of youth impact expectations?

Projections for 2007 were relatively cautious. Lack of experience, particularly at receiver and offensive line, caused concern, but our record of 33–5 over the last three season, plus having a third-year starter at quarterback deterred major-drop-off predictions. The Birmingham News returned us to our normally assigned slot of second in the western division, behind LSU. The initial AP poll ranked us 18th. Stewart Mandell of Sports Illustrated put us one spot higher, at 17th.[d] The general consensus was that we needed strong performance from unproven players, but that our program was led by a proven coach. Those factors would balance each other, producing a good, but not great, season. Let's take a look.

The 2007 Season

The season opener was uncomfortable, to say the least. Kansas State led 13–9 with 4:26 left in the game. Fortunately, at that point we started the sequence that brought us so much success in 2006. After a great punt by Ryan Shoemaker, our defense forced a three-and-out. The Wildcats punted, giving our offense the ball at our 43-yard line. Brandon Cox then completed five of six pass attempts on a seven-play touchdown drive, giving us a 16–13 lead with two minutes remaining. K-State's attempt to answer was quashed when Quentin Groves hit their quarterback, causing a fumble that was returned by Antonio Coleman for a touchdown. Final: Auburn 23 – Kansas State 13. The mood afterwards was far different than the response to last season's opening-night domination of Washington State.

"We knew we'd struggle on offense with a young offensive line. We're very fortunate. We won it on pure guts."[e] Tuberville's assessment applied especially to his quarterback's guts. "He's a tough young man. He took a beating."[f] Cox also acknowledge the price of victory. "I took a few good shots. I'm going to be really sore."[g] Cox was sacked five times in the game. He was sacked 34 times in 2006. Moving forward, we wondered if he could survive another hit parade. The first chance to correct the protection problem would come against the South Florida Bulls.

Confusion

Talk of South Florida beating Auburn started in the spring. It played well, of course, especially on Birmingham radio. The refrain repeated so frequently over the summer months that Jim Dunaway finally had to explain, "It's not an upset if everyone's picking it." Unfortunately, this time *the public* was right. Given that we turned the ball over five times, Tuberville said, "We were very lucky to even be in it."[h] The game ended with a South Florida touchdown pass in overtime: USF 26 – Auburn 23. The next week the Tigers would start conference play. At least we would still be at home, which is supposed to be a good thing.

The struggle against Kansas State was still a win; and the loss to South Florida might have been seen as a fluke. The 2007 Mississippi State game, however, was a sure sign that the Golden Age of Tuberville was winding down. This game introduced something Auburn fans had not seen since 2002—a quarterback controversy. Kodi Burns entered the game in the first quarter. Brandon Cox had already thrown two interceptions, and we were down 10–0. With Burns in the game we scored two touchdowns and led 14–13 at the half. When it came time to do or die, however, we gave the ball back to Cox. Down 19–14 in the final five minutes, he led us 67 yards on eight plays to the State nine. Once we had first and goal, I was sure Tuberville would bring Burns back in. The whole stadium would know the play, but could State stop it four times? The world will never know. Cox threw three incompletions and one completion for no gain. End of game.

By mid-September the Tigers had lost as many games in 2007 as we had the entire 2006 season. Where do we go from here? For one more week we stayed at home. The next game was worrisome for a moment—we led New Mexico State only 21–20 at the half. Thankfully, we showed up after the break and won 55–20. What happened next in the 2007 season might have otherwise been called aberrant or anomalous. In the Tuberville era it was just Auburn being Auburn.

Gigging the Gators Once Again

After beating New Mexico State, the Tigers were 2–2 and 0–1 in conference, but a funny thing happened on the way to Shreveport—a scheduled detour to Gainesville. The fourth-ranked Gators were chomping for us. They wanted revenge for the sole loss in their 2006 BCS championship campaign. Vegas said they would get it. The Tigers were 17-point underdogs. That number figured into score—just not in the way expected.

Auburn scored a touchdown in each of the first two quarters and led 14–0 at the half. Each team kicked a field goal in the third quarter before Tim Tebow threw for one touchdown and ran another in the fourth quarter. With the game tied 17–17 late in the final period, our defense once again gave our offense a chance to win the game.

Florida's last possession started at their 42, but our defense pushed them back six yards on first down, and the Gators punted two plays later. The Tiger offense took over at our 39. We ran Ben Tate straight at the Gators, seven times for 19 yards on a nine-play drive. The other two plays were completions by Cox to Prechae Rodriguez and Rodgerigus Smith. After Tate's final rush, true freshman and native Floridian Wes Byrum came on to attempt a 43-yard field goal with three seconds remaining. The execution was perfect. Tuberville began walking toward midfield; Urban Meyer did not.

Meyer had called a timeout—supposedly just before the snap for the kick. Both teams, and Tuberville, retreated to the sidelines momentarily before resetting the play. Byrum's second kick wasn't quite as strong, but it was just as good: Auburn 20 – Florida 17. Apparently, Byrum was the only guy on our team not worried about making the kick a second time. Brandon Cox: "I was on the sideline about to throw up; I was so nervous."[i] Tuberville: "He absolutely has ice water running in his veins. I couldn't even breathe, and he had to kick two of them."[j] Byrum: "The second was right down the middle. I knew it (was good) when it left my foot."[k] The big upset on the road gave our team new energy and new life. Suddenly, the two early losses seemed a long time ago. It was just what the doctor ordered, and the good vibe came home with us to face Vanderbilt.

Auburn is always supposed to beat Vanderbilt. Three weeks into 2007, even that maxim seemed in question. Fortunately, the Tigers who played the Commodores looked more like the ones who beat Florida than those who lost to South Florida. We scored 28 points in the first half, and seven in the second. Vanderbilt did not score until the final five minutes of the game: Auburn 35 – Vanderbilt 7. The home stay was brief. Now 2–1 in conference play, we headed to Fayetteville.

Escaping Fayetteville

The 2007 game at Arkansas tells us something important about the *Hawg Hex*—it only shows up when it can really cost us. Regardless, the way our defense played might be considered *hexproof*. With strong line play from Antonio Coleman, Josh Thompson, Pat Sims and Sen'Derrick Marks, and effective tackling by linebackers Tray Blackmon, Craig Stevens and Chris Evans, our D held Arkansas running backs Darren McFadden and Felix Jones to a combined 85 yards. It was the Auburn running game that kept the chains moving. We made 21 first downs to the Hogs' 11; our time-of-possession advantage was 35:53 to 24:07. None of that would have mattered if we couldn't move the ball one more time at the end.

Arkansas quarterback Casey Dick threw a touchdown pass to Lucas Miller, giving the Hogs a 7–6 lead with just 1:36 left in the game. On the ensuing kickoff, they just popped the ball down to our 25, and Brad Lester returned it to our 47. Four plays later Cox hit Robert Dunn over the middle; Dunn turned it into a 30-yard gain down to the Arkansas 12. We ran Ben Tate at them three times, and then Wes Byrum—two of four attempts in the game to this point—hit an extra-point-length field goal for the win: Auburn 9 – Arkansas 7. A season that once seemed unsalvageable was now showing considerable promise. Tuberville cautiously acknowledged the progress. "I don't know if we're good enough to get to Atlanta or win in Atlanta, but the good thing is, we are getting better."[1] There's a troublesome stop between Fayetteville and Atlanta, of course—Baton Rouge.

Squandered via Squibble

For the second time in four games, the Tigers faced a highly-ranked SEC opponent on the road. Again, we were double-digit underdogs, and again we took control early. We led LSU 17–7 at the half, but the corndogs came back with three field goals and a touchdown to take a 23–17 lead. That was the score when we started our last drive of the game, at our own 17 with eight minutes left.

Over the next nine plays, Cox connected on four of six pass attempts. He also ran for four yards. Lester added an eight yard run, and then on first-and-goal Ben Tate carried five yards down to the LSU 3. On second-and-goal Cox threw to the back shoulder of Rodgerious Smith, who detangled himself from an LSU defender and made the catch in the end zone. Auburn leads 24–23. It should have been good enough for a win.

What happens next cracked my skull open in disgust like nothing else in the Tuberville decade. We sort of squibbed the kickoff. I never like squib kicks. When there is less than a minute remaining, I understand. In this instance, there was still 3:13 left to play. The kick traveled only 30 yards, giving LSU the ball at their 42-yard line. Byrum surely meant to drive the ball farther, but I place the blame on Tuberville opting to shorten the field. Tuberville's mistake that lost the game was overshadowed by Les Miles' mistake that won the game.

After the kickoff, LSU worked the ball down to our 22—close enough for a makeable field goal. On third-and-seven, with one timeout still available, they let the game clock run down to eight seconds, and then snapped the ball and dropped back to pass. LSU receiver Demetrius Byrd caught the ball in the end zone. Our defender, Jerraud Powers, had tight coverage and tried to break up the pass. The receiver managed to hold on, and with a single tick left on the clock, LSU led 30–24, and that was the final. My brain bled the rest of the season.

"We wanted to keep it away from their returner, like we did all game. We gave them about 10 more yards than we needed to."[m] What might have happened had we kicked it deep? Their returner could have scored a touchdown. Fine: then we get the ball back with two minutes—instead of one second—with two timeouts. Their returner could have brought it down to our five-yard line. Ok—only so much time they can burn before scoring from there. Or, their returner could have brought it out to their 40. They got the ball there anyway.

Part of the reason I got so upset about squibbing this game away was because ESPN showed Cox on the bench after our final touchdown. He had given our program so much over three years; and he had been through a lot in that season—even being benched and having to win his job back. In the shot of him on the sideline after the score he looked so happy—like it had all been worth it, even just for that one drive at Baton Rouge; a drive that should be a game-winning drive and a keystone in the Brandon Cox Auburn lore. Instead, we squibbed; and with the burden of losing to the mad hatter came home to face a native Cajun.

The Final Stretch

Ed Orgeron coached the Ole Miss Rebels from 2005–2007. He did not have the success at Oxford that Tuberville did; and he never beat Tuberville while coaching the Rebel Alliance Blackbear Ackbars. The 2007 matchup was undecided until the final four minutes, when Cox beat an Orgeron blitz with a hot route to Rodgeriqus Smith, who found his way to the end zone for the final score of the game: Auburn 17 – Ole Miss 3.

The next week's game against Tennessee Tech went according to plan. Cox sat out the second half; Kodi Burns, Blake Field and Neil Caudle all took snaps: Auburn 35 – Tenn. Tech. 3.

The following week, nothing went according to plan, at least not for the Tigers. We traveled to Athens to face the Bulldogs, who were 7–2 and ranked 10th. We made them look better than that.

Wes Byrum kicked a field goal to give us a 20–17 lead with 6:45 left in the third quarter. Georgia then scored touchdowns on each of their next four possessions. We did nothing: Georgia 45 – Auburn 20. In terms of points allowed, this game is the worst loss in Tuberville's Auburn career. The defeat, in combination with LSU's win over Mississippi State on the same day, eliminated the Tigers from western division championship contention. After the way we opened conference play against State, who would have thought we would be alive in November? Once again, though conference aspirations were unfulfilled, there was still something to play for—the Streak.

The Thumb Plus One

By 2007, the Streak had been an active, living thing for at least a couple years. Everyone in the state, and elsewhere, on both sides of the rivalry lived it throughout the year, each year. While the Streak's place in societal memory was already established, Tuberville had to win no. 6 to make himself stand alone as the Auburn coach with the most consecutive wins over Alabama. In the first quarter, it looked like he would do so with ease. Our defense forced a three-and-out to open the game, and then our offense drove 65 yards on 12 plays for a 7–0 lead. We kicked a field goal on our next possession for a 10-point lead. Unfortunately, we did not maintain this pace.

Alabama answered our field goal with a touchdown, and then our offense cooled off. The Tide had two more scoring opportunities in the first half, but failed to convert either. First they missed a field goal. Then, with 24 seconds left in the half Alabama quarterback John Parker Wilson delivered a fine pass into the end zone, but his receiver bobbled it into the waiting hands of Jerraud Powers, who quickly secured possession before stepping out of bounds, preserving our three-point half-time lead.

The second half was mostly an old-school Iron Bowl—the two teams exchanging several punts. Things got shaken up a bit, however, when Auburn's Robert Dunn returned a punt 31 yards to Alabama's 44. Our offense took advantage of the short field, covering the distance in nine plays. Cox finished the drive with a one-yard sneak for a touchdown. Alabama then put together a good drive, but only got a field goal out of it. We recovered the ensuing onside kick and ran out the clock: Auburn 17 – Alabama 10 – Tuberville 6. Tuberville successfully became the first Auburn coach to beat Alabama six consecutive years. The celebration of this historical achievement was muted—for some—by distractions pertaining to Tuberville's future.

The Duckhunter

Dennis Franchione—whom Tuberville beat in game one of the Streak—had a disappointing 2007 as the head coach at Texas A&M. Talk of Franchione possibly being fired started up in late September after a 34–17 loss to Miami of Florida. Tuberville, who was defensive coordinator at A&M in 1994, was soon rumored to be Francione's replacement. Reliable as always, the loudest reporters and pundits pushed the rumors as if they were a story. As Tuberville put it in early October, "It's good media talk."[n] The talk persisted and intensified to the point that, prior to the Georgia game, Auburn fan Warren Tidwell felt the need to launch paytuberville.com, a website from which he encouraged the Auburn Family and the University to pay Tuberville "the respect he deserves and the money he's worth."[o] After the Alabama game, many Auburn fans paid Tuberville the compliment of being worried sick about the possibility of him leaving, and many Alabama fans paid him the respect of being giddy at the thought of him going elsewhere—they were sick of losing to him. The latter, of course, is why the rumors played so well in the Birmingham media.

The "story" of Tuberville's eminent departure might have died the Monday after the Alabama game when Texas A&M named Mike Sherman their new head coach. Fortunately for the "journalists" who cater to Alabama fans, Houston Nutt resigned as Arkansas' coach the same day; the Birmingham News promptly reported that Arkansas would court Tuberville.[p] This idea—regardless of any connection to reality—really took off because Tuberville is an Arkansas native. A coworker of mine at the time, also an Arkansas native, told me he expected Tuberville would make the move. "I think he's coming home." The next week WJOX radio in Birmingham reported that someone in Arkansas was reporting that Arkansas and Tuberville had agreed in principle to the terms of his contract, and the deal would be announced in the next few days. You could feel it in the air driving around bammerham; Christmas was coming early—Tuberville was finally leaving!

There was news in the next few days—when Tuberville announced on December 4 that he had agreed to a contract extension with Auburn. The next day he said, "there was never any doubt I was coming back . . . I was never contacted by anybody else. There's no reason to go out and address something that's really not happening."[q] The new contract extension—interestingly enough—was to run through 2013. Tuberville was not leaving Auburn, but someone who had played a significant role in his success was.

A few days after announcing his new contract with Auburn, Tuberville accepted the resignation of offensive coordinator Al Borges. After the incredible 2004 season, our offense began a gradual decline, until in 2007 we ranked 101st nationally. That our team could win eight regular-season games with that little offense is incredible. How many games might we have won had we ranked, say, 65th? The departure of Borges was regrettable, even if predictable. Obviously, his role in Auburn's 2004–2007 run, during which we averaged better than ten wins per season, is undeniable. Borges is a very likeable guy, and he fit in well at Auburn and on Tuberville's staff. The next guy? Well . . .

Trojan Tony

Tuberville made a gear change—to say the least—in hiring Borges' replacement. Have you ever shifted gears without pushing in the clutch?[1] Tuberville hired Tony "The System" Franklin as his new OC in time for Franklin to be at practices for the upcoming Chick-fil-A Bowl against Clemson. Initially, Franklin said he

---

[1] I did once—an old Toyota. Those things are tough.

would mostly just observe the bowl preparations. "If I've got a suggestion, maybe a wrinkle or two, that would be good. I just want to try to see what the players are like and get around them and let them get to know me."[r] Franklin's role continually increased over the next two weeks until he had installed some portion of his offense and been designated the play-caller for the Chick-fil-A Bowl. The results were promising.

Franklin's offense delivered a considerable change of pace. Against Clemson, the Auburn offense ran a total of 90 plays; the per-game average for the regular season was 67. Points, however, were still relatively scarce. Ben Tate scored on a one-yard run to tie the game at 17 with 8:27 left in the fourth quarter. The two teams traded punts for the rest of regulation. Clemson got the ball first in overtime and kicked a field goal. We moved the ball effectively on our overtime possession and ended the game with a seven-yard Kodi Burns touchdown run: Auburn 23 – Clemson 20. Tuberville sounded happy with his new hire.

> A new offense in eight days? I think that's magnificent. Overall, it was a good game. We gave the people their money's worth. Nine wins and 50 for the seniors. That's a great sendoff. . . . We haven't had 423 yards in awhile. That's a pretty good day.[s]

The 2007 season ended on a high note. As stated above, it lacked the near-perfection (or even near-miss) quality that 2005 and 2006 possessed. At the same time, if we could have beaten LSU, we would have played in the SEC championship game—even with the losses to Mississippi State and Georgia—as LSU lost inexplicably to Kentucky, and again at season's end to Arkansas. The Bayou Bengals ultimately played in—and won—the BCS championship game. So, relative to the competition, 2007 is on the same level as its two predecessors—one win away from post-season championship contention. Furthermore, 2007 does include certain Tuberville trademarks: a hard-fought, conference road win (at Arkansas); a win over a top-ten team (Florida, also on the road); and, of course, another win over Alabama. For those reasons, we do count 2007 as part of a special period that began with 2004.

On December 31, 2007 the future looked bright. Tony Franklin's system produced impressive numbers and a win against Clemson. Tuberville seemed almost to have reinvented himself; bringing much needed diversity of ideology to the program. We were ready to move forward. Unfortunately, about a half hour after Kodi Burns crossed the goal line in Atlanta, the clock struck midnight, both on 2007 and on the Golden Age of Tuberville.

16

2008

The last six chapters have been pretty fun. Half of them were a lot of fun! The other half were mostly fun, but also possessed a certain agony of the near-miss—the what could have been . . .[1] This chapter? Well, it is almost enough—maybe it is enough—to make one wish Tuberville had gone to A&M or Arkansas or the Dallas Cowboys or wherever after winning game 6 of the Streak.[2] I do not mean to say 2008 overshadowed the previous nine years of Tuberville's tenure. Rather, only that I wish it could have ended on a high note. I wish this chapter of Auburn history closed with a strong season and a win over Alabama plus a bowl win. Of course, such is the nature of college football—and much else; the stories do not usually have the happiest endings. If things had been happy enough, the story would have gone on.

---

[1] For the ultimate in Auburn fan so-close-but-so-far turmoil, see chapters 21, 22 and 24 of Coach Dye's book, In the Arena. Dye announced in 2013 he is writing a new book, and will in part revisit his coaching days. I'm afraid with even greater hindsight (maybe 20/20 by now), the close will be even closer.

[2] . . . and taken Tony Franklin with him!

The influence of the Tuberville era upon the Auburn Family lives on, but the story of Tuberville's tenure at Auburn ends in 2008. We will look at this final season only as closely as our investigation requires. The final season—like all the others, of course—begins with the yearly changeup in personnel.

Once again, Tuberville's defensive coordinator—this time Will Muschamp—left Auburn for the same position at Texas. Tuberville hired Paul Rhoads as Muschamp's replacement, finally luring Rhoads away from Pittsburgh; he had offered him the position in 2002, but Rhoads declined. The 2008 season would be Tuberville's first since 2002 with new coordinators for both offense and defense. The new offensive coordinator, Tony Franklin, was hired before 2007 was even in the books. Franklin brought with him—or so he must have thought—the successor to Brandon Cox at quarterback, Chris Todd. There was uncertainty concerning Todd, however, from the beginning.

"It's a mystery to him. It's a mystery to me. He doesn't have pain, but he can't throw. He doesn't have any zip on the ball. He had better zip when he was in middle school than he does now."[a] When spring practice started, Todd's shoulder health was an enigma to both Franklin and the doctors. Had Todd been healthy, perhaps there would have been no quarterback controversy in 2008. As it was, Kodi Burns took most of the snaps in spring practice. Still, going into the summer, Franklin hinted at his logical preference for Todd.

> We hoped he [Burns] would get that good, and he has. He's gotten better. Chris has made him better. That's the good thing. Competition makes you better if you're a great player . . . We've got a wonderful problem.[b]

Some people say when you have two quarterbacks, you have none. Franklin called it "a wonderful problem." Tuberville attempted to describe our recruiting in 2008 using a similar idea.

The Tigers' starting lineup for the 2007 Chick-fil-A Bowl featured only five seniors. The projection for 2008 was that the team would be young, but experienced. When our recruiting class for 2008 was ranked 19th by Scout.com, and 20th by Rivals, Tuberville, while still declaring that his staff does their own evaluations and does not worry about rankings and recruits to meet needs, also explained that recruits were turned off to Auburn on account of our wealth of young talent. That is, we had so many good, young players already that we could not push playing time as a selling point: "A lot of the high-profile players think, I can go to this place [somewhere besides Auburn] and play sooner, which is fine. That has happened for us before."[c] How well was this young, talented team expected to perform?

The voters at SEC media days picked Auburn to win the western division.[d] Such confidence seems misplaced in a team without a starting quarterback in late July. Perhaps the pundits saw enough of Kodi Burns and Tony Franklin in the Chick-fil-A Bowl to know Auburn could win with that combination. If Todd won the job over Burns, even better. As noted above, apart from Brandon Cox, virtually all the playmakers—on both sides of the ball—were returning. Maybe the media just figured Auburn was due—after being a game away three consecutive seasons—for a trip to Atlanta. Tuberville and Franklin had still not named a starter when the preseason AP poll was released; the Tigers were ranked 10th. I usually love it when Auburn proves the experts wrong. In 2008, I wish they had been right.

The 2008 Season

We opened 2008 against Louisiana-Monroe. It was the most disappointing 34–0 win in the history of football. The offense looked nothing like what we expected. As noted in the previous chapter, we ran 90 offensive plays to end 2007 in the Chick-fil-A Bowl. Our offense then ran six plays in the first two minutes of the 2008 A-Day game. That kind of pace was what everyone wanted to see. Instead, we repeatedly ran up to the line as if we were going to run a play quickly, but then everyone rose up and looked to the sideline. This approach has been called the "prairie dog" offense. To the fans, this routine got old quick. It was also disconcerting— why was it so important that we adjust our play call to the defense against La. Monroe? The other pending question was: are we really going to have a two-quarterback system?

Burns played the first two series, and then Todd came in. At day's end Todd had attempted 18 passes, and Burns nine. Kodi also ran six times. With the first Saturday of 2008 in the books, we were 1–0, but all shaking and scratching our heads. The mood was chipper enough when I got a phone call from my Dad while walking back from the stadium: "Alabama's going through Clemson like a knife through butter." Welcome to 2008.

A few days after the game Tuberville announced we would not continue splitting the snaps between two QBs. He named Todd the starter for the next week—against Southern Miss—but added, "There's going to be a battle all year long, and, hopefully, they'll stay close because it'll make them and the team better."[e] Tuberville had recruited Kodi Burns, and Burns' commitment was a highlight—if not the highlight—of the 2007 class. Todd was Franklin's guy. What could go wrong? Division is a well known killer of else wise successful football teams. For the first two games in 2008, I experimented with my own nuance of division.

I wore a bright yellow Golden Eagles shirt to our game against Southern Miss. I also wore our opponents' colors to the first game of the season. Allow me to explain. In 2007 the ULM Warhawks defeated Alabama and their great golden god, Nick Saban. When I saw that the La. Monroe athletics department was selling shirts that read, "ULM 21 Bama 14," I could not—well, I chose not to—resist. I thought it would be fun to take it to work and hang it outside my cubicle for the benefit of passersby. It was. When it came time for us to play ULM in 2008, I figured I would wear the shirt, just for anyone who might get a kick out of it (meaning myself). Now, as for the next week . . .

My wife is a Southern Miss graduate. I thought it would be fun—I'm full of these ideas if you need any—to surprise her on game day by wearing a Southern Miss shirt. It went over pretty well.[3] Sarah enjoyed watching the fans around us, who were visibly perplexed by this guy wearing a Southern Miss shirt who cheered loudly the whole game for Auburn. Did our team need cheering that day? Yes.

We beat USM 27–13. Things still did not look just right. The Golden Eagles scored touchdowns late in the third quarter, and early in the fourth, cutting the lead to 11. It seemed as though the game was for sale. The Golden Eagles could have it if they just paid the price. We kicked a field goal to make the lead 14, but later USM drove to our 25 before turning it over on downs (on fourth and one). It was uneasy. Fortunately, we did seem to have the quarterback situation relatively settled. Todd completed 21 of 31 attempts for 248 yards. No one would look that good the next week.

---

[3] Sarah pointed out to me that the shirt I purchased was the USM equivalent of Tuberville orange. The Golden Eagles' colors are black and gold. This shirt was neither—it was more of a cautious, but proud, canary.

Our third game of 2008 was played at Starkville. This is one of those games where prior to the opening kickoff the ball falls off the tee—literally, figuratively, spiritually. Nobody won this game, but when the clock read 0:00, we had three points, and State had two (from a safety via holding penalty in our end zone). Tuberville stuck to the coach speak as if it had been any other unimpressive win, rather than an embarrassment to the sport. "It was ugly, but we'll take 3–2 every game we play this year." He also spoke gingerly about the offense. "Offensively, obviously, we need to go back to the drawing board a little bit."[f] No need for urgency, however; next up is only no. 6 LSU.

The Wagon is Wobbling

I went to this game, too. I did not wear purple and gold; maybe I should have. We led the Bayou Bengals 14–3 with nine minutes left in the third quarter, at which point we made a critical error—we knocked their quarterback out of the game. On a second-and-nine play, Andrew Hatch kept the ball on a pistol-option, and Jerraud Powers popped him high. Hatch's feet instantly swung up to head-level; his body dropped to the turf. Hatch was done. Coming off the field, he couldn't keep his mouthpiece in. It's a wonder he walked to the right sideline. We would have been better off had Powers just hit him in the gut and drug him to the ground.

LSU also had some quarterback uncertainty in early 2008. Hatch started the game, but Jarrett Lee relieved him in the second quarter. On a first-down play from the LSU 27, Lee carelessly attempted a swing pass, which was intercepted by Auburn defensive end Gabe McKenzie. The once-and-future tight end easily returned the interception for a touchdown. It seemed that this error sent Lee to the bench for good, until Powers rearranged Hatch's skull contents.

Once Hatch found the bench, Lee came in and promptly threw for a first down. Three plays later he threw a 39-yard touchdown pass, cutting our lead to 14–10. LSU continued to move the ball with Lee at quarterback. They closed the third quarter with a halfback-pass touchdown to take a 17–14 lead, and later kicked a field goal to make the score 20–14. Then our offense responded.

Wide receiver Tim Hawthorne turned a completion from Todd into a 58-yard gain, setting us up at the LSU 16. Todd then threw a pretty pass to Robert Dunn in the end zone. Auburn leads, 21–20.

Our defense shut down LSU's ensuing possession, giving our offense the ball with 5:32 left in the game. A couple of first downs and a good punt may have been enough for the win. Instead, we went three-and-out and punted 25 yards to the LSU 46. Lee then directed a seven-play touchdown drive. After a failed two-point conversion attempt, LSU led 26–21, and that is how the game ended.

Who can say what might have happened had we kept it together the final five minutes against LSU? Perhaps a win would have only delayed the inevitable. Or, maybe our team would have taken on new confidence, enabling a decent season. Even as it was, the loss to LSU was not officially the end; we dropped from no. 10 to just no. 15 in the AP poll. People still thought we could get it together. In reality, the season was already on the edge.

Tuberville's Last Conference Win

After LSU we hosted Tennessee. This game was like the trip to Starkville—neither team looked good. In the end, the Vols looked a little worse. As noted above, Todd was promoted from co-starter to starting quarterback after his performance against Southern Miss. At that point in the season Tuberville said the previous two-quarterback system partly accounted for the offensive ineptitude: "Obviously, you can't do that and get any kind of rhythm."[g] Consistent with that philosophy, Burns played little to none against

Mississippi State and LSU. Against Tennessee, however, Burns came into the game in the second quarter. He ran three times and attempted four passes on a nine-play drive that ended with a missed field goal. Todd played most of the second half, but Burns came back in for our final two possessions. With 2:14 left in the game Burns threw a ten-yard completion to Montez Billings on third-and-five. Without that first down, we would have been punting from our own ten-yard line. As it was, we ran out the clock for a 14–12 win.

At 4–1 and ranked 13th, nobody really knew how we had won four games, nor how we would win any more. Who was the quarterback? Why did Burns play against Tennessee? Todd was 9 for 12 when Burns first relieved him. After the game, Tony Franklin said Tuberville had decided to practice Kodi and make him part of the game plan. "He [Tuberville] felt like we needed a boost."[h] Franklin continued to defend his quarterback's performance, saying that against Tennessee,

> The first 28 snaps before Chris came out of the
> game, he had 27 perfect plays. He had 27 snaps that
> he was perfect— that he did every single thing that I
> would ask him to do. The only play he didn't was a
> fumbled snap from center . . .

Franklin also hinted that Todd would play better if he was our no. 1 and only. "It's hard on a young man to come into boos and people screaming the other guy's name and all that stuff. That's hard on any human being."[4] With our quarterback controversy and

---

[4] Franklin also said after the Tennessee game that he did not blame the fans for booing him; that the product on the field was poor, and that if he was a fan, he would boo himself. Furthermore, Franklin, per his own account, inadvertently made a quasi-Christological comment to Todd, "They don't hate you. They hate me . . ." (cf. John 15:18) GOLDBERG, CHARLES. "Franklin says he deserves the boos Doesn't blame fans for being upset." *Birmingham News (AL)* 29 Sep. 2008, SPORTS: 1-C. *NewsBank*. Web. 28 Jun. 2013.

our unpopular offense and even our psychoanalysis we traveled next to Nashville, to play a team that had not beaten us since 1955.

The Wheels Are Off

We had our opportunities against the Commodores. On our first possession of the game we drove to the Vanderbilt one, but then ran Ben Tate for no gain on both third-and-goal and fourth-and-goal. We scored touchdowns on our next two possessions (passes by Todd to Rod Smith and Mario Fannin), but Wes Byrum missed the PAT following the second TD; we led 13–0.

Our offense did little the rest of the game. Vanderbilt scored two touchdowns and won 14–13.

Kodi Burns summarized the state of affairs: "This isn't the Auburn I saw when I was recruited. This isn't the Auburn I saw last year. I don't know what's going on. We've got to figure something out."[i] Receiver Rod Smith was asked after the loss about Tuberville's post-game comments to the team. "He just said it's on him. He's going to carry the burden and we've just got to go back to work and make a lot of changes. I don't know what kind of changes he's going to make . . . probably be drastic changes."[j] Yes, I think we can agree the now imminent change qualifies as "drastic."

A Tiger No More

Before practice on Tuesday Franklin told the offense they would be seeing a different side of their coach. Rod Smith described the change this way: "The intensity he had at practice today was just crazy."[k] Whatever Franklin was trying to do with the new enthusiasm was not enough. On Wednesday he was fired.

"They told me to get lost."[l] Things now looked as pitiful—as un-Auburn—off the field as they did between the lines. Video of Franklin schlepping stacks of books and what not out of the athletics department offices and into his car made the rounds on the internet. Tuberville offered predictable explanations. "After evaluating where we are at this point of the season offensively, I felt it was in the best interest of the Auburn football program to make this change . . ."[m]

Tuberville did add that Franklin's firing was not the result of any personal conflicts, and that,

> It had nothing to do with X's and O's. He's a heck of a football coach. It was about getting it done on the practice field and to the game field—we're all responsible to that.[n]

Tuberville also announced that, even without Franklin, we would remain committed to the spread offense. He assigned play-calling duties—just as he had the last time we tried to run an offensive coordinator's offense without the coordinator—to Steve Ensminger; and that previous coordinator was now the head coach of our next opponent.

Given our identity crisis on offense, Arkansas should have been an ideal next opponent. The Hogs came to Jordan-Hare having given up 159 points in their previous three games. It did not matter. We made enough plays—including a 97-yard kickoff return for touchdown by Tristan Davis—to stay in the game, but Arkansas scored last, and won 25–22.

Tuberville took some responsibility for the situation. "It's been a tough week. I put our guys in a tough situation." At 4–3, it wasn't a losing season yet, but it already had the feeling of a lost one. He added some philosophy: "We're going to find out the character of our team. We're going to have to dig deep. We're going to have to dig hard. We're not playing very well right now. We're not coaching very well."[o] I think most of us knew by this point the time for digging deep had passed us by.

Unless I went to the Georgia game and somehow don't remember it, the loss to Arkansas was the last home game I attended in the Tuberville era. At game's end we saw a morbidly obese gentleman holding a cardboard sign that read, "Will coach offense for food." I heard someone in the crowd point out the paradox: "Doesn't look like he's missed many meals."

We used both quarterbacks in the loss to Arkansas, but only Burns played in our next game, at Morgantown against West Virginia. He threw one touchdown and ran for another. At the half we led 17–10. Everything unraveled after that, and we lost 34–17.

The blown-lead-blowout exacerbated talk of 2008 being Tuberville's last season at Auburn. Jay Jacobs made the obligatory statement:

> As I do with every coach, I evaluate their job performance based on the body of work. That being the case, we will continue to support Coach Tuberville and the program as we always have, and are looking forward to the next four games.[p]

There proved to be little reason to look forward. Nonetheless, on to Oxfordtown.

I saw a different side of Oxford on my second trip. In 1994 Vaught-Hemingway was filled with red dresses and Rebel flags. In 2008 we happened to drive through a neighborhood near the university. Every other yard had an Obama-Biden sign. The results on the field were equally disparate.

The story of this game—both good and bad—was the quarterback play of Kodi Burns. He completed 27 of 43 pass attempts for 319 yards, a performance that surely would have been good enough for a win had he not thrown three interceptions in the second half. The second interception came early in the fourth quarter on a third-and-twelve play from the Ole Miss 19. We trailed 10–7 at the time. If Burns had pulled the ball down and run, or thrown it away, Wes Byrum or Clinton Durst or Morgan Hull could have missed a potential game-tying field goal. As it was, Ole Miss scored once more and won the game 17–7. Three games remain.

Tuberville's Last Win

Our last non-conference opponent of the season was Tennessee-Martin. The Skyhawks came to Jordan-Hare with a record of 7–2 (5–1 in the I-AA Ohio Valley Conference). I did not know that at the time. I had heard we would be wearing white jerseys so that it didn't look like we were playing ourselves. Tennessee-Martin switched uniform suppliers in 2007, from Nike to Russell.[9] The Skyhawks had previously worn royal blue jerseys, but, when they switched to Russell, their new supplier provided uniforms identical in colors and design (apart from logos) to the ones Russell previously made for Auburn. In other words, they looked just like us. If we had worn our regular home blue jerseys (for homecoming, no less), and UTM had worn their white road jerseys, the game would not have counted, because it would have been A-Day. Fortunately, the Skyhawks also had orange jerseys available. There was nothing weird—or ironic—about that at all.

We walked away from Russell under Tuberville's leadership in 2006. In 2008—Tuberville's final, sad season—he had to face the jilted clothier; he (we) even had to face our old jerseys. We had to face ourselves. Moreover, Tuberville was the man who made Jordan-Hare orange. Now, on homecoming, we wore our road jerseys, and our opponents wore our jerseys, except they were orange. On that day, orange was their color. Anyway . . .

I fell asleep sometime shortly before kickoff. It had been a long day already. I did a kicker tryout that morning for the

Columbus Lions.[5] When I woke up, Sarah said, "Auburn's winning." Good, I thought; but then I saw the score: 20–13 does not count as *winning* against UT–Martin. The Skyhawks scored first in the second half to tie the game at 20. Fortunately, they did not score again. Wes Byrum hit a field goal, and Kodi Burns made touchdown runs of 31 and 58 yards. We *won* 37–20. Next up: 13th ranked Georgia.

Almost a Really Bad Day for Georgia

The 2008 edition of the Deep South's Oldest Rivalry was a weird game. Initially, it was weird that we were in it; then, it was weird that we did not win it—or, it would have been weird in any other season; in 2008, nothing worked.

We scored the first points of the game on a touchdown pass from Kodi Burns to Mario Fannin. Unfortunately, we botched the snap on the PAT and only led 6–0. Georgia scored a second-quarter touchdown and a third-quarter field goal. The Dawgs led 10–6 with 15 minutes left to play.

On the kickoff return after Georgia's field goal we were penalized for illegal blocking; our ensuing drive began at our own 10-yard line. Four plays later we converted a fourth-and-one from our own 19 (Kodi Burns got just the one yard we needed). We covered the rest of the field in sizable chunks, the last 35 on a touchdown run by Mario Fannin to take a 13–10 lead.

What happens next is quintessentially 2008. Morgan Hull sent the kickoff out of bounds, giving Georgia the ball at their 40. On first down, Georgia receiver Mohamed Massaquoi runs an out-pattern from the slot. Our defender, Jerraud Powers, hand checks Massaquoi as he makes the cut. This contact happens on virtually every play when a receiver runs this route. Massaquoi easily

---

[5] I made most of the kicks. A couple of guys made all of them.

separates himself from Powers and gets open. Matthew Stafford then throws the ball well behind his receiver, and high. Massaquoi turns all the way around and reaches back and up towards the ball with one hand, but it is uncatchable. Powers is falling down; he makes no contact with Massaquoi as the ball sails past. You know why I am breaking the play down like this. A flag is thrown—pass interference, defense, no. 8 (Jerraud Powers). The JP broadcast shows Tuberville watching the replay on the big screen; after seeing it, he goes ballistic, so much so that he incurs a delay-of-game penalty. Now, since our second touchdown, Georgia has not *gained* a single yard, but they have first down and five at our 40. Stafford ultimately throws a 17-yard touchdown pass to A. J. Green. Georgia leads 17–13.

Georgia returns the favor of kicking the ball out of bounds. We then drive down to their 21. The drive stalls, and Tuberville sends out the kicking team, with Morgan Hull instead of Wes Byrum, who had been up-and-down all season and missed a 42-yard attempt in the first half. Tuberville changes his mind and calls timeout. We then fail to convert on fourth-and-three. Of course, a field goal would have only pulled us within one. Had we made the extra point after the first touchdown, however, it could have been a game-tying attempt.

Our defense forces Georgia to punt, and we get the ball at our 20 with 1:44 left in the game. On the next 11 plays, we drive 66 yards, to the Georgia 14. On fourth-and-one, Burns' pass to Ben Tate falls incomplete: Georgia 17 – Auburn 13.

The Streak Dies

There's not much to tell from the last game of the Tuberville era. Our defense kept us alive in the first half, but our first five possessions of the game ended with punts. The sixth—and final possession of the first half—provides the only point of interest. On fourth-and-one at the Alabama 23, with five seconds left in the half, Tuberville sends his kicking unit onto the field. Wes Byrum remains on the bench. It will be Morgan Hull's first collegiate field goal attempt. The snap and hold are good. Hull's approach is steady and sure. He swings easy, and the ball jumps off his foot like a drive off Tiger's tee. It sails down the middle, as high as the tops of the uprights. The kick would have been good from close to 60 yards, but it did not count. Alabama had called timeout just before the snap. Everyone resets. The second attempt looks nothing like the first. Something is wrong with the line at the snap. This time Hull's approach is hurried, and he tries to punch the ball out as quickly as possible. Multiple Alabama defenders are crashing through the line; one of them gets a hand on the low kick; and that's as close as Tuberville came to not being shut out in his final game as Auburn's coach.[6] Alabama won 36–0.

The end of the Streak was difficult for me to accept. It had been a while—better than a fifth of my life at the time—since we had last lost to Alabama. I watched most of the second half alone in my parents' basement. Not that I'm bad company when Auburn is getting beat . . .

I don't remember how I felt after the game regarding whether Tuberville would—or should—be our coach the next season. I do remember thinking Jay Jacobs' press conference the following Thursday seemed odd—a little like he had shuffled

---

[6] Coincidentally (?), Pat Dye called for a field goal trailing Alabama 17–0 late in his last game. Scott Etheridge's 48-yard attempt fell short. Thus, both Dye and Tuberville had field goal opportunities that, had they been made, could have spared the coaches from ending their Auburn careers with shutout losses to Alabama.

For Dye, it was actually his only time to be shutout as Auburn's coach—that's right, almost 12 full seasons without being shutout. How many shutouts did Auburn's defense deliver during Dye's tenure? Thirteen. The 1988 defense blanked three consecutive opponents (Akron and Mississippi State at home; then at Florida).

pages from two different scripts. But, let's not get ahead of ourselves.

Resigned, Fired, Something

When Auburn president Jay Gogue was asked in early November about Tuberville's job security, he explained that he meets with the head coaches for all the school's sports before and after each season. Tuberville's postseason meeting with Gogue took place Monday morning. The two reportedly discussed the coach's plan for turning things around. The University released a statement that officially placed Tuberville—and thus our whole program—in limbo:

> Further conversations between Jay Jacobs and Coach Tuberville will take place in the following days to discuss Coach Tuberville's plan to make improvements for the program moving forward under his leadership.[r]

Yes, the statement implies Tuberville will be the coach in the future, but such statements are never needed when a coach's job is secure. Tuberville met with Jay Jacobs on Tuesday. Gogue had previously said Jacobs would make a recommendation to him regarding the football program, and that Gogue would likely act on that advice. After the Tuesday meeting, Jacobs said nothing more specific than, "we'll meet again over the next several days."[s]

The next meeting happened the next day, starting at lunch, and that is when, per Jacobs, Tuberville first expressed a desire to resign.[t] Jacobs and Tuberville both released statements Wednesday night.

> Tommy and I have had the opportunity to discuss the direction of the program. Through those discussions, Tommy felt it would be in his and the program's best interest to step aside as Auburn's

216

head football coach. We appreciate everything Tommy has done for this program, this university and the Auburn community over the last 10 years. He has established a strong foundation to build upon and we thank him for the standard he set. We wish Tommy and his family—wife Suzanne, and sons Tucker and Troy—nothing but the best.[u]

The last 10 years have been a great time in my life, both professionally and personally. It's been a great place to coach and live, and we've had a lot of success along the way. I'm going to remain in Auburn and help the Auburn family however I can. I'm very appreciative of the coaches, players, staff and Auburn fans over the last decade.[v]

On Thursday, Jacobs held a press conference.[w] Per Jacobs, Tuberville told him on Wednesday that he wanted to resign. "He [Tuberville] said, 'Ten years is a long time.' He said he would talk to Suzanne and think about it. He came back yesterday and said he thought the best thing for him and his family was to resign."[x] Jacobs then told the press he asked Tuberville three times to reconsider. "After three times of asking him would he change his mind, he convinced me that the best thing for him and his family and for this football program was for him to possibly take a year off and take a step back."[y] Jacobs said he then went to the president's office and told Gogue of Tuberville's decision. Gogue responds by instructing Jacobs to tell Tuberville he wants him to stay. Jacobs tells the president, "I've already done that three times." Jacobs then goes back to the athletics department offices and calls Gogue on speakerphone with Tuberville. Tuberville says he wants to sit down with Gogue. The three get together, and

Gogue tells Tuberville that, if he does not want to coach anymore, Gogue still wants him to be part of the Auburn Family.

The reporters at the press conference isolated the issue of whether Tuberville resigned, was fired, or something in between.

> Question: Just to clarify—he was not forced out; this was his decision?
> Jacobs: Completely his decision.

> Question: Was he given a mandate to fire his coaches—his entire staff?
> Jacobs: No, not at all. He wasn't given any mandates at all.

> Question: If Tommy hadn't resigned yesterday, would he be the coach at Auburn next year?
> Jacobs: Absolutely; absolutely.

The statement released by the University on Wednesday night stipulated the following:

> The buyout portion of Tuberville's contract will be fulfilled, from which no state or university funds will be used. All assistant and contractual staff will be paid according to their respective contracts.[z]

This information created some confusion. The general understanding of a buyout is that it has to be paid by the party who walks away from a contract. If Tuberville was resigning, then he was the one walking away. Why would the University pay his buyout? This point also prompted questions at the press conference.

> Question: Did you have the option to not pay his buyout? If he resigns, technically, you're not on the hook for that.

> Jacobs: "Well, you know, there's a lot of technical things. But, the president and I—with Tommy, what he's done for this program the last ten years, him wanting to stay here at

Auburn and help the president, we have two [rules]—one is to tell the truth and treat people the way you'd like to be treated; we just thought that was the best way to treat him.

Question: So the buyout will be paid because you guys think it's the right thing to do?

Jacobs: Exactly; and his willingness and assurances that he wants to stay here and help us move forward and transition.

Jacobs was also asked if Tuberville would have been paid the buyout if he had indicated he was going straight to a new job at another school. Jacobs responded that he told Tuberville if he had another opportunity lined up, the buyout would be "irrelevant;" that Tuberville [or, presumably, a new employer] would not be required to pay it.

So, according to Jacobs' press conference answers, Tuberville was paid the buyout even though he was not fired, and if someone had hired him away, they would not have been required to pay a buyout. What are we to make of this generosity/hypothetical magnanimity? One interpretation is just to say Auburn actually did fire Tuberville, or that they forced him out by making some demand he was not willing to meet. Of course, if either was the case, Jacobs lied to us—boldly and frequently—in his press conference. At least one person close to the situation took that position the week after the press conference. Tuberville's mother, Olive, was quoted by the Opelika-Auburn News as saying, "He didn't resign. He was fired." Jacobs says he resigned; his mother said he was fired. What did Tuberville say?

Tuberville's last day as Auburn's coach was, expectedly, an emotional one. "I'm doing fine, but then you suddenly realize you're not a coach anymore. I had a tough time with the players. I almost didn't get through it."[aa] Tuberville went home Wednesday evening to a house full of food and friends. "It was as close as you can come to going to your own funeral. It was like somebody died. I guess something has died. Something inside of you has died."[bb] In response to that description by Tuberville, Kevin Scarbinsky of the Birmingham News posed our question this way: Was it a murder or a suicide? I have not been able to find a categorical statement by Tuberville from 2008 on whether or not he was fired. We have to infer what we can from comments like these:

> Right now, I want to help the healing process, if there needs to be one, with me leaving. I'm not saying people are disappointed I'm leaving, but anytime there's a change, there could be a division. We've had huge support. We're fortunate, very blessed, to have been here 10 years.[cc]

Tuberville later spoke about his departure in a compilation of Auburn memoirs, published in 2010, titled What It Means to be a Tiger.

> After 10 years I knew a lot about this program and how it worked, the successes, the failures, and I just thought in 2008 there was a lot of dissension. I was a blue-collar guy and not aligned with some people who wanted to control the football program. We were not headed in the right direction. Somebody had to give, and I knew those certain people were not going to give.
>
> I was making $3 million a year and knew if something didn't happen, the program was going to hit the bottom. If it took somebody to leave, I was going to do it. I hated it; I still hate it. I should still be the coach, but there were a couple of factions, and I didn't want to see the program suffer. If they had left, I would have stayed. They had been controlling it for years.[dd]

We can interpret even the above statement a number of ways. He still does not expressly say, "I was fired," or "It was completely my decision." What is our best guess as to the question of whether Tuberville was fired? Some consider the University's willingness to pay the buyout as an uncontestable answer—he was fired. I do not believe he was. Here is my interpretation.

It all hangs on Jacobs' answer to the question about whether the University was required to pay the buyout: "Well, you know, there's a lot of technical things . . ." My interpretation is that the answer lies in the technical things; that somewhere in Tuberville's contract, there was a stipulation that if a certain condition existed, then Tuberville would have the option to resign and still be owed the buyout. This hypothesis explains why Jacobs asked Tuberville three times to stay—he was asking the coach to not put the University in a position where we had no coach, and owed an outgoing coach $5.1 million. It also works with Jacobs' statement that paying the buyout was "the right thing to do," because honoring one's contractual obligation is the right thing to do. This explanation does not require us to accept that Jacobs lied through his teeth to the Auburn Family in a vulnerable moment. I do not mean to imply that Jacobs is incapable of lying, but, "I asked him three times?" I hope he would not have chosen the strategy of telling a lie so ridiculous that it has to be thought true.

One may argue I have discovered the empty cookie plate and concluded Santa must be real. Perhaps. What can I say? I fired Tuberville many, many times. I choose to believe Auburn did not. Maybe I choose this belief because in 2008—for one moment—I was a member of the barbeque crew.

Sarah and I got married on A-Day, 2008. On the day before I had lunch with my groomsmen at Byron's Smokehouse. We placed our orders, settled into our tables, and then noticed who was lounging in the corner—Tommy Tuberville. How did coach look on the day before A-Day? Relaxed. Very relaxed. It makes me think of Andy Dufresne, alone in the shade while the rest of the roofing detail guzzles beer and cuts jokes in the sun—totally content; a smug half-grin on his face—well aware that Todd's shoulder is shot and Burns can't run Franklin's *system*, but, who cares? It's Friday. The ribs are perfect. He's comfortable.

I'm being unfair—and overly imaginative—I know. Somehow much of my frustration from 2008 gets focused onto my observation from that day. Furthermore, it's a bit hypocritical for me to speak ill of Tuberville regarding that encounter. After all, he was willing to take a picture with me.

The author with Tommy Tuberville, who is wearing a darker, but not quite burnt, orange.

17

Conclusion

At the beginning of this book I claim that the events of the Tuberville era impacted the Auburn Family in such a meaningful way that the effect is still active today. What is the connection between everything we have just examined and who we are today? Allow me to begin answering this question with a fundamental assertion.

Auburn is different. Really, Auburn is not just different; Auburn is unique. One might argue there are supporters of many schools who think their institution is unique. I am not sure that is true. There are plenty of people who think their respective schools are special, but they understand that everyone thinks his or her own college is special, and thus none of them are truly unique. Auburn is different. I have loved Auburn all my life; so I cannot objectively make this claim. Subjectivity, however, does not necessarily exclude correct judgment.[1] Many readers of this book

---

[1] When a six-foot-tall person walks into a room full of five-foot-tall people and says, "I am the tallest person in this room," he or she lacks full objectivity, but the assessment is still correct.

already understand Auburn is unique. Those readers, too, might face accusations of subjectivity. How then, might we convince an unenlightened individual of the unique quality of Auburn?

We could make our case based on voluminous history, with information about *The Deserted Village*, George Petrie, Katharine Cooper Cater and thousands of other exhibits; or, we could simply take the jury to Toomer's Corner. The Oaks that once stood there provide as much evidence of Auburn's uniqueness in their absence as they did when present. Just as no other school has a tradition quite like rolling Toomer's Corner—from which the Oaks emerged as a living symbol of the Auburn Spirit—so, of course, no comparable community has lost such a symbol by the means that we have. I am not saying that the rolling of Toomer's Corner is what makes Auburn unique. Rather, the ritual and the symbol represent what is unique about the Auburn Spirit. Just what is it that makes the Auburn Spirit unique? To answer that question let us review what we have seen in our history of the Tuberville era.

Out of the Fire

The lasting impact of the Tuberville decade begins on the tarmac. When the *Jetgate* conspirators decided they knew best for Auburn—that they could work for Auburn's best interest even while acting contrary to the Auburn Spirit—they stole something of the integrity of the Auburn Family. Once the crime was discovered, the Auburn people responded with a passionate demand that the integrity of the University be restored. The people rallied behind their head coach, whom even David Housel, one of the conspirators, had previously called "the leader of the people."[2] Tuberville worded his appreciation for the people's support wisely, so as not to make it about himself. "I've never seen a group of people rally around a cause like they have the past week. I want to

---

[2] cf. page 3.

thank them for their thousands of e-mails and faxes and phone calls and all the love that they've shown." Of course, Tuberville was right. It was not strictly about him, but rather for the cause of restoring the University's integrity. The love, however—yes, that was for Tuberville; for everything he had done to restore Auburn's integrity after the Bowden/Oliver debacle.

The theme for recovery from *Jetgate* was unity. When Tuberville announced he would remain Auburn's coach, he emphasized solidarity. "I have no ill feelings toward anybody. We're all in this together. When you win, you win together. When you lose, you lose together."[a] Governor Bob Riley released a statement the same day. Its concluding sentence reads, "Finally, as we work to correct this process, I agree with Coach Tuberville's sentiment that this is a time for the Auburn family to come together for the good of the university."[b]

For a community as large and geographically dispersed as the Auburn Family, coming together is a deep-level phenomenon—discernible on the small scale, but generally hidden on the macro level; unless, of course, 86,000 of us wear the same t-shirt at the same time and at one place. It was Tuberville who first asked us to do that, in 2000, and with greater encouragement in 2001. But it was in July 2004, prior to the first football season after *Jetgate*, that the All Auburn All Orange program was launched. The program involved selling a specially designed t-shirt, and a portion of the proceeds went to Tiger Habitat—the Auburn University chapter of Habitat for Humanity.[3] The purpose of the program was "to create unity and spirit among the Auburn student body, alumni, fans and student-athletes at events throughout the

---

[3] In 2006 the beneficiary for All Auburn All Orange was changed to the Auburn SGA's Big Event, a student-led volunteer day involving 2,400 students and faculty in 197 community service projects.

school year."[c] So, as we worked to move on from 2003, we started a program based on dressing for game day the way Tuberville asked us to in the name of unity and spirit. Keep that in mind.

What happened after *Jetgate*? We won every game in 2004. The moral of the story was clear: when we come together to stand up for the Auburn Spirit—when we emphasize our unity—good things happen. Of course, Auburn is different—winning every game did not afford us the same opportunity that it has any other BCS conference team. How did we face the injustice? We maintained our belief in the Auburn Spirit and in each other. We focused on our unity. We celebrated another perfect season.

The 2004 undefeated season occurred, of course, in the middle of the Streak. The perfect season allowed us to celebrate what we can do. The Streak allowed us to celebrate who we are. The Streak provided a sustained period of time during which Auburn indisputably owned the State of Alabama. This sustained dominance—and Tuberville's personal celebration of it—gave us heightened incentive to celebrate something that is always true regardless of who wins in November: they have their tradition; and we have the Auburn Spirit and the Auburn Family and its unity.

We began this chapter with the assertion that Auburn is different; that Auburn is unique. What is it that makes Auburn unique? The answer can be seen in the experiences of the Auburn Family from 1999–2008. The impact of the Tuberville decade that is still seen today is that during those ten years the Auburn Family came to understand the uniqueness of Auburn more expressly in terms of our unity. By unity, we do not mean we always agree on everything, but that we possess a shared loyalty to something we love.

In the preceding chapters we have seen Tuberville's role in this development of our self-understanding. And we have looked at the entire Tuberville decade—to some extent—through navy-tinted glasses, that is, from the perspective of a fan who learned to love Auburn football during the Pat Dye era. The two men were very different Auburn coaches in some ways. The game—or, more so everything that goes with it—was changing very quickly in the six years between Dye's Auburn career and Tuberville's. To just observe that Dye is older than Tuberville shows their differing locations on the timeline of history, but does not fully convey their respective places in the chronology of college football. Here is a comparison that makes it clearer. Dye was an assistant coach for nine seasons at Alabama under Paul Bryant. Tuberville was an assistant coach for eight seasons at Miami under Jimmy Johnson and Dennis Erickson. These two coaches are not, however, totally unalike.

Both Pat Dye and Tommy Tuberville understand the Auburn Spirit. Allow me to quote both coaches, on seemingly disparate subjects, to show a common thread. Firstly, Tuberville on the reality of what it takes to be an Auburn fan.

> The alumni and fans have a piece of Auburn in their hearts. It's not just that they want somebody to pull for, to root for on Saturdays, it's a part of them. That's what it means to be a Tiger.

> Alabama is going to get 70 percent of the media attention and have all the advantages, so to be an Auburn person you have to have it deep in your heart that you are going to support this team no matter what.[d]

Now, here is a comment from Pat Dye in response to the allegations made by Eric Ramsey.

He said one true thing. He said football practice was hell at Auburn. If it's not, it's meant to be. And when you get out there across the line of scrimmage from the big, tough, fast, smart, angry boys from Florida, and Georgia, and Alabama, where there is no quality of mercy on the ground and no place to hide, you know why practice is hell at Auburn.[e]

What is the common thread here? In these statements both coaches express one of the beliefs of the Auburn Creed. Just as the two men are at opposite ends of the coaching spectrum in some regards, so did they emphasize beliefs from opposite ends of the Creed. Dye was more known for his emphasis on the first tenet of the Creed, specifically, "I believe in work, hard work." Tuberville more so displayed his understanding of the last line of the Creed: "And because Auburn men and women believe in these things, I believe in Auburn and love it."

Tuberville understood how we love Auburn, and we could see that he understood it. So when he called for unity, we responded. When we saw what our unity produced, we came to better understand that the unity of the Auburn Family is what makes us unique. Now, how is this understanding still evident today?

We can answer this question by asking another: what has happened in the life of the Auburn Family since Tuberville's departure? The answer is, of course, a lot! But in the context of assessing the Tuberville era's lasting impact, the first thing to recognize is that ever since December 2008 the Auburn Family has been under attack.[4] Really, the Auburn Family is always under attack to some degree or another. The reason why stems from what we said at the start of this conclusion—Auburn is unique. Just as

---

[4] *Oh, no—here he goes . . .*

the Auburn people know the Auburn Family is unique, so does, really, most everyone who has looked at us with any discerning eye. Some such observers simply respond, "Good for them; they have what they have and we have what we have." Others cannot so graciously accept the uniqueness of Auburn. To the contrary, it makes them absolutely sick because they would rather believe their community is the one that is unique.

The envy of many of our opponents is why the attacks against Auburn were so intensely mean-spirited in 2010. Auburn is already unique; and now we dared to be champions, too? Unacceptable. The reader may respond by asking whether I am really claiming that the incessant slander against Auburn in 2010 was driven by other fans' jealousy for the uniqueness of Auburn. My response is that their jealousy may not have been the origination of the first accusations, but it is why ESPN and other media outlets rode the non-story all season—because the jealousy of many drove television ratings and internet page views. But, what does all this have to do with the Tuberville era? The answer lies in our response.

The Auburn people responded to the challenges of 2009–2011 by going All In. Yes, All In is inseparable from Gene Chizik—Auburn's head coach from 2009–2012, who was Tuberville's defensive coordinator from 2002–2004. Chizik somehow lost effectiveness in 2012 and was fired, and now we are moving on. Now is a new day. But, for a moment, let's remember 2009–2011. All In was very real in its moment of greatest necessity and strength. What does All In mean?

All In means two things; we can see what they are by emphasizing either of the two words. Let's start with the latter word. When we say all *IN*, we emphasize the depth of commitment to a cause—that is, being All In means total commitment, total investment with no concession to turning back or giving up. When we say *ALL* in, we emphasize the breadth of commitment—that is, it's got to be everybody, all of us. In other words, there has to be unity. Coach Chizik expanded the All In philosophy from the team to the larger Auburn Family at a pep rally in September 2010.

> I just got done with practice, and the speech I gave our football team was simply this: It's Wednesday night. I don't need 'em ready to play tonight. I need 'em ready to play Saturday night. But here's what I need right now. I need every guy on that team all in. I need everybody on that field all in. And here's my message to you: I need each one of you all in on Saturday.[f]

Chizik made this speech before the media publicized the baseless allegations against Auburn regarding the eligibility of our quarterback, Cam Newton. Chizik chose All In as a keyword/ideology for moving the team from good (2009) to great (2010). But when those who hate Auburn—and the media outlets who pander to the haters—launched their assault, the Auburn Family amplified our adoption of All In because we learned from the Tuberville decade that our unity is the strength by which we can overcome any challenge.

Tuberville was right. This unity shows up on TV better when we all wear bright orange t-shirts. TV, of course, is a snapshot from one perspective of one facet of the indefinable something we call Auburn. It transcends navy blue and orange of any hue. We go along, as a family, all the time both making it and learning what it is. We learned something in the experiences of the Tuberville decade about the importance of our unity in the Auburn Family. The impact of those experiences now plays a role in shaping just how it is that we "believe in Auburn and love it!"

AFTERWORD

It's the way things go sometimes. I start writing a book called Orange Is Our Color and, by the time I finish it, the first signs of *Tuberville orange* fading can now be seen.

Take a look at the merchandise wherever you buy Auburn gear. Blue is making a comeback. Furthermore, allauburnallorange.com now redirects to auburnloveitshowit.com. Indeed, the writing appears to be on the virtual wall. Consider this verbiage from an Auburntigers.com page titled *Auburn Announces Gameday Weekend Events*:

> . . . the annual All Auburn, All Orange game has been scheduled for Nov. 16 vs. Georgia, when Auburn fans are encouraged to wear orange to Jordan-Hare Stadium.

Almost sounds like we're only encouraged to wear orange to one game, doesn't it? The announcement continues, providing the real kicker:

> The Iron Bowl will be the True Blue game.[a]

In 2013, we'll be True Blue for the biggest game of the year. Of course, we now have our second coach since Tuberville, and Tuberville is at his second school since Auburn. Perhaps it is time. That we are finally—if gradually—letting go of *Tuberville orange*, does not affect my thesis and conclusion. Still, I will not fight to drag it into the present if it more accurately answers a question pertaining to 2009–2012.

Today is a new day. We welcome it. New Auburn head coach Gus Malzahn says we have to get our edge back. That admonition makes me think of running gassers until guys are throwing up blood and quitting the team. It also makes me think of Coach Dye running a second, private A-day game, a "first-class bloodbath" to "find out who wants to play ball next fall."[b]

I hope when our team takes the field in 2013 we will see evidence that we have gotten our edge back. It's in my blood to believe we will. I believe we will win the True Blue game.

W A R   E A G L E

SOURCES

Chapter 1

[a] Opelika-Auburn News. "Game Notes." *Opelika-Auburn News* (August 31, 2000): 3.

[b] Dann, Lori. "New-look Jordan-Hare Greets Tigers." *Opelika-Auburn News* (September 1, 2000): 4B.

[c] "ORANGE CRUSH AUBURN'S TUBERVILLE LOVE AFFAIR PAYING OFF." *Birmingham News (AL)* 21 Sep. 2000, SPORTS: 01-C. *NewsBank.* Web. 10 Aug. 2013.

Chapter 2

[a] Goldberg, "Tuberville Tells AU Alumni to Keep the Faith," 1-D.

[b] Kevin Scarbinsky. "AU PICKS OFF NO. 1 GATORS ARE TIGERS BEST IN LAND? BELIEVE IT, BOWDEN SAYS." *Birmingham News (AL)* 16 Oct. 1994, SPORTS: 01-01. *NewsBank.* Web. 23 Jul. 2013.

[c] NEAL SIMS. "ALUMNI SEE TUBERVILLE REPAIRING IMAGE." *Birmingham News (AL)* 29 Nov. 1998, SPORTS: 06-B. *NewsBank.* Web. 22 Jul. 2013.

[d] The Associated Press, "Ole Miss hires Tuberville as its new head coach," *The Gainesville Sun* (December 4, 1994): 16.

[e] Charles Goldberg, "Fan Day at Auburn has Feel of Fresh Start," *Birmingham News* (August 16, 1999): 1-C.

[f] Goldberg, "Evans Eager to Run for Tigers," 1-D.

[g] Goldberg, "AU's Robinson: "It was hard . . . I dealt with it"," 1-D.

[h] Goldberg, "Gabe's the Man: Tuberville Names Gross Starting Quarterback - For Now," 1-D.

[i] Kirk, "AU Victory Offers Hope for Season," 12-B.

[j] Kirk, "AU Victory Offers Hope for Season," 12-B.

[k] Kirk, "AU Victory Offers Hope for Season," 12-B.

[l] Kirk, "AU Victory Offers Hope for Season," 12-B.

[m] Adam Winslow, "Safety Net Fails: Tigers late-game strategy leads to Bulldogs come-from-behind win," *The Gadsden Times* (October 10, 1999): B1.

[n] Charles Goldberg, "Tuberville Pleased with Progress, Sets Goals," *Birmingham News* (November 22, 1999): 1-C.

° Charles Goldberg, "Tuberville Dismisses LSU Job Reports," *Birmingham News* (December 1, 1999): 5-D.

ᵖ CHARLES GOLDBERG. "Tuberville's plan revived two programs Coach's changes breathed new life into Mississippi, Auburn teams." *Birmingham News (AL)* 26 Aug. 2007, SPORTS: 15-P. *NewsBank.* Web. 21 Jun. 2013.

q Pate, Rob. *A Tiger's Walk: Memoirs of an Auburn Football Player.* Sports Publishing, 2004. Kindle edition, location 1031.

ʳ Pate, Rob. *A Tiger's Walk: Memoirs of an Auburn Football Player.* Sports Publishing, 2004. Kindle edition, location 1043.

ˢ Williams, Chette, and Dick Parker. *Hard Fighting Soldier: Finding God in Trials, Tragedies, and Triumphs.* Decatur, Ga: Looking Glass Books, 2007, 96.

ᵗ Williams, Chette, and Dick Parker. *Hard Fighting Soldier: Finding God in Trials, Tragedies, and Triumphs.* Decatur, Ga: Looking Glass Books, 2007, 110.

Chapter 3

ᵃ Birmingham News, "AU's Summer Practices Have Veterans, Newcomers almost '100 Percent' Ready," *Birmingham News* (August 4, 2000): 1-C.

ᵇ Frank Couch, "Laying It On the Line: Get-Tough Tuberville Wants No Paper Tigers," *Birmingham News* (July 27, 2000): 1-D.

ᶜ Charles Goldberg, "College Beat," *Birmingham News* (August 9, 2000): 5-D. Tuberville made this statement when addressing the Birmingham-Jefferson County Auburn Club.

ᵈ Sports Illustrated, "The Master List," n.p. [cited November 18, 2012]. Online: http://sportsillustrated.cnn.com/football/college/2000/preview/si/masterlist2/.

ᵉ Charles Goldberg, "Tuberville Pleased with Progress, Sets Goals," *Birmingham News* (November 22, 1999): 1-C.

ᶠ Gregg Dewalt, "Tommy's Next Test: Auburn Coach Tuberville Returns to Ole Miss with Strong, Hungry Tigers," *Times Daily* (September 6, 2000): C-1.

ᵍ Jimmy Smothers, "The Coach Must Return: Auburn's Tuberville may Face a Bitter Crowd in Host Ole Miss," *The Gadsden Times* (September 6, 2000): D-1.

ʰ Mike Freeman, "Pro Football; Bugel Out in Oakland; Belichick Could Be In," n.p. [cited November 22, 2012]. Online: http://www.nytimes.com/1998/01/07/sports/pro-football-bugel-out-in-oakland-belichick-could-be-in.html.

ⁱ Bobby Hall, "Coach Wants Flag Waived - Tuberville Disavows Reb Symbol," *The Commercial Appeal* (September 26, 1997): D-1.

[j] Hall, "Coach Wants Flag Waived," D-1.

[k] Charles Goldberg, "Tuberville Pulls Out of AU Race," *Birmingham News* (November 12, 1998): 8-D.

[l] Birmingham News, "Sweet Ride for Tuberville: Tigers Help their Coach Celebrate Win over Old Team," *Birmingham News* (September 10, 2000): 1-B.

[m] Birmingham News, "Auburn Runs Over LSU: Tigers Snap Eight-Game SEC Losing Streak at Home," *Birmingham News* (September 17, 2000): 1-B.

[n] Birmingham News, "Tigers in Tailspin Will Go Back to Basics," *Birmingham News* (October 16, 2000): 1-C.

[o] Birmingham News, "Rudi's Big Day Makes his Season Grand," *Birmingham News* (October 22, 2000): 12-B.

[p] Charles Goldberg, "Tigers Go to 8-2, Sat in Running for SEC West Title," *Birmingham News* (November 12, 2000): 1-B.

[q] Kevin Scarbinsky, "Tigers Sack T-Town: Auburn Shuts Out Crimson Tide to Nail Down SEC West Championship, Trip to Atlanta," *Birmingham News* (November 19, 2000): 1-B.

Chapter 4

[a] Matt Tidmore, "Williams: 'AU Close Second'," *Birmingham News* (January 10, 2001): 1-D.

[b] Matt Tidmore, "Etowah's Williams Says It's Auburn," *Birmingham News* (January 30, 2001): 1-D.

[c] Charles Goldberg, "Cobb Outplays QB Rivals, Emerges No. 1," *Birmingham News* (April 15, 2001): 1-B.

[d] Charles Goldberg, "AU Coaches still not sure on Starter at QB," *Birmingham News* (August 16, 2001): 1-C.

[e] Charles Goldberg, "Soup's On: Campbell is Tigers's QB," *Birmingham News* (August 19, 2001): 1-B.

[f] Kevin Scarbinsky, "Shhhh! Tigers will let Talent do the Talking," *Birmingham News* (August 27, 2001): 1-C.

[g] Charles Goldberg, "Tiger Offense Plans to Step Up for LSU," *Birmingham News* (September 10, 2001): 1-C.

[h] Charles Goldberg, "Alabama, Auburn, UAB Waiting to Hear if They'll Play," *Birmingham News* (September 12, 2001): 1-D.

[i] Charles Goldberg, "SEC to Take the Field - UAB-Pitt Game Reset for Dec. 1; Other State Schools will Play," *Birmingham News* (September 13, 2001): 1-D.

[j] http://www.nytimes.com/2001/10/14/sports/college-football-Auburn-jolts-no-1-florida-with-10-seconds-left.html. Accessed April 14, 2012.

[k] Glier, Ray. *What It Means to be a Tiger*. Kindle edition: Position 1029.

[l] Charles Goldberg, "New Year's Eve Toast - Valiant Tigers Defense Can't Overcome Inept Offense," *Birmingham News* (January 1, 2002): 1-D.

Chapter 5

[a] Casey McCall in Dan Williams, "'We Believe in Tommy' - The AD Says AU's Coach Isn't on the Hot Seat; Some Fans Agree, Some Don't," *Birmingham News* (August 25, 2002): 12-P.

[b] Charles Goldberg, "Tuberville Thinks Recruits are Best Yet," *Birmingham News* (January 24, 2002): 1-C.

[c] Charles Goldberg, "Tigers' Cobb, Campbell Jockey in QB Duel," *Birmingham News* (July 30, 2002): 1-C.

[d] Charles Goldberg, "Cobb, Campbell Share Co-starter Status at QB," *Birmingham News* (March 19, 2002): 6-C.

[e] Charles Goldberg, "Opening Day QB: Cobb - Grasp of Petrino's Offensive Scheme Tips Scales to Senior," *Birmingham News* (August 21, 2002): 1-D.

[f] Charles Goldberg, "New Coordinator Chizik a Textbook Hire for AU," *Birmingham News* (February 8, 2002): 3-B.

[g] Charles Goldberg, "New QB Cox Redshirted; He Calls it Chance to Learn," *Birmingham News* (August 5, 2002): 1-C.

[h] Charles Goldberg, "Young Gun - Josh Sullivan is the New Horse in Auburn's QB Stable and He's Moving Up the Depth Chart," *Birmingham News* (August 9, 2002): 1-C.

[i] Charles Goldberg, "Cox Leaves Football Team; Former Hewitt Star Misses Drills, Fan Day," *Birmingham News* (August 11, 2002): 1-B.

[j] Pete McEntegart, "23. Auburn," n.p. [cited Janury 8, 2013]. Online: http://sportsillustrated.cnn.com/football/college/features/2002/preview/Auburn/.

[k] Kevin Scarbinsky, "Tuberville Goes High Profile in Los Angeles," *Birmingham News* (September 2, 2002): 1-B.

[l] Charles Goldberg, "Cobb Gains Role as Team Leader - Quarterback Wins Confidence of Teammates," *Birmingham News* (September 27, 2002): 1-E.

[m] Charles Goldberg, "Cobb Ready to Return to Face Razorbacks," *Birmingham News* (October 7, 2002): 1-C.

[n] Charles Goldberg, "AU Staff gets Critical during Off Week," *Birmingham News* (October 10, 2002): 1-C.

[o] Fred Talley, 21/241; Matt Jones, 6/66; Mark Pierce, 5/62.

[p] Charles Goldberg, "Auburn Needs to Get Fast Start to Finish LSU," *Birmingham News* (October 25, 2002): 1-E.

[q] The Auburn Plainsman, "Tuberville Discusses Upcoming Season," *The Auburn Plainsman* (August 30, 2001): 8.

Chapter 6

[a] Charles Goldberg, "AU's Chizik back on Old Turf again - His Challenge: Containing Penn State's Johnson," *Birmingham News* (December 31, 2002): 7-C.

[b] Charles Goldberg, "'Wow' - Defense Steals Show as Auburn Upsets No. 10 LSU," *Birmingham News* (October 27, 2002):1-B.

[c] Charles Goldberg, "'Wow' - Defense Steals Show as Auburn Upsets No. 10 LSU," *Birmingham News* (October 27, 2002): 1-B.

[d] Charles Goldberg, "Tigers Take Fight to Tide; Execute Near-Perfect Plan," *Birmingham News* (November 24, 2002): 4-I.

[e] Charles Goldberg, "Tigers Take Fight to Tide; Execute Near-Perfect Plan," *Birmingham News* (November 24, 2002): 4-I.

[f] Doug Segrest, "Can't Run, Can't Hide - Penn State's Larry Johnson Disses Auburn Defense that Holds Him to 72 Yards Rushing," *Birmingham News* (January 2, 2003): 6-C.

[g] Charles Goldberg, "Death Hushes Familiar Voice of Seasoned AU Announcer," *Birmingham News* (May 16, 2003): 1-A.

[h] Charles Goldberg, "Death Hushes Familiar Voice of Seasoned AU Announcer," *Birmingham News* (May 16, 2003): 1-A.

Chapter 7

[a] Charles Goldberg, "Tigers Dream Big for 2003 - Aim to Build on Win in Bowl," *Birmingham News* (December 27, 2002): 1-C.

[b] Kevin Scarbinsky, "Auburn Looks Forward with Grand Ambition," *Birmingham News* (December 31, 2002): 7-C.

[c] Charles Goldberg, "AU may Promote from Within," *Birmingham News* (December 29, 2002): 1-B.

[d] Charles Goldberg, "AU may Promote from Within," *Birmingham News* (December 29, 2002): 1-B.

[e] Charles Goldberg, "What's Up with Tiger Play Calling? - Tuberville Confident in System, Nall, Ensminger," *Birmingham News* (September 3, 2003): 1-D.

[f] Charles Goldberg, "Dansby: High Rankings made Tigers Relax," *Birmingham News* (September 10, 2003): 1-D.

[g] Charles Goldberg, "Grounding the Hogs - Tigers Hold SEC's Top Rushing Attack to 173 yards, Field Goal," *Birmingham News* (October 12, 2003): 8-B.

[h] Charles Goldberg, "AU Coaches See Game as Waste, One of Worst," *Birmingham News* (November 3, 2003): 1-C.

[i] Chuck Williams, "Close but No Completion - Obomanu: 'I misjudged it. It Hit Me in the Wrong Place, I guess. It Hit Me on my Hands.'," *Birmingham News* (November 9, 2003): 10-B.

[j] Charles Goldberg, "What's at Stake - Coaches Looking Forward; Cadillac in Reverse," *Birmingham News* (November 17, 2003): 1-C.

[k] Steve Irvine, "On All Cylinders - Carnell 'Cadillac' Williams' 204-Yard Night Powers Auburn," *Birmingham News* (November 23, 2003): 3-P.

Chapter 8

[a] Associated Press, "Williams rushes for 204 yards," n.p. [cited July 13, 2012]. Online: http://espn.go.com/ncf/recap?gameId=233260002.

[b] Charles Goldberg, "It's Mum on the Plain - No Word Yet on Tuberville's Future at Auburn," *The Birmingham News* (November 24, 2003): 1-C.

[c] Charles Goldberg, "AU President Won't Reveal 'Inclination' - But List of Possible Replacement Candidates Beginning to Emerge," *The Birmingham News* (November 25, 2003): 7-B.

[d] Charles Goldberg, "Auburn Interviews Petrino - AU Officials Visit with Louisville Coach Two Days before Iron Bowl," *Birmingham News* (November 26, 2003): 1-B.

[e] Steve Irvine, "Pro-Auburn Interview Gets Bama Cheerleader Dropped from Squad," *Birmingham News* (November 25, 2003): 7-B.

[f] William F. Walker, "Walker's Statement," *Birmingham News* (November 27, 2003): 3-D.

[g] Charles Goldberg, "'Search Firm' was One Individual – Tuberville, Assistants Ready to go Recruting Today and Monday," *Birmingham News* (November 30, 2003): 1-B.

[h] Charles Goldberg, "'Search Firm' was One Individual – Tuberville, Assistants Ready to go Recruiting Today and Monday," *Birmingham News* (November 30, 2003): 1-B.

[i] All quotations in this paragraph taken from Jimmy Smothers, "Tuberville Emotional as He Announces He's Staying," *The Gadsden Times* (December 2, 2003): B-1, 5.

[j] Charles Goldberg, "Tubberville Gives Thanks while AU Mulls his Fate," *Birmingham News* (November 23, 2003): 3-P.

[k] Tom Arenberg, "For Tuberville, Timing Really was Everything," *Birmingham News* (November 30, 2003): 20-B.

[l] John Zenor, "Auburn Coach Remains in Limbo," *The Gadsden Times* (November 25, 2003): B-7.

[m] "AUBURN NOTEBOOK." *Birmingham News (AL)* 23 Nov. 2003, Sports: 5-P. *NewsBank*. Web. 1 Aug. 2013.

[n] Goldberg, "Tubberville Gives Thanks," 3-P.

[o] Zenor, "Auburn Coach Remains in Limbo," B-7.

[p] Goldberg, "AU President Won't Reveal 'Inclination'," 7-B.

[q] John Zenor, "Auburn Coach Remains in Limbo," *The Gadsden Times* (November 25, 2003): B-7.

[r] Goldberg, "Auburn Interviews Petrino," 1-B.

[s] Dye and Logue, *In the Arena*, 2.

[t] Charles Goldberg, "'I'm Looking Forward to Being Around Here for a Long Time.' - Coach Seeks Unity," *Birmingham News* (December 2, 2003): 1-A.

[u] Charles Goldberg, "Tiger Time Begins for Tuberville - Tuberville Era Begins at Auburn - Official Announcement Over, Coach Starts Earning Salary," *Birmingham News* (November 29, 1998): 1-A.

[v] Johnson, Suzanne. "In His Own Words." *Auburn Magazine* 19 (3 2012): 29-33.

[w] Phillip Marshall, "Ex-Auburn great Mengelt set up Petrino meeting," *The Huntsville Times* (December 1, 2003): D-1.

[x] Associated Press, "Tuberville to remain as Auburn coach," n.p. [cited July 13, 2012]. Online: http://www.usatoday.com/sports/college/football/sec/2003-12-01-Auburn-tuberville_x.htm.

Chapter 9

[a] Thomas Spencer, "Auburn Put on Probation - Penalty a Step Short of Lost Accreditation," *Birmingham News* (December 10, 2003): 1-A.

[b] Richard Y. Bradley, "Report of Special Investigation Conducted at Auburn University for the Southern Association of Colleges and Schools, Inc," n.p. [cited April 20, 2013]. Online: http://www.ocm.Auburn.edu/sacs_specinvest.html.

[c] Kent Faulk, "Alum Officials Urge Resignations," *Birmingham News* (December 14, 2003): 21-A.

[d] Kevin Scarbinsky, "Tuberville Won't Be Quick to Pull Trigger," *Birmingham News* (December 31, 2003): 1-D.

[e] Charles Goldberg, "Looking for Redemption," *Birmingham News* (December 31, 2003): 1-D.

[f] Charles Goldberg, "One More Year for Tiger Trio - Williams, Brown, Rogers Bypass NFL," *Birmingham News* (January 15, 2004): 1-C.

[g] Charles Goldberg, "One More Year for Tiger Trio - Williams, Brown, Rogers Bypass NFL," *Birmingham News* (January 15, 2004): 1-C.

[h] Charles Goldberg, "Alumni Group Renews Call to Oust Tiger AD," *Birmingham News* (January 18, 2004): 1-D.

[i] Charles Goldberg, "Tuberville Continues Shuffling - Latest Move Sends Ensminger from Coaching QBs to Tight Ends," *Birmingham News* (February 17, 2004): 1-C.

[j] Charles Goldberg, "Tigers Go West Coast - Campbell Working with Fourth Offensive Coordinator in Four Years," *Birmingham News* (March 1, 2004): 1-C.

[k] Charles Goldberg, "Auburn's AD Housel will Retire in January - 'It's been a Very Gratifying Day'; More Athletics Changes Expected," *Birmingham News* (March 17, 2004): 1-A.

[l] Charles Goldberg, "TV Host Phil Snow Learns of Removal from Media Guide - Bramblett Replaces Longtime Host," *Birmingham News* (August 3, 2004): 1-B.

Chapter 10

[a] Charles Goldberg, "SEC Media Days Notebook," *Birmingham News* (July 30, 2004): 7-D.

[b] Charles Goldberg, "How SEC West Looks," *Birmingham News* (August 29, 2004): 20-P. Stuart Mandell, "SEC Preview," n.p. [cited April 29, 2013]. Online: http://sportsillustrated.cnn.com/2004/football/ncaa/specials/preview/2004/sec.preview/.

[c] Charles Goldberg, "College Football Beat," *Birmingham News* (November 8, 2002): 5-E.

[d] Charles Goldberg, "Tigers Plan to Play Cox - Campbell Still No. 1 QB, but Redshirt Freshman will See Action, Too," *Birmingham News* (September 1, 2004): 1-B.

[e] "TIGERS NOTEBOOK." *Birmingham News (AL)* 19 Sep. 2004, Sports: 15-C. *NewsBank.* Web. 8 May. 2013.

[f] DVD, Fighting Soldiers: The Story of the 2004 Auburn Tigers. Presented by Movie Gallery.

[g] Segrest, Doug. "BEAT VOLS AND AU WILL CONTEND FOR NATIONAL TITLE." *Birmingham News (AL)* 26 Sep. 2004, Sports: 10-C. *NewsBank.* Web. 7 May. 2013.

[h] KYLE VEAZEY. "ROCKY STOPPED - LED BY ROSEGREEN'S FOUR INTS, TIGERS SMOTHER VOL FRESHMEN, OFFENSE." *Birmingham News (AL)* 3 Oct. 2004, Sports: 6-C. *NewsBank.* Web. 8 May. 2013.

[i] Williams, Chette, and Dick Parker. *Hard Fighting Soldier: Finding God in Trials, Tragedies, and Triumphs*. Decatur, Ga: Looking Glass Books, 2007. 144-147.

[j] "DARE AUBURN DREAM OF A NATIONAL TITLE?." *Birmingham News (AL)* 3 Oct. 2004, Sports: 1-C. *NewsBank.* Web. 9 May. 2013.

[k] Goldberg, Charles. "Tuberville: Put top four teams in a playoff." *Birmingham News (AL)* 4 Nov. 2004, SPORTS: 1-D. *NewsBank.* Web. 11 May. 2013.

[l] Goldberg, Charles. "Show time for No. 3 Tigers AU has chance to shine on national TV." *Birmingham News (AL)* 8 Nov. 2004, SPORTS: 1-C. *NewsBank.* Web. 11 May. 2013.

[m] CHARLES GOLDBERG. "'Ready to jump' Williams, Tigers hope convincing win moves them past Oklahoma." *Birmingham News (AL)* 14 Nov. 2004, SPORTS: 1-D. *NewsBank.* Web. 13 May. 2013.

243

[n] CHARLES GOLDBERG. "'Ready to jump' Williams, Tigers hope convincing win moves them past Oklahoma." *Birmingham News (AL)* 14 Nov. 2004, SPORTS: 1-D. *NewsBank.* Web. 13 May. 2013.

[o] CHARLES GOLDBERG. "'Ready to jump' Williams, Tigers hope convincing win moves them past Oklahoma." *Birmingham News (AL)* 14 Nov. 2004, SPORTS: 1-D. *NewsBank.* Web. 13 May. 2013.

[p] Ibid.

[q] Marc Weiszer, "No sanctions forthcoming on Rosegreen," n.p. [cited May 13, 2013]. Online: http://onlineathens.com/stories/111604/dog_20041116027.shtml.

[r] Dick Weiss, "AUBURN LOOKS LIKE TOP DAWG ROUT HARD TO IGNORE IN BCS," n.p. [cited May 13, 2013]. Online: http://www.nydailynews.com/archives/sports/Auburn-top-dawg-rout-hard-ignore-bcs-article-1.592111.

[s] "SOUND OFF Reader's predictions for the big game." *Birmingham News (AL)* 19 Nov. 2004, SPORTS: 4-P. *NewsBank.* Web. 4 Aug. 2013.

[t] CHARLES GOLDBERG. "'Just do your thing'." *Birmingham News (AL)* 21 Nov. 2004, SPORTS: 2-K. *NewsBank.* Web. 15 May. 2013.

[u] Glier, Ray. *What It Means to Be a Tiger: Pat Dye and Auburn's Greatest Players* (Chicago: Triumph Books, 2010), Kindle edition, location 3950.

Chapter 11

[a] Stephen Atkinson, "Festive Crowd Celebrates Unbeaten Football Season," n.p. [cited June 8, 2012]. Online: http://Auburn.scout.com/2/342286.html.

[b] Goldberg, Charles. "COLLEGE FOOTBALL BEAT." *Birmingham News (AL)* 6 Jan. 2005, SPORTS: 6-C. *NewsBank.* Web. 17 May. 2013.

[c] Lynn Zinser, "U.S.C. Loses Its 2004 B.C.S. National Championship," n.p. [cited May 19, 2013]. Online: http://www.nytimes.com/2011/06/07/sports/ncaafootball/usc-stripped-of-2004-bcs-national-championship.html.

[d] Mark Schlabach, "Tuberville: Auburn should be '04 champ," n.p. [cited May 19, 2013]. Online: http://sports.espn.go.com/ncf/news/story?id=5273313.

[e] Tim Wendel, "College football's annual asterisk," n.p. [cited May 31, 2013]. Online: http://usatoday30.usatoday.com/news/opinion/editorials/2005-01-05-college-edit_x.htm?csp=34.

Chapter 12

[a] CHARLES GOLDBERG. "Perfect repeat won't be easy task." *Birmingham News (AL)* 5 Jan. 2005, SPORTS: 1-B. *NewsBank.* Web. 17 May. 2013.

[b] CHARLES GOLDBERG. "AU's McNeill, Mix will be back Bama's Ryans also ignores appeal of going pro." *Birmingham News (AL)* 13 Jan. 2005, SPORTS: 1-C. *NewsBank.* Web. 17 May. 2013.

[c] CHARLES GOLDBERG. "Chizik takes coordinator's job at Texas Coaching vacancy attracts many callers at Auburn." *Birmingham News (AL)* 18 Jan. 2005, SPORTS: 1-C. *NewsBank.* Web. 17 May. 2013.

[d] CHARLES GOLDBERG. "Fast defenders, role players fill out AU's 'great' recruiting class." *Birmingham News (AL)* 3 Feb. 2005, SPORTS: 1-C. *NewsBank.* Web. 17 May. 2013.

[e] CHARLES GOLDBERG. "Tigers' 2005 class has 'quality' that Tuberville likes." *Birmingham News (AL)* 2 Feb. 2005, SPORTS: 1-C. *NewsBank.* Web. 17 May. 2013.

[f] CHARLES GOLDBERG. "Stepping up Cox perseveres to get his shot as QB." *Birmingham News (AL)* 31 Jul. 2005, SPORTS: 1-D. *NewsBank.* Web. 20 May. 2013.

[g] CHARLES GOLDBERG. "SEC champs open fall drills with RB problem Tigers, suddenly short on running backs, move speedy DB to backfield." *Birmingham News (AL)* 3 Aug. 2005, SPORTS: 1-C. *NewsBank.* Web. 20 May. 2013.

[h] "Breaking down the West." *Birmingham News (AL)* 5 Jun. 2005, SPORTS: 4-C. *NewsBank.* Web. 17 May. 2013.

[i]

http://sportsillustrated.cnn.com/2005/writers/stewart_mandel/08/30/power.rankings/1.html

[j] CHARLES GOLDBERG. "Looking for another FULL HOUSE Star backfield, 13-0 record will be a tough act to follow." *Birmingham News (AL)* 28 Aug. 2005, SPORTS: 4-P. *NewsBank.* Web. 20 May. 2013.

[k] "TIGERS NOTEBOOK." *Birmingham News (AL)* 11 Sep. 2005, SPORTS: 9-C. *NewsBank.* Web. 20 May. 2013.

[l] CHARLES GOLDBERG. "Tuberville impressed with team's execution." *Birmingham News (AL)* 3 Oct. 2005, SPORTS: 1-C. *NewsBank.* Web. 21 May. 2013.

[m] CHARLES GOLDBERG. "Five is a lonely number Vaughn hopes to bounce back from five missed field-goal attempts vs. LSU." *Birmingham News (AL)* 24 Oct. 2005, SPORTS: 1-C. *NewsBank.* Web. 21 May. 2013.

[n] John Kaltefleiter, "On a road to recovery," n.p. [cited June 11, 2013]. Online: http://onlineathens.com/stories/111205/gameday_20051112003.shtml.

[o] CHARLES GOLDBERG. "Sweet redemption Vaughn's 20-yard field goal caps off Tigers' rally." *Birmingham News (AL)* 14 Nov. 2005, SPORTS: 1-D. *NewsBank.* Web. 21 May. 2013.

[p] CHARLES GOLDBERG. "Sweet redemption Vaughn's 20-yard field goal caps off Tigers' rally." *Birmingham News (AL)* 14 Nov. 2005, SPORTS: 1-D. *NewsBank.* Web. 21 May. 2013.

[q] CHARLES GOLDBERG. "Tigers put up little fight against Badgers Alvarez goes out a winner as Calhoun tears through Auburn's respected defense." *Birmingham News (AL)* 3 Jan. 2006, SPORTS: 1-C. *NewsBank.* Web. 10 Jun. 2013.

Chapter 13

[a] CHARLES GOLDBERG. "Tigers picked to win SEC; that's not good." *Birmingham News (AL)* 29 Jul. 2006, SPORTS: 1-C. *NewsBank.* Web. 10 Jun. 2013.

[b] CHARLES GOLDBERG. "Appreciative but cautious Tigers don't make a big deal about being ranked fourth." *Birmingham News (AL)* 19 Aug. 2006, SPORTS: 1-B. *NewsBank.* Web. 10 Jun. 2013.

[c] CHARLES GOLDBERG. "AU rides 'The Horse' Irons' career-best 223 yards carry Tigers past Cougars." *Birmingham News (AL)* 3 Sep. 2006, SPORTS: 1-D. *NewsBank.* Web. 11 Jun. 2013.

[d] Melick, Ray. "Auburn began LSU planning months ago." *Birmingham News (AL)* 10 Sep. 2006, SPORTS: 6-D. *NewsBank.* Web. 11 Jun. 2013.

[e] JON SOLOMON. "Tuberville rolls the dice and wins." *Birmingham News (AL)* 29 Sep. 2006, SPORTS: 9-D. *NewsBank.* Web. 11 Jun. 2013.

[f] Van Allen Plexico and John Ringer, "The Hawg Hex – and How to Break It," n.p. [cited June 18, 2013]. Online: http://www.thewareaglereader.com/2010/10/the-hawg-hex-and-how-to-break-it/#.UcETVZy0QbA. See also Plexico, Van Allen and John Ringer. *Decades of Dominance: Auburn Football in the Modern Era.* White Rocket Books, 2013.

[g] CHARLES GOLDBERG. "Stealing Hogs Arkansas bamboozles No. 2 Tigers; national title hopes crippled." *Birmingham News (AL)* 8 Oct. 2006, SPORTS: 1-C. *NewsBank.* Web. 11 Jun. 2013.

[h] CHARLES GOLDBERG. "Stealing Hogs Arkansas bamboozles No. 2 Tigers; national title hopes crippled." *Birmingham News (AL)* 8 Oct. 2006, SPORTS: 1-C. *NewsBank.* Web. 11 Jun. 2013.

[i] CHARLES GOLDBERG. "AUBURN VS. FLORIDA Tebow mania Tigers defense must keep Gator freshman in check; UF trying to do the same with

fans." *Birmingham News (AL)* 11 Oct. 2006, SPORTS: 1-C. *NewsBank.* Web. 11 Jun. 2013.

[j] DOUG SEGREST. "Little man Tate plays big Rarely used freshman rushes for career-high 156 yards, TD." *Birmingham News (AL)* 22 Oct. 2006, SPORTS: 8-C. *NewsBank.* Web. 11 Jun. 2013.

[k] CHARLES GOLDBERG. "Tigers win ho-hum game with Georgia, Bama looming Tuberville promises harder workouts before SEC challenges." *Birmingham News (AL)* 5 Nov. 2006, SPORTS: 1-C. *NewsBank.* Web. 17 Jun. 2013.

[l] CHARLES GOLDBERG. "COLLEGE BEATS." *Birmingham News (AL)* 6 Nov. 2006, SPORTS: 6-C. *NewsBank.* Web. 17 Jun. 2013.

[m] CHARLES GOLDBERG. "BCS dreams Dawg-gone Georgia limped into Auburn but left Tigers licking their wounds." *Birmingham News (AL)* 12 Nov. 2006, SPORTS: 1-C. *NewsBank.* Web. 17 Jun. 2013.

[n] Predestination, The Unsharable, and Shakers in Shreds: Five seasons of Auburn Football

http://www.thewareaglereader.com/2011/01/predestination-the-unsharable-and-shakers-in-shreds-five-seasons-of-Auburn-football/#.UgHFyG2YeFB

[o] Plexico and Ringer, *Decades of Dominance*, 90.

[p] Melick, Ray. "Auburn began LSU planning months ago." *Birmingham News (AL)* 10 Sep. 2006, SPORTS: 6-D. *NewsBank.* Web. 11 Jun. 2013.

[q] "QUOTEWORTHY - AUBURN 34, MISSISSIPPI STATE 0." *Birmingham News (AL)* 10 Sep. 2006, SPORTS: 7-D. *NewsBank.* Web. 11 Jun. 2013.

[r] "QUOTEWORTHY - AUBURN 34, MISSISSIPPI STATE 0." *Birmingham News (AL)* 10 Sep. 2006, SPORTS: 7-D. *NewsBank.* Web. 11 Jun. 2013.

Chapter 14

[a] The Auburn Plainsman, "Tuberville Discusses Upcoming Season," *The Auburn Plainsman* (August 30, 2001): 8.

[b] "SPORTS BUZZ." *Birmingham News (AL)* 23 Nov. 2005, SPORTS: 2-B. *NewsBank.* Web. 21 May. 2013.

[c] Scarbinsky, Kevin. "Tuberville shirt helps fan flames of AU-UA rivalry." *Birmingham News (AL)* 1 Jan. 2006, SPORTS: 1-C. *NewsBank.* Web. 21 May. 2013.

[d] "SPORTS BUZZ." *Birmingham News (AL)* 23 Nov. 2005, SPORTS: 2-B. *NewsBank.* Web. 21 May. 2013.

[e] Scarbinsky, Kevin. "Tuberville shirt helps fan flames of AU-UA rivalry." *Birmingham News (AL)* 1 Jan. 2006, SPORTS: 1-C. *NewsBank.* Web. 21 May. 2013.

[f] Scarbinsky, Kevin. "Tuberville photos serve as Tide motivation." *Birmingham News (AL)* 15 Nov. 2006, SPORTS: 1-C. *NewsBank.* Web. 21 Jul. 2013.

[g] RAPOPORT, IAN R.. "Bama players get constant reminders of streak - even in their own locker room." *Birmingham News (AL)* 17 Nov. 2006, SPORTS: 1-I. *NewsBank.* Web. 17 Jun. 2013.

[h] Scarbinsky, Kevin. "Tuberville makes himself at home at Bryant-Denny." *Birmingham News (AL)* 19 Nov. 2006, SPORTS: 3-S. *NewsBank.* Web. 22 Jul. 2013.

[i] DOUG SEGREST. "Thumb plus one Auburn extends Iron Bowl streak; Tuberville first Tigers coach to beat archrival six straight." *Birmingham News (AL)* 25 Nov. 2007, SPORTS: 3-I. *NewsBank.* Web. 28 Jun. 2013.

Chapter 15

[a] CHARLES GOLDBERG. "Tigers have holes to fill as senior class says good-bye No rest for the weary; team starts spring practice next month." *Birmingham News (AL)* 3 Jan. 2007, SPORTS: 1-C. *NewsBank.* Web. 17 Jun. 2013.

[b] CHARLES GOLDBERG. "Signed and delivered TOP 10 CLASS Auburn's group of 30 players is one of Tigers' best in years Burns, Ziemba big catches in AU's top 10 class." *Birmingham News (AL)* 8 Feb. 2007, SPORTS: 1-C. *NewsBank.* Web. 21 Jun. 2013.

[c] Fairley failed to qualify academically and enrolled in a junior college. He was, nonetheless, originally a Tuberville signee who later played—rather well—for Auburn.

[d]

http://sportsillustrated.cnn.com/2007/writers/stewart_mandel/08/28/power.rankings1/1.html

[e] CHARLES GOLDBERG. "Tigers rally in season opener Cox hits McKenzie for go-ahead score; Coleman's fumble return caps off rally." *Birmingham News (AL)* 2 Sep. 2007, SPORTS: 1-C. *NewsBank.* Web. 25 Jun. 2013.

[f] CHARLES GOLDBERG. "Tigers rally in season opener Cox hits McKenzie for go-ahead score; Coleman's fumble return caps off rally." *Birmingham News (AL)* 2 Sep. 2007, SPORTS: 1-C. *NewsBank.* Web. 25 Jun. 2013.

[g] "QUOTEWORTHY - AUBURN 23, KANSAS STATE 13." *Birmingham News (AL)* 2 Sep. 2007, SPORTS: 7-C. *NewsBank.* Web. 25 Jun. 2013.

[h] "QUOTEWORTHY - SOUTH FLORIDA 26, AUBURN 23 (OT)." *Birmingham News (AL)* 9 Sep. 2007, SPORTS: 6-C. *NewsBank.* Web. 25 Jun. 2013.

[i] DOUG SEGREST. "Freshman kicker Byrum knew moment he kicked it, it was good." *Birmingham News (AL)* 30 Sep. 2007, SPORTS: 4-C. *NewsBank.* Web. 27 Jun. 2013.

[j] CHARLES GOLDBERG. "It's good - twice Auburn shocks No. 4 Florida with game-ending field goal." *Birmingham News (AL)* 30 Sep. 2007, SPORTS: 1-C. *NewsBank.* Web. 27 Jun. 2013.

[k] DOUG SEGREST. "Freshman kicker Byrum knew moment he kicked it, it was good." *Birmingham News (AL)* 30 Sep. 2007, SPORTS: 4-C. *NewsBank.* Web. 27 Jun. 2013.

[l] "QUOTEWORTHY - AUBURN 9, ARKANSAS 7." *Birmingham News (AL)* 14 Oct. 2007, SPORTS: 5-C. *NewsBank.* Web. 28 Jun. 2013.

[m] "QUOTEWORTHY LSU 30, AUBURN 24." *Birmingham News (AL)* 21 Oct. 2007, SPORTS: 9-C. *NewsBank.* Web. 28 Jun. 2013.

[n] GOLDBERG, CHARLES. "AU's Tuberville addresses rumors by pushing Auburn." *Birmingham News (AL)* 11 Oct. 2007, SPORTS: 1-C. *NewsBank.* Web. 28 Jun. 2013.

[o] Scarbinsky, Kevin. "Auburn fan fires up site to keep Tuberville." *Birmingham News (AL)* 9 Nov. 2007, SPORTS: 1-E. *NewsBank.* Web. 28 Jun. 2013.

[p] CHARLES GOLDBERG. "Coach, AD meet Tuberville, Jacobs eye improvements for AU program." *Birmingham News (AL)* 27 Nov. 2007, SPORTS: 1-C. *NewsBank.* Web. 28 Jun. 2013.

[q] CHARLES GOLDBERG News staff writers, ANDREW GRIBBLE. "'Never any doubt' Tuberville was returning." *Birmingham News (AL)* 6 Dec. 2007, SPORTS: 1-C. *NewsBank.* Web. 28 Jun. 2013.

[r] CHARLES GOLDBERG. "Fast and furious New offensive coordinator Tony Franklin bringing the no-huddle to the Plain." *Birmingham News (AL)* 13 Dec. 2007, SPORTS: 1-C. *NewsBank.* Web. 28 Jun. 2013.

[s] CHARLES GOLDBERG. "Burns, baby, Burns Freshman QB scores winning touchdown in overtime." *Birmingham News (AL)* 1 Jan. 2008, SPORTS: 1-B. *NewsBank.* Web. 28 Jun. 2013.

Chapter 16

[a] CHARLES GOLDBERG. "Scrimmage chance for Burns to shine." *Birmingham News (AL)* 1 Mar. 2008, SPORTS: 3-B. *NewsBank.* Web. 28 Jun. 2013.

[b] CHARLES GOLDBERG. "Burns makes his case to start." *Birmingham News (AL)* 3 Apr. 2008, SPORTS: 1-C. *NewsBank.* Web. 28 Jun. 2013.

[c] CHARLES GOLDBERG. "AUBURN FILLS NEEDS Tigers' class heavy on defensive linemen, backs Tigers miss on impact player on signing day." *Birmingham News (AL)* 7 Feb. 2008, SPORTS: 1-C. *NewsBank.* Web. 28 Jun. 2013.

[d] CHARLES GOLDBERG. "RELUCTANT FAVORITE Tigers prefer the role of the underdog." *Birmingham News (AL)* 26 Jul. 2008, SPORTS: 1-C. *NewsBank.* Web. 28 Jun. 2013.

[e] CHARLES GOLDBERG. "TODD'S THE MAN . . . FOR NOW Tuberville hopes either Todd or Burns grabs hold of No. 1 QB job." *Birmingham News (AL)* 3 Sep. 2008, SPORTS: 1-C. *NewsBank.* Web. 28 Jun. 2013.

[f] CHARLES GOLDBERG. "STARKVILLE, RAVING MAD Defense pulls Tigers through on crazy night in Mississippi." *Birmingham News (AL)* 14 Sep. 2008, SPORTS: 4-C. *NewsBank.* Web. 28 Jun. 2013.

[g] CHARLES GOLDBERG. "TODD'S THE MAN . . . FOR NOW Tuberville hopes either Todd or Burns grabs hold of No. 1 QB job." *Birmingham News (AL)* 3 Sep. 2008, SPORTS: 1-C. *NewsBank.* Web. 28 Jun. 2013.

[h] CHARLES GOLDBERG. "TIGERS WIN DEFENSIVE DUEL Burns' clutch third-down pass clinches victory." *Birmingham News (AL)* 28 Sep. 2008, SPORTS: 4-C. *NewsBank.* Web. 28 Jun. 2013.

[i] CHARLES GOLDBERG. "VANDY EXTENDS AU MISERYCommodores beat AU for first time since 1955; changes coming for Tigers." *Birmingham News (AL)* 5 Oct. 2008, SPORTS: 6-D. *NewsBank.* Web. 28 Jun. 2013.

[j] CHARLES GOLDBERG. "VANDY EXTENDS AU MISERYCommodores beat AU for first time since 1955; changes coming for Tigers." *Birmingham News (AL)* 5 Oct. 2008, SPORTS: 6-D. *NewsBank.* Web. 28 Jun. 2013.

[k] CHARLES GOLDBERG. "Franklin more hands-on Players see more intense, 'crazy' coordinator in practice." *Birmingham News (AL)* 8 Oct. 2008, SPORTS: 1-B. *NewsBank.* Web. 28 Jun. 2013.

[l] CHARLES GOLDBERG. "'THEY TOLD ME TO GET LOST' AU offensive coordinator gets punted at midseason." *Birmingham News (AL)* 9 Oct. 2008, SPORTS: 1-C. *NewsBank.* Web. 28 Jun. 2013.

[m] http://blog.al.com/spotnews/2008/10/franklin_packs_up_leaves_aubur.html

[n] CHARLES GOLDBERG. "'THEY TOLD ME TO GET LOST' AU offensive coordinator gets punted at midseason." *Birmingham News (AL)* 9 Oct. 2008, SPORTS: 1-C. *NewsBank.* Web. 28 Jun. 2013.

[o] CHARLES GOLDBERG. "'IT'S BEEN A TOUGH WEEK' Offensive woes continue as Petrino, Hogs deal No. 20 AU second straight loss." *Birmingham News (AL)* 12 Oct. 2008, SPORTS: 6-C. *NewsBank.* Web. 28 Jun. 2013.

[p] "COLLEGE BEAT." *Birmingham News (AL)* 30 Oct. 2008, SPORTS: 9-C. *NewsBank.* Web. 28 Jun. 2013.

[q] http://www.uni-watch.com/2007/12/11/%E2%80%99hawks-copycats-of-tigers/

[r] CHARLES GOLDBERG. "Tuberville, Gogue talk about season Decision on coach's future will follow additional meetings." *Birmingham News (AL)* 2 Dec. 2008, SPORTS: 1-C. *NewsBank.* Web. 8 Jul. 2013.

[s] CHARLES GOLDBERG. "No resolution for Tuberville at AU." *Birmingham News (AL)* 3 Dec. 2008, SPORTS: 1-B. *NewsBank.* Web. 8 Jul. 2013.

[t] RAY MELICK. "'AUBURN FAMILY' SAYS THANKS But some wonder if Tuberville lost desire." *Birmingham News (AL)* 4 Dec. 2008, SPORTS: 1-C. *NewsBank.* Web. 8 Jul. 2013.

[u] http://www.Auburntigers.com/sports/m-footbl/spec-rel/120308aaa.html

[v] http://www.Auburntigers.com/sports/m-footbl/spec-rel/120308aaa.html

[w] As of July 12, 2013, video of the press conference was available online at http://blip.tv/Auburnundercover/athletics-director-jay-jacobs-on-tommy-tuberville-s-resignation-12-4-1546799.

[x] CHARLES GOLDBERG. "Tuberville plans to swap hot seat for an easy chair For now his focus is on being husband, father." *Birmingham News (AL)* 5 Dec. 2008, NEWS: 1-A. *NewsBank.* Web. 8 Jul. 2013.

[y] CHARLES GOLDBERG. "Tuberville plans to swap hot seat for an easy chair For now his focus is on being husband, father." *Birmingham News (AL)* 5 Dec. 2008, NEWS: 1-A. *NewsBank.* Web. 8 Jul. 2013.

[z] http://www.Auburntigers.com/sports/m-footbl/spec-rel/120308aaa.html

[aa] CHARLES GOLDBERG. "TUBERVILLE OUT AT AU Auburn's final loss of year is its head coach." *Birmingham News (AL)* 4 Dec. 2008, NEWS: 1-A. *NewsBank.* Web. 8 Jul. 2013.

[bb] Scarbinsky, Kevin. "Dead coach walking: Murder or suicide?." *Birmingham News (AL)* 5 Dec. 2008, SPORTS: 1-C. *NewsBank.* Web. 8 Jul. 2013.

[cc] CHARLES GOLDBERG. "Tuberville plans to swap hot seat for an easy chair For now his focus is on being husband, father." *Birmingham News (AL)* 5 Dec. 2008, NEWS: 1-A. *NewsBank.* Web. 8 Jul. 2013.

[dd] Glier, Ray. *What It Means to Be a Tiger: Pat Dye and Auburn's Greatest Players* (Chicago: Triumph Books, 2010), Kindle edition, location 3979.

Chapter 17

[a] CHARLES GOLDBERG. "'I'M LOOKING FORWARD TO BEING AROUND HERE FOR A LONG TIME.' - COACH SEEKS UNITY." *Birmingham News (AL)* 2 Dec. 2003, News: 1-A. *NewsBank.* Web. 10 Aug. 2013.

[b] CHARLES GOLDBERG. "MOVING FORWARD - HOUSEL, WALKER OFFER APOLOGY, SUPPORT TO TUBERVILLE AFTER STORMY WEEK." *Birmingham News (AL)* 2 Dec. 2003, Sports: 7-C. *NewsBank.* Web. 10 Aug. 2013.

[c] "COLLEGE FOOTBALL BEAT." *Birmingham News (AL)* 21 Jul. 2004, Sports: 3-C. *NewsBank.* Web. 15 Aug. 2013.

[d] Glier, Ray. *What It Means to Be a Tiger: Pat Dye and Auburn's Greatest Players* (Chicago: Triumph Books, 2010), Kindle edition, location 3957.

[e] Pat Dye and John Logue, *In The Arena* (Montgomery, AL: The Black Belt Press, 1992), 7.

[f] Chizik, Gene, and David Thomas. *All in: What It Takes to Be the Best.* Carol Stream, Ill: Tyndale House Publishers, 2011, 211.

Afterword

[a] http://www.Auburntigers.com/sports/m-footbl/spec-rel/080113aan.html
[b]

http://sportsillustrated.cnn.com/vault/article/magazine/MAG1183588/3/index.htm **VIA** http://www.thewareaglereader.com/2013/04/first-class-bloodbath-that-time-pat-dye-made-Auburn-play-two-a-day-games/#.UgczeD-YeFB